THE SEASONS OF MY MOTHER

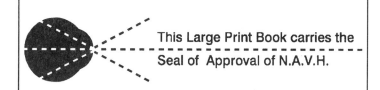

This Large Print Book carries the
Seal of Approval of N.A.V.H.

THE SEASONS OF MY MOTHER

A MEMOIR OF LOVE, FAMILY AND FLOWERS

MARCIA GAY HARDEN

THORNDIKE PRESS

A part of Gale, a Cengage Company

Lewes Public Library
111 Adams Ave.
Lewes, DE 19958
302-645-4633

 GALE
A Cengage Company

Farmington Hills, Mich • San Francisco • New York • Waterville, Maine
Meriden, Conn • Mason, Ohio • Chicago

Thorndike Press, a part of Gale, a Cengage Company.

**LIBRARY OF CONGRESS CIP DATA ON FILE.
CATALOGUING IN PUBLICATION FOR THIS BOOK
IS AVAILABLE FROM THE LIBRARY OF CONGRESS**

ISBN-13: 978-1-4328-5445-4 (hardcover)

Published in 2018 by arrangement with Atria Books, an imprint of Simon & Schuster, Inc.

Printed in the United States of America
1 2 3 4 5 6 7 22 21 20 19 18

*This book is dedicated to
my amazing mother, Beverly Harden,
who fills the world around her with beauty.*

*And to Alvin Sargent, who inspired me
to write in twenty-minute stretches.*

*And to my remarkable children,
Eulala, Julitta, and Hudson,
without whom my stretches would
have been interminable.
Your grandmother is an
extraordinary woman.*

CONTENTS

fuubutsushi: Japanese (n.) the things — feelings, scents, images — that evoke memories or anticipation of a particular season.

■ ■ ■ ■

PROLOGUE:
MY MOTHER'S
FLOWER PATH

■ ■ ■ ■

A mother is the truest friend we have, when trials heavy and sudden fall upon us; when adversity takes the place of prosperity; when friends desert us; when trouble thickens around us, still will she cling to us, and endeavor by her kind precepts and counsels to dissipate the clouds of darkness, and cause peace to return to our hearts.

— WASHINGTON IRVING

Washington Irving, the author of the beautiful quote above, also wrote the wonderful short story "Rip Van Winkle" about a man who goes to sleep in the Catskill Mountains for several decades, and when he wakes up, the world around him has drastically changed. He has slept through the death of his wife, the growth of his daughter, life has transformed around him, yet he has no

15

memory of the passing of time. I read that story as a kid, and hated it. Beautifully written, yes, but what an unbearable loss it seemed.

My mother too has spent many wonderful days in the Catskill Mountains while visiting my family on our property in upstate New York. She has played with my kids, canoed on the lake, planted in the garden, and slumbered on the hammock. Unlike Rip Van Winkle, however, my mother hasn't slept through life's momentous events. In fact she has participated fully in the growth of her children, the death of her husband, the births of her grandchildren, and all of the miraculous moments that life has gifted her, but she also has no memory of the passage of time. She has Alzheimer's disease. I will never stop yearning for her to wake up and simply need an update on the last twenty years, rather than an update on her entire life. In this book, I do for my mother what she can no longer do. I remember.

My memories are not fact. Science says our memories change each time they are recalled, and that no two people's memories are the same, even if they are recalling the same event. Memories are affected by emotion and perspective. As one of five children, I am grateful to have shared so many wonderful childhood experiences with my siblings, but I know these don't necessarily translate into duplicate memories. So these memories are mine, of my adventures with my mother.

This is not a disease where one can "make lemonade from lemons," there is nothing good about Alzheimer's, and I resist even a nod toward accepting its ravages. But I will say that my beautiful mother has managed to teach me, even through the destruction of her capabilities and creativity, that there *is* such a thing as indestructible spirit. Pursue your dreams, now. Be in the moment, now. Fill your head with good loving thoughts, now. These are gifts from my mother, learned over the years, but especially poignant as the one place she lives the most fully is in the "now." She cannot remember the past. She cannot imagine the future. But she is fully aware of the *now.* Through a daughter's eyes, I share her stories in hopes of keeping her legacy alive.

Grief and loss have cycles, like the seasons. Sometimes loss can spur the planting of new seeds and give birth to a creative rush. Sometimes, however, loss can crush a seed, or force it to lie dormant for years. My mother and I were to experience both of these as we embarked upon the journey for this book.

In December 2003, our lives were about to turn upside down. Mom got on a plane, returning from a great stay at my home in the colorful Catskills to her homeland of Southlake, Texas. She had been busy filming her hoped-for idea of a show — we would call it *The Flower Path* — and in it she would take people all over America (indeed, the world) exploring various exotic flower gardens and occasionally arranging an ikebana flower arrangement, as she had learned how to do so masterfully when Dad was stationed in Yokohama, Japan. While Dad was at sea, Mom, perhaps to stifle her boredom at raising five kids, had taken a Japanese flower-arranging class and discovered an outlet for her spirit.

She had learned that the roots of ikebana were over a thousand years old, and were associated with the the ritual offering of flowers by monks to Buddha, and so the ideas surrounding ikebana were about spiritual harmony. She was told that by placing an arrangement in her home, she could transform the space into one of spiritual reflection and beauty. That certainly sounded appealing to an often single mother of five rugrats all under the age of eleven! She also learned that ikebana was used to mark the seasons, and so, with each arrangement, she celebrated the seasons and events of our lives. She discovered that ikebana is both a spiritual ritual and a fine art, just like painting or sculpture, and that the arrangements follow specific rules. The most important rule being that ikebana flower arrangements form an assymetrical triangle, and the three main stems of the triangle are called *shin, soe,* and *hikae,* meaning heaven, earth, and man.

In wonderment at this art that so majestically captured the entire universe in its philosophy, she curved the gentle line of *shin* and thought of galaxies, she slightly bent the *soe* line, and meditated on Mother Earth, and as she placed the last line, the *hikae,* she thought of mankind, and vowed to preserve the beauty of our natural world. With this cosmos as her guide, she wove chrysanthemums and lavender, pussy willow and hydrangea, roses and driftwood into abstract triangular arrangements. She planted them in ceramic vases of various sizes, bright orange and black, flat and round or tall and crystal, square or modern shapes. She used the kenzan, a metal pronged flower holder, to weigh down the arrangements, spiking the slanted cuts of the calla lilies and laurel branches into its sharp prongs, and what emerged was a piece of Mom herself. Something so stately and lovely and complicated, something so wonderful and full of emotion, a flower arrangement so expressive that it often seemed to undulate with the toil of my mother's particular day, and beckon to me to simply sit, and stare.

I came to think of these arrangements as living sculptures, though, in truth, they weren't really alive. Yet, at the same time, they *were* alive. The branches were still green, the velvet catkins not yet dropped from the willow, and some flowers had yet to bloom and open, causing the arrangement to transform. The Stargazers had yet to crane their creamy necks to the sky.

So, that fall Mom and I were excited to be collaborating, and eager to bring these arrangements and their philosophy together in a flower book and a television show. We were filming in the glorious rust-colored Catskills. It was late October, early November, and Mom had been pulling actor's hours trying to create a ten-minute "pilot" for her garden show, *The Flower Path*. I was producing and writing with her at night, and in the morning we would don our various caps and set about the day, sometimes being makeup artist or prop master, vase puller or vase creator. My then husband, Thad, would review the day's shots and scope light and locations. Mom was arranging flowers she had gathered on the land, or brought in from the New York flower market. She was tramping around the three-hundred-acre property, drinking in the crisp oranges and yellows and red colors of East Coast fall that she missed so much. Early rising at 6:00 a.m. to canoe down to the battered marsh, sneaking up on the beaver dam as the mist slowly rose on the flat and placid surface of the lake, and laughing because in the stillness she actually heard a beaver fart. I can't think of too many people who can claim as much. She was excited, walking down to the dam in Hunter rain boots and a brown Driza-Bone, reaching for the furry cattails that would be featured in an arrangement we would shoot later in the day. We filmed all of it, Thad and I. I did Mom's makeup and fed her the lines. Thad captured the beautiful images and landscape, and my lovely mom.

I fully supported the possibility of a show, but I was surprised when Mom began to express concern about her memory. She would quietly say to me, "Something is

21

wrong. I'm afraid I'm forgetting the simplest of things." She was very private and didn't want anyone to know. Mom had always said she wanted to grow old with a sharp mind, so memory loss was one of my greatest fears for her, too. I tried to dismiss her concerns when I was with her — I certainly hadn't seen anything unusual in her behavior — but I worried that this seed of frailty would prevent her from really being able to carry a show.

For the most part, however, we were in good spirits. I was pregnant and spinning pots in clay-covered overalls and a bandanna, Mom was arranging flowers, the weather was cooling off as November settled in, and we felt the possibility of a bright future — a new beginning for Mom, who had spent the last many months mourning the loss of my father. *The Flower Path* would be a much needed spring awakening, and what better time to plant the bulbs than fall?

Dad had died in 2002 and took with him a trove of pain, and a trunk of love, that he had shared with his beautiful bride, as he so often called her. He had suffered for many months with congestive heart failure, and Mom and my sisters had tirelessly cared for him both at home and in the hospital. He was the toughest man I ever knew, a navy captain and battle commander of ships, and it seemed impossible that a little bacteria he had picked up in the hospital, MRSA, would finally take his life. But it did. It was a punch-in-the-gut loss, his death. He was smart, funny, artistic, brave, domineering, bawdy, and very sentimental. In many ways, my parents were polar opposites, Mom the delicate Dallas lady, Dad the rough and tumble El Paso cowboy turned naval officer. But they were also the yin to each other's yang. There is a moment that perfectly sums up my father. Once, in high school, I was heading out on a date. My father insisted that the young man who was to take me to the movies come in, shake hands, and pay his respects to the father of the house — no curbside pick-up for this officer's daughter! However, at the very moment my date arrived, Dad was in the middle of listening to the opera *La traviata* on the stereo, and he was leaning back in his armchair, swirling his brandy, and waiting in anticipation for one of his favorite arias. "Sit down!" he commanded. We glanced toward the kitchen to see if Mom would save us, but she was busy loading the dishwasher, so we did as we were told and sat on the couch awkwardly, not daring to speak — the room was silent except for the opera. "Listen to the counterpoint," Dad instructed. Then he began translating the Italian: "*piacere . . . amore . . . amore,* now this . . . ," he threw a piercing look right at us and said, "This . . . is about pleasure, and love." My date hunched down deeper into the couch. He wasn't prepared to hear my father talking about love or pleasure. I'm sure it almost seemed a setup. He scooted several inches farther down the couch, away from me. Dad got quieter as the aria approached. "Here it comes . . . here it comes . . . annnnddd." He was now quite literally mouthing the words, attempting the tune, softly, in a sort of accompaniment with the opera singer. He began conducting, his hand swirling the empty air, the other hand swirling the brandy, all the while fully reclined in his armchair. "Annnnd . . . here it is!" His baton hit the down beat and the aria began. Dad's head now fully arched backward and tears were streaming down his face. My date took a sidelong look of desperate confusion at me, but there was nothing we could do; there was certainly no escape, so the three of us sat in the den and listened to Maria Callas fill the air with spectacular song while my dad conducted and sang along. I could see Mom standing still in the kitchen, her head tilted to the side, listening. When it was over, Dad lumbered out of his reclining armchair, wiped his tears, and bellowed, "That's the best Goddamned aria I've ever heard!" Those three words have perhaps never been put together before: *best, Goddamned, aria,* but there it was, the soldier and the artist, in one sentence. "Nice to meet you, lad! Carry on!" Dad said. "Love you, honey," Mom chimed in, and we were sent on our way, with a little bit better appreciation of music and Maria Callas. That was my dad, always learning, always teaching, and seemingly indefatigable.

But by the end of his life, he had been sick for a long time, and had become weak and fragile — and in pain. He was practically a shell of himself, reduced to tubes and hospital beds and homogenous gowns. Far from the navy captain we all knew so well, he was almost unrecognizable. So it was also a terrible, bittersweet relief, his death. I felt guilty to be grateful that he was no longer suffering; I kept hearing his voice, "Pull yourself up by the bootstraps, Marcia Gay." It was hard to let him go.

Mom numbly made her way through the funeral. She sat with composure as the honor guards draped the flag over his coffin, and then pride gave way to tears as they ceremoniously folded the red, white, and blue into a triangle and handed it to her. Finally, as the volley of shots burst forth, so too did her grief. Many empty weeks followed. Feeling an aching loss of companionship, stumbling over disrupted patterns, shocked at habits not necessary anymore, and lonely for purpose and partnership, Mrs. Beverly Harden tried to piece together her past, and look forward to her future. "Step over the cracks; step back into your life," she told herself. She turned to her children, and to her garden club, and to her flowers.

So this leafy air and wood-smoked smell of the iron stove in the pottery studio, this filming and belief in her talent and in the possibilities of a show, this driving companionship that was enjoyed when people worked and created together, was a fuel of gold for Mom, and for me, too. I wanted her to do well. I wanted to help her have a season of blush and rush and highs and work. I wanted her to come home exhausted at the end of the day, sated with accomplishment. I wanted her to meet someone, a dapper sober man, and have sex, slow and romantic and hot and fast. I wanted her to have a fantastic, lively last twenty years.

The memory loss was a nagging concern,

but the burn of it only drifted around the edges of reality at this time. So we could put it off while we worked on our show, and Mom was to return to Texas to come up with twelve months' worth of arrangements so we could write a calendar flower book called *Beverly's Blooms* that we would market along with the show.

She got on a plane to return to Dallas–Fort Worth, and she went home to a quiet, dark house in Southlake. She turned the lights on one by one and prepared for bed, then got the call that no one wants to get. The call that began with "Are you sitting?" The call that broke her heart, as she learned that my brother's children, Audrey Gay and Sander, had tragically died in a fire in New York, along with their mother, Rebecca, my brother's ex-wife. Silence. Grief. A black hole. At the center of this chasm of despair sat my brother. Bearing, bearing, bearing unbearable loss. Mom returned to New York, the family gathered one by one, and nothing has ever really been the same since. Audrey and Sander were two of the most beautiful children, inside and out, that I have ever known, and their brutal deaths shattered our entire family. It was a devastating loss that we are all still processing, and probably will *be* processing for the rest of our lives. What I will say, however, is that now, at the center of this tragic loss, no longer sits my brother; he stands. He is a fierce survivor, and over the years his determination to heal has shone a light for all of us. With strength and resilience he has moved forward. He has heroically rebuilt his life and shown that the human heart is capable of much, and that the human spirit grows toward love.

But healing is a long, complicated, and uncharted road. Unexpected loss turned, for me, into abject fury. Furious that the sun continued to rise. Furious at my helplessness. Furious at my sorrow. The show idea soon washed away, slowly disappearing, like a forgotten spill on the counter. Gone.

Over the last few years, my mother's Alzheimer's disease has mimicked that evaporating spill. That's what the memories seem to do, evaporate. One minute a person's face, or the function of a spoon, is known. The next minute, it has disappeared and is replaced with confusion, or frustration, or amusement. Language tumbles out in no particular shape sometimes, words intersperse that at once make sense but don't. There is a stealthy, cowardly, dangerous protein in my mother's brain neurons that is malfunctioning, causing the toxic buildup to remain in her brain's neural cells rather than being washed away.

In science photographs, this protein often looks like an unruly, tangled flower, but it is not a flower. It is a weed called tau. It covers the path of neural connection like a weed run wild, slowly choking the path of memory. It is this toxicity that seems to be the cause of Alzheimer's, and though mice have been restored to memory in Australia with sound therapy, to date there is no cure for humans. Millions of men and women suffer this barren brain devastation, and the brutality of it enrages me. Rich, fertile minds, PhDs and scientists, plumbers and dancers, doctors, presidents, inventors, teachers, and firemen. Minds that gave birth to life-changing devices and ideas, minds and bodies that raised children and said prayers, and grew old hoping to sit around a fireplace, cozy in an overstuffed couch with their children, slicing into turkey and mashed potatoes, catching up on lives, sharing memories — these minds . . . these people . . . are now deprived of the validation of *the memory* of their lives. They don't remember who they were. Their grandchildren will never know who they were. The histories of these minds become muted, evaporated, and exist only in the storytelling and memory of family, friends, and children.

This is a disease with no dignity, yet my mother has somehow managed to keep hers. Her appreciation of beauty remains as a purifier for her spirit. She notices the cardinals, the blue jays, the mallards, the squirrel hanging upside down on the feeder swinging like a member of the circus. She notices the seasons as they advance, the water rippling on her dark Texas lake, the bluebonnets and Indian paintbrush in April. She is pleased to see her Japanese woodcuts and embroidered peacock pictures on the walls. My mother always made a beautiful home: she filled a space with light and color and aroma, with silk pillows and Japanese tansus made of cherrywood, with marble-covered dressers, with jazz records, and, of course, with lovely flower arrangements that greeted you like a deep curtsy, and a warm hug, when you entered the room.

At her lake home in Texas, we light a fire and watch a movie and I say, "That's me, Mom. In the movie. It's called *The Spitfire Grill*."

She makes the connection between me and the film, and she smiles and nods. "Wonderful," she demurs.

"You visited me on that set, and on Mother's Day we woke up and looked out the window of the old cabin I was renting, and saw my Jeep Grand Wagoneer completely covered in jonquils! Hundreds of them!" I imagine I see a spark of recognition, and go on. "My ex covered the car in jonquils on Mother's Day — maybe two hundred of them!" She laughs, happy to imagine this scene. "He was trying to impress *you, Mom!*"

"Well, he did," she responds, then adds: "That's the happiest flower in the garden, the daffodil." I am thrilled that she had made the connection between *daffodil* and *jonquil.* For some reason I always call them *jonquils,* maybe because once I heard Katharine Hepburn call them that, but Mom prefers *daffodils.* Yes! She has remembered that they are the same thing! A small but important victory. Mom had once described this sweet yellow flower to me. "The daffodil seems to be smiling at me. It is proud to be up and blooming and greeting everyone it sees. It has on a beautiful new petticoat and a bonnet, it must be the happiest flower in the garden, ready to start the new year," she said. I tell her that, and remind her that she also taught me how to slide a wet pipe cleaner made of chenille inside the daffodil stem, so that it could bend to one's whim in an arrangement. "Oh, that would be a good idea," she says.

Time is full of telling my mother who she was, and the information sits on the periphery of her brain, dangling like a girl's swinging feet off of a bridge. There is a moment of lift as she relates the story to herself, yet it swings there in the air, not connecting to any path.

Unbearable loss. I want to plant her feet firmly on the path.

"Mom, you used to be president of Ikebana International in Washington, DC."

"Oh . . . that's nice."

Rip Van Winkle, go to hell. I want to write a different story, a defiant story, where my mother's legacy will not be sleep, but rather the resilience and beauty of her spirit and a celebration of her art.

"Mom, we are writing a book about flowers."

"Oh . . . that's nice. If they'll let us."

At first, I'm not sure who she means by "they," but then I realize that "they" is all of it — all of *loss,* all of the ravages of time: the deaths of loved ones, aging, divorce, relocating, broken hearts, sorrow, trauma — all of the shit that "loss" puts in the way of following our dreams. But Mom and I are ready to embrace this journey. I am, after all, the daughter of a woman with an unbreakable spirit; strong and resilient and ever growing toward love, and we have picked up the notes and pieces of the book we had started so many years ago in the Catskills. We have gathered vases and flowers, and unearthed memories. Let us walk with *shin, soe,* and *hikae.* Let us take you on a journey through the seasons of my mother's flower path.

.

SPRING

■ ■ ■ ■

My Mother is
a Brightly
Ribboned Maypole

■ ■ ■ ■

It is may day. It's my first memory of my mom and her love of flowers.

Standing on tippie toes, I peek through the window and watch the morning light slide down the street. The block is quiet. The chatter of crickets slowly fades as dawn stealthily creeps across dew-drop-green lawns, then slithers over curbs and sprinklers. Soft rays now pool in small puddles, like golden mercury, and are reflected momentarily in the still water next to the battered neighborhood hoses. Sunlight advances over a sleeping dog twitching on the patch of threadbare grass, then glides between forgotten plastic garden toys scattered around the cul-de-sac. Now swirling in eddies like sun-melting butterscotch, the golden mercury spreads relentlessly, then seems to evaporate. I gazed mesmerized as glorious light gently drifts higher and higher up the trunks of swaying palms, over the tops of trees and houses. Nests of baby robins blink in surprise, awakened by the passing floodlight. The light is softer than the glare it will soon become — here in this small ranch house neighborhood, just west of Disneyland, in Garden Grove, California.

The sun peeks through the window of our house. It chases me across the carpet and lands on my toe for one second before climbing the wooden table leg and washing over what seems to be a garden spread amongst spoons and Lucky Charms–filled bowls.

My older sisters each have a cluster of bouquets: iris, roses, a bird-of-paradise, some dandelion stuck in by the smallest of hands. We children call dandelion balls a "magical weed." We take delight in blowing the fluffy cotton buds and chasing "the fairies" as they are released and drift through the air, blowing until their stem stands alone, stripped naked. *Naked fairies* — it seemed so forbidden.

The night before, my sisters and I had gathered all the flowers with Mom. Dressed in our cotton pajamas, Mom in her nightie, we had separated the sprigs into little piles so that we would each have an equal crafting opportunity. Some flowers had come from the garden, like the lavender, rose, and azaleas; some had come from Ralph's grocery store, like the puffy angel's breath; and some had come from the roadside, like regal Queen Anne's lace. With store-bought white doilies we created cones, then glued blue and pink and yellow and green silk ribbons to the cones to make a handle. We had made the tags using crayons, and stapled them to the handle. Some years, when money was tight, we would use little strawberry baskets instead of cones, and the bunches of flowers had garden leaves included instead of store-bought angel's breath. But regardless of how much money we did or didn't have, we always carried out the tradition of May Day.

The brightly ribboned nosegays are carefully laid out in a cardboard box.

Mom, wearing a blue A-line skirt and white button-up-the-front blouse, and for jewelry a blue stone necklace but no earrings — because, as she was taught in her elegant Dallas home, "pierced ears are for cheap girls" — begins to sort the clusters.

Her soft drawl: "One for the Kraufchecks. One for the Joneses. One for the Kolariks. One for the Morgans. One for that house on the end of the loop — I don't know what her name is, but she is old and really nice."

Mom was like that, always looking out for others, always wanting to include people,

41

especially old ladies, in the niceties of life. And a May Day bouquet was definitely one of the niceties of life, sure to bring a smile and a spot of beauty into someone's humble home.

The tradition was always the same: knock knock. Wait. Silence. Stomachs lurch. Knock knock. Nothing. Then . . . distant footsteps fall, clicking the parquet flooring on the other side of an oaken door. Knock knock . . . again, quickly now, and little hands hang the ribbon on the doorknob, lavender and white angel's breath spraying out the top, and garden flowers peeping out of the doily cone so carefully glued just hours before. A happy may day tag carefully written in cursive crayon dangling from the ribbon.

"RUN!" Giggle. "GET DOWN!" Giggle giggle. "HIT THE DIRT!" We wait: the door creaks open and the mother of the house discovers the bouquet. We keen as she murmurs "How niiice," then loudly proclaims to the morning dew, "I wonder just *who* could have left this pretty little bouquet on my porch?" Our giggles sneak in the crack of her door as it closes, and we run on to the next house, and the next, and the next, until our cardboard box has only a crushed flower or two scattered in its bottom.

It is a tradition I have enjoyed since I was five years old — one that I passed along to my own three children, and one that they will pass along to theirs (or so they say). Few people remember this little holiday, but when I lived in Harlem and my kids and I were running up and down the block leaving aromatic bouquets, some of the old-timers nodded with delight and said, "Ahh, yes . . . May Day! Now just *who* could have done left this little bunch of pretty flowers on my stoop!?" My kids and I giggled just as I had once giggled with my own siblings. We hid behind the cars parked on the street and ran on to the next brownstone once the old-timers' wrought iron gates had squeaked shut.

How did this tradition start, this ritual that has become such a sweet little part of my life? How did my mom start doing it? Did she and her mother, Coco, run through her Dallas neighborhood leaving garden gifts on the first of May in the 1940s? Or did she walk slowly with her stately grandmother, Mammy Riddler, who wore pearls even in the morning? Why do I not know so many things that could fill out and enrich the story of my mom? How can I tell my kids exactly *who* my mom was — and thus, who I am — and *why,* in this age of instant communication and technology, do I have so little record of the past?

I know that, historically, the ancient Romans may have been the first celebrators of May Day, with the festival of Floralia occurring sometime in April and celebrating the Roman goddess of flowers, Flora. I know May Day marks the beginning of spring and is often celebrated with dances around a ribboned maypole, young girls and boys weaving in and out of each other in a circular rhythm, the crowning of Queen May, and the giving of little anonymous baskets of sweets or flowers. And I know that since we were doing this May Day activity in California *before* we moved to Japan, Mom's love of flowers and gardening didn't begin with ikebana — the Japanese art of flower arranging that she learned several years later — but, in fact, predated it.

The innocence of the virgin village girls dressed in white with flowers in their hair and jasmine necklaces drooping around their necks and scenting their breasts and bodies, is something that would have appealed to my mom. She liked traditions, celebration days, sensuality, purity, virginity.

She liked gathering community together through the arts, beauty, and flowers. She was my Bluebird leader; she took us camping under the stars, and skating at the roller rink; she helped organize Campfire Girl fun for my sisters. She liked activity, joyous activity. And it's funny, because in some ways the maypole festival is pure and virginal and uncomplicated — a simple act of dancing with ribbons, wrapping them around a pole, and celebrating spring and new beginnings — but in many ways the underbelly of May Day is just the opposite. It is also a celebration of mating and fecundity and all the birthing and blossoming that explodes in the spring. I wonder what happened in ancient times when the sun set on May Day. Did the festival transform? Did feasting and drinking dominate the night? Did the dance of the virgins arouse men, the young boys, the girls themselves?

Would what happened after dark have scared my gentle mom — the feeling of being preyed upon, of being defenseless in the wake of lust and uncontrolled desire? Nightlights were always scattered around our house in the hallways and the bathrooms. Perhaps the dark represented a scary freedom that my mom never knew, and possibly, never wanted to know.

■ ■ ■ ■

She was brought up in the age of no birth control. Which I can't even imagine — birth control is such an obvious game changer for women. The difference between my mom's generation and mine concerning women's sexual freedom, attitudes, and presence in the workplace feels more like the difference between a hundred years than just a mere twenty years. Social mores allocated the word "slut" to a woman who enjoyed sex, and "stud" to a man who enjoyed the same. Just the *feeling* of desire seemed to be condemned: if a woman (especially a wife or daughter) was flirtatious, or dancing wildly, or dressed even minutely in a sexy or formfitting way, she was looked down upon. "Loose, tramp, and whore" were the reputations of women who were independent and sexual in the fifties. So it makes sense that my mom never spent much — or any — time as a "single" woman exploring her sexuality while slightly inebriated, as so many of our young girls do today. (Or as I did in college . . .) Instead, she settled down at nineteen years of age, after two years of attending the University of Texas. She married her college sweetheart, NROTC candi-

46

date Thad Harden, and ten months later she gave birth to her first child, a beautiful girl named Leslie. Within ten years, she had five children. With my dad away at sea, much of her "nightlife" was spent changing diapers, attending to her bustling household, and likely falling exhausted into bed at 9:30 p.m. Mostly on her own, with very little help, she did laundry and schoolwork and made breakfast, lunch, and dinner. She cleaned and shopped, and she locked the doors at night to keep us all protected. We didn't have a home security system as so many people do today. We had a brass chain that mom slid in the door as the stars rose in the night sky. She shut and locked the windows, and she drew the curtains closed so the Peeping Tom in the neighborhood couldn't see her, or her children. In the mornings, she threw the curtains open and let in fresh light and fresh air and sunshine creeping across the floor, glad to have made it to another beautiful California day. Maybe that's why she now loves the sunshine so much. And toothy bright smiles and unfettered joy. And yellow kitchens, and the song lyric "Blue skies smiling at me . . ." She loves the *good* things of life, the pleasant scents, the positive, the seen, the known.

She was, and is, one of the bravest women

I have ever met. And even as the pitch-black darkness of this hideous disease called Alzheimer's advances, the core of my mom has remained the same. I think of it as her light that cannot be extinguished. She has forgotten so much, sometimes her own childhood or even the names and faces of her children, yet she has not forgotten her own personality. It possesses her, it clothes her, and bleeds with her, it shines all around her. She didn't suddenly become someone who could condone, for instance, a messy home. She knows that she likes polite children. And beds that are made up. She loves birds, and classical music, and she hasn't suddenly developed a tolerance for, let's say, AC/DC. The Beach Boys, Gary Puckett & the Union Gap, Petula Clark — this is her music. She is neat, almost prim, and as her memory fades, it is remarkable to see how the foundation of her *character* remains intact.

Sometimes it's hard to know where my mother leaves off and I begin. We love so many of the same things. We are, I am forced to admit, old-fashioned. Which is okay for my mom, but for me? *Yikes.* There was always the desire to be hip, somewhat cool, certainly tough, and definitely edgy. (I'm an actress, for God's sake! Am I not glamorous? Shouldn't I at least insist upon *vegan* marshmallows in my hot chocolate?) And yes, while I am all those things, I am also my mother's daughter, and share almost exactly in the delights and pleasures that she does. Not only do I share in them: I pass them down to my own daughters and son. I replicate the nighttime reading in bed, the notes from the tooth fairy and fairy godmother, the planting of tulips in the spring.

My mother loves spring. She loves Mother Goose and church bells. She loves warm water between her toes on clean bright sand. She loves pretty hair and ladies in dresses and pearls. She loves tulips, and aromatic Stargazers, and night-blooming jasmine. At least I *think* she loves night-blooming jasmine — but maybe that's just me. If I ask her, she'll say, "Oh, yes . . . of course!" But she won't really remember. She loves cherry blossoms and the Fourth of July. Fireworks and Gregorian chants and Dave Brubeck. She loves family and puns. She loves magazines. She loves arched eyebrows and clean skin. She loves travel. She loves to move. She loves to teach. She is all these things she loves, and so much more . . . and so much more that I don't know.

Does she feel heartache from the confines

of her wheelchair as she struggles to remember her *self*? I do. I feel it. While visiting Mom in Texas, I think of something Peter O'Toole once said in a rather melodramatic movie I did with him called *Christmas Cottage,* about the painter Thomas Kinkade. "Don't get old." That's what his character said. Several times. Once with periods after each word. "DON'T. GET. OLD." I think of it now, with Mom. She is stooped, bending over her red walker and walking with such an enormous effort that it hurts to simply watch. The effort for her is not the walking itself, but to remember what to do. To remember where to put her foot; how to move it forward. She wills herself to accomplish the journey, and then moves one slippered foot toward the red leg of the walker. Then, the other foot moves an inch. And so we go. The flowered legs of the walker, and then Mom's own two legs — until ten minutes later she finally sits, exhausted, safe in the wheelchair. She sits quietly and waits, hoping for a hummingbird to pass through the view of the window. A victory to have made it to the dinner table. She watches the cardinal and the blue jay flit to the bird feeders, which my sister Leslie has positioned perfectly outside the window, ensuring that Mom can always have a happy view. I watch her smiling at the birds and remember May Day. Her energy flows into me like the mercury sunlight seeping across the lawns: For a moment she looks up and smiles, and in that tiny glimmer I know *she* knows she is loved. Nothing else matters for a while.

Later that day, I am happily reminded that though she is losing her memory, she hasn't lost her wit. She is still funny, with a crackpot sense of humor, and she has a great time ribbing me. In the afternoon, when I say "Mom, I am going to turn your chair around so that instead of facing the coffee cup, you can face *me* as I dust these pictures on your tansu! See, Mom, I will shake my butt and dust just for you!" And I demonstrate a rousing and lascivious version of me dusting and wiggling my butt. She responds, "I would rather take the coffee," and we laugh and laugh.

There are facts I know only because I was told them. The facts are attached to vague pictures in my head — snapshots, really — and then feelings get attached to these snippets of memory. And then there is memory itself.

Fact: I was born in La Jolla, California, in Scripps Memorial Hospital in a room with a view of the sea. It was the only room they had left. The previous patient hadn't wanted it because of the sound of the waves; she thought them bothersome. But my mom was thrilled to hear the waves and see them crash as she awaited the final hours of her pregnancy. I even have a painting that my great-grandmother did of the La Jolla cliff that my mom could see from her hospital window.

(Parenthetical fact: As my marriage was coming to an end in 2011, I was performing *God of Carnage* in Los Angeles and was spending the time between performing the play and homeschooling my kids, crying and in denial that my marriage was over. During my kids' Easter break, we joined my sister Stephanie's family at a resort in La Jolla, and I accidentally fell off a single bed as one of my children unexpectedly jumped across the expanse from the other bed to hug me. My daughter landed in my arms and threw me off balance, and we started to fall toward the opposite bed. Time slowed down. We were falling and her head was aiming for the lower metal rail of the bed with 140 pounds of me on top of her. I could see the rail coming, almost in slow motion, and in that split second I knew that if she hit her head she would be seriously hurt, and somehow I managed to twist around so she was on top of me, and hit the back of my neck on the rail instead. I slammed into the rail and lay on the floor, breathless. The wind had gotten knocked out of me and it took me a few minutes to recover. I stood up, weak-kneed, and almost passed out. I went to the bathroom, and didn't have the strength to pull my pants down, so my sister helped me.

On the way back to the bedroom to get my keys so I could begin the drive back to Los Angeles — I had a performance of the play that night — I slowly hugged my children good-bye, brightly assuring them that I was fine, and then I full-on fainted. I was taken by ambulance to the same hospital where I had been born, Scripps Memorial. I woke up as we pulled into the hospital, the scream of the sirens now slowing down to a low growl, and realized that I was on my own, and that my husband wasn't in love with me anymore, and that in some ways this small brush with oh my God *death* was a kind of rebirthing for me. Hopefully I wasn't damaged from the fall. Hopefully I could make the drive back to downtown LA and perform that night. Hopefully I could accept that my marriage was over, start anew, give my kids a great life, and eventually find love somewhere. I was wheeled into a curtained cubicle, and in tears in the emergency room I sobbed to the doctor that I had been born there, and how weird it was that here I was again and I hoped I wasn't going to die there, and how crazy that my marriage was *really* over, and wasn't this a funny full circle to be back in this hospital, and also was I okay to drive? An hour later, still in tears, now sobbing to the technicians that my marriage was over and what were the results of the scan — and oh by the way did I have brain damage? Two hours and several ice packs later, with technicians and doctors waving good-bye in the loading dock wishing me good luck in my "over with" marriage and also the play, I swallowed the aspirin with codeine that I was to take only when I got to the stage, buckled up with a *very* stiff neck, and began the three-hour drive from La Jolla to downtown Los Angeles. I vowed not to call my husband, but to wait for him to call me. Right out of the driveway I immediately dialed his number, looking for sympathy (perhaps my near-death experience would save my marriage?). He said how sorry he was that I was hurt, and then, quite clearly, that he thought we should proceed with a divorce. I passed Laguna Beach in a blur.

Heartache heartache heartache.

Now what? I called my mom. She said God must've put me in that same hospital, in that same place, with a big hit on my head, to help me realize that my marriage was over. She said I had always had to learn the hard way, and I should be grateful that God had hit me on the head. She asked why did I think I was doing a play called *God of Carnage* about a marriage that was ending? She said it meant something that I had been taken to same hospital where I had been born, and I should take it very seriously. She said it was to be a rebirth. Rebirth. That notion seemed so scary, at fifty-one years of age. Scary, but hopeful.) That's the end of my parenthetical fact. I did take it seriously.

Fact: Back at Scripps Memorial hospital, I came into the world as my mother was laughing. The hour was 2:00 a.m., and the doctor was sleeping. My father stormed off to get him, commanding my mother to "hold it, Beverly!" The madder my dad got, the more my mom laughed. "Goddamned son of a bitch, where is that Goddamned doctor?" he cursed. "Damnit! Hold it, Beverly!" She winced, then laughed. I was coming and wouldn't be held back, and with a great degree of ease Mom delivered me just as the doctor arrived. That was part of the reason that my middle name turned out to be Gay: the merriment of my mother during that moment had to be honored.

Fact: Speaking of names, I was the middle child of five children, each with their own special nickname. There was Leslie, nicknamed Lezle, then one year later Sheryl, nicknamed Sheryl-Bird, then one year later, me. Somehow I earned the nickname "Marcia-Mutt," which my sisters later shortened to Marcia-Mudd, then just Mudd. A few years later, my brother Thaddeus Mark was born, but he was always called Mark because my dad was already Thad. And finally, a few years after Thaddeus, came the youngest of us, Stephanie. I loved her nickname, which Dad would sing: "Stephanie Deeee Diiinggg DONNNGG." That was our big little family: Mom and Dad, Leslie, Sheryl, me, Mark, Stephanie, and a cat named Elmer.

Fact: We lived in La Jolla, then Carmel-by-the-Sea, where I have a vague memory of the woods and a rope swing and going into the woods alone with a girlfriend and her brother when I wasn't supposed to. It is a little bit of a creepy memory — and exciting, because we all swung on the huge rope swing and ran back from the woods when we heard my mother calling. I got in trouble for that one. There is a vague memory of a disastrous Easter when I couldn't find any eggs. A vague memory of chasing my sisters on a bike, all the while jealous that they were faster. Glimpses of feelings, a snapshot of going to a funeral with my mom, a snapshot of accompanying Mom to a trailer park where we dropped off our ironing to a wispy, brown-haired woman in a polyester T-shirt who smiled a chipped-tooth smile. A body memory of pushing a doll on a swing. A body memory of spanking the doll, because she was a "bad girl" and had fallen off the swing. A feeling that my mom liked me, even loved me, but the absolute knowledge that she wasn't partial and didn't play favorites. A sketchy memory later verified by Mom of me coming out so proudly one morning and announcing "I got dressed all by myself!," and indeed the clothing was matching, it was a job well-done. Remembering Mom not wanting to praise me too much because it might go to my head. And a physical memory of being hugged and enveloped by a kind black woman. Apparently we had had a babysitter when I was three or four, and I just loved her. She was a plump woman with large breasts, and she would wrap me up in her arms and hold me tight, with her head thrown back, laughing. It is perhaps the safest I have ever felt. Even if I do not fully recall the woman, I recall the emotion.

But real memories of visual clarity don't really begin until we moved to Garden Grove, California. I was five years old.

I remember a girl with a barking German shepherd up the street. I remember when she tried to fondle me in the ditch in the park near Ralph's grocery store. I remember when my sister told me Santa wasn't real, and she got in trouble because I was inconsolable. (I felt horrible that she got in trouble. And I felt horrible that Santa was dead. And I felt horrible that I couldn't stop crying.) I remember ants in the backyard. I remember a summer plastic blow-up pool, and I remember stubbing my toe in the driveway and Mom putting stinging iodine on it, soothing me with her cool voice and cooler hands. I remember going to the beach with my family and getting covered in tar, then using turpentine and a hose in the driveway to get it off.

And I remember my mom, not yet as a friend, but more as a presence, a presence of love and gentleness and resigned discipline. A presence of beauty. A stabilizer. A tuck-you-in-at-night mom. A woman making her home and garden beautiful, creating a practical nest for her chicks. She didn't do it to compete with the neighbors for the "prettiest yard" award; she did it because as she put her steel key in the front door, she loved the smell of the gardenia in bloom, and she would angle her brown curly hair toward the plant, inhaling for a second before she dragged the paper bags of groceries across the floor in the foyer.

In the California neighborhood of our May Day sneak-a-thons, the Garden Grove moms could be seen on weekends in cotton shorts and collared yet sleeveless cotton shirts planting spring bulbs. This was the midsixties, no T-shirts for these middle-class moms, no sweatpants, canvas shorts, or jeans. To school, their daughters wore dresses, or skirts and blouses (always tucked in, *thank you very much*), skipping in white socks and two-toned shoes or penny loafers or Keds. So their mothers were not sloppy in their gardens, even as they planted. They consumed icy tall glasses of lemonade on their breaks, with perhaps a sprig of mint for garnish.

We lived in a small neighborhood of three-bedroom ranch houses, of cul-de-sacs and side streets and loops that wove out to the main artery where Ralph's and McDonald's and Jack in the Box beckoned. On our street, serendipitously called Beverly Lane, there were cement-block fences, green grass, rubber trees, cactus, and flowers. Our neighbors — the Kraufchecks — had an orange and a lemon tree, and we had our gardenia bush. There were also succulents and tropical bushes and trees in our yard, and to the right of our sidewalk hopscotch game, we had a palm tree.

Today, I have a snobbery about cul-de-sacs, a distaste for small ranch houses. The seeming sameness makes me feel hopeless; I feel like I am trapped, almost drowning, going round and round the dead-end circle looking for the exit. The dark windows of the houses scare me, and I get an overwhelming sense of *We will never get ahead. We will never be special if we live in that house where I can see all the walls, where the ceiling is low. Where the lights are off. Where I am like everyone else.* I panic. I can't seem to pass these houses without wondering about the lives within. I get quite melancholy, wondering if the inhabitants are happy, and as I drive by I think, "That's not me. Nope, that house isn't me. Nor that one." As if the house defines the person. As if I will become a person whose eyes need washing like the windows need washing, whose porch needs painting, whose yard needs mowing, whose trash need emptying. Or if I lived in a wealthier neighborhood, I would become a white-bread conservative with 3.2 kids. So I look for treehouses, boathouses, stone cottages, Japanese designs and colonial pillars, something to define the quirk of the home, something to insist on personality. Most of which is too expensive for me to afford, so I stay in my third-floor walk-up and lug suitcases up and down the stairs when we travel, and so for now I am that girl, that mom, the one who lives in an anonymous third-floor walk-up and lugs suitcases up and down the stairs, and barks at her children to help. The one who lives near the beach and is satisfied that the beach itself provides the quirk, even though I don't really surf and only sometimes ride my bike on the boardwalk. My aversion to certain houses is rather ridiculous, really, certainly inexplicable, because I do believe we were happy as kids in our little neighborhood in Garden Grove. Happy in our little house. Jumping on the bed and playing pirates as we walked the gangplank. Pretending we were heading out to sea.

Long Beach marked the beginning of my father's voyages to sea. He had been on a navy path to become a pilot, but that had come to an abrupt end when a small plane he was flying during training in San Francisco lost both engines and began hurtling toward the Bay Bridge. The plane stood a good chance of hitting the structure, and my father had to make a split-second decision: should he abort the plane and parachute out, saving his own life but risking the lives of others, or should he stay with the plane, steering it clear of the bridge and crash into the water, and almost surely die? He crashed. And saved lives. And, miraculously, survived. He claimed that his training had simply taken over, that he hadn't thought about it, that the moment he hit the water, he had begun an automatic series of movements to unbuckle his belts and eject from the plane. There is a picture of him looking so handsome in a hospital bed with a bandage on his head, and my mom sorrowfully leaning into him. I just know she was begging him *not* to be a pilot, to change, to go to sea instead. Which he did, perhaps begrudgingly, but soon he came to love the ocean with a passion.

In Garden Grove, we were close to Knott's Berry Farm and close to brightly colored Disneyland, and closer still to the gray steel ships in the Long Beach harbor, where my father drove to work.

When he was called to duty, we had the departure ritual. After breakfast, Mom cleaned the kitchen and supervised our getting dressed. Then as Dad sat impatiently in the car drumming on the wheel, Mom finished picking up and locking all the windows. We spent the morning crowded in the station wagon, all five kids, elbows purposefully poking into whomever we were sitting next to. The hard elbows were a way of defining space: "DON'T you DARE touch me! This is MY imaginary line!" "Stop it!" would be fiercely whispered because God forbid Mom or Dad should get involved. Even in the way back, bandaged knees and elbows remained rigid as the last two kids divided up the rear spaces, each of us searching for something to call our own.

Driving the few miles to port, smoothing wrinkles in my green and gold plaid skirt and white blouse with the lace collar, I watched my mom as her eyes darted with the moving landscape. Was she happy? She was playing the role of Military Wife beautifully. Here we all were, dressed so spiffily, and she had her hair perfectly waved and a green cotton checked dress on, and she was preparing for him to be at sea for three months? Or maybe even six months? She would be on her own, probably not so lonely — because five kids is a lot of distraction from loneliness — but then still . . . lonely.

Lonely for love and for a man and for the jazz music that they played together. Lonely for naps. Once I walked into their room during a nap. Mistake. Blurry shapes and noise . . . Dad barked at me to "shut the Goddamned door." *Gulp.*

Lonely for naps, she would be.

When we arrived at the dock I felt so special as we were waved in by official navy personnel. Dad parked the car and we all spilled out, pulling up socks and tucking in shirts so that we would be presentable as the five children of Lieutenant Commander Thad Harden. The dock smelled of pine and hemp and tires and tar. We gathered on the pier, black water ominous through the cracks of the wood, and stared up at the immensity of the ship, imagining it protecting him during a bombing, or, God forbid, maybe not protecting him at all, maybe sinking with the sharks! And we waved and waved good-bye to our brave heroes on top of the ship, waved till our arms hurt, hundreds of arms waving on the dock, hundreds of other wives and children waving farewell, farewell to their husbands and brothers and fathers. A sea of hands waving on one side, and on the other side, sailors and officers lined up on the deck of the ship with white hats disappearing into the white clouds and white gloved hands folded behind their backs, legs apart and eyes straight ahead, men going off to sea. Men going off to war. Music played. A horn blasted three times and we all jumped. The ship began to inch away. The men didn't flinch. The ladies cried. The kids wiggled. Some were relieved because military dads were notoriously strict, but they hid it, the relief, and tried to look sad. The band played a lively tune, sunlight glinting off of tubas and shiny jet wings, and sometimes we watched until the ship was a tiny speck on the horizon. Then we climbed back into the car, Leslie in the front passenger seat because she was the oldest, and we drove away with more space, and relaxed elbows, studying my mom's face in the mirror as she carefully eased her car onto the highway, watching to see if she was crying or not.

We returned home, remembering how the night before we had all gone to Taco Bell as a special occasion because it was Dad's last night and he was leaving for the sea and we wouldn't see him for maybe five months or maybe forever, so we had splurged on beef tacos "TO GO." Dad played Herb Alpert & the Tijuana Brass band in the living room when we got home. The album was *Whipped Cream & Other Delights,* and on the front was a beautiful Spanish lady sitting in a white gown made entirely of whipped cream. Even the white flower on her head was whipped cream, and I could tell it was sexy, that the picture on the album was sexy. She was brown-skinned and naked under the creamy gown, her brown breasts scented with whipped cream — unlike the jasmine scented white virgin breasts of the maypole dancers. Her flower you could lick off of her dark brown hair. This *mamacita* was unlike any woman I had ever seen! And then I imagined my own mamacita naked, covered in whipped cream, smiling at the camera. It was such a racy thought, it made me giggle. I remembered "shut the Goddamn door," and naps.

Dad was proud of the picture on the album, I could tell, and he was proud of the speakers and stereo they had bought. The speakers were a big piece of furniture, and flanked the long stereo cabinet, and when the music was loud it was fun to dance in front of them, my eardrums pounding with the Mexican beat. I danced pretending I was the whipped cream lady, swirling my hips and flinging my hair, stamping out a kind of salsa. Then Mom played another album. We stared at the spinning black record . . . and in anticipation said, "Wait for it . . . wait for it" . . . the needle scratching around for a few seconds . . . "Wait for it!" . . . YES! She put on our favorite song. It was "Tequila"! She turned it up really, really loud: it was the Wes Montgomery version, and we all danced in the living room. Waving our brightly colored napkins like the ribbons of a maypole, we sang "Da da da da da da da dummm, da da da da da da DAHHHH," and shouted "TEQUILA!" at the top of our lungs. We danced behind the speakers, and popped out on "Tequila!" It became an impromptu game of hide-and-seek: we hid behind the couch, popping out on "Tequila!," we hid and looked for each other down the hallway and in the bedrooms, music blaring through the small house, shouting "come out, come out, wherever you are," and we screamed with delight when one of us popped out of the coat closet, perfectly timed to "Tequila!" Still in the living room, Mom and Dad danced in little salsa whipped cream steps, then stood in the kitchen and drank Dos Equis beer because it was from Mexico, and we kids drank milk because, well, we were kids, and we danced around them both, swinging our napkins and shouting "TE-QUILA!," shaking our bums, and dancing wildly, wrapping our napkins around them like a Mexican maypole.

Years later, in Texas, I sit at the gleaming dining room table, with mom in her wheelchair. I play the old song for her on my iPhone. They say music from the past can spark memories in Alzheimer's patients, and so I amplify the sound through my small portable Bose speaker. She is astonished at the technology, even though I have shown her this speaker, and played music off of it several times before. Just the day before I had played Pachelbel's Canon, and she was mesmerized with the repeating melody, and astonished at the Bose technology. She is always astonished anew. Now she smiles, and taps her stocking foot to the beat. My heart aches, in rhythm to the beat, and in sync with her small cold foot. *Heartache, heartache, heartache. Tap tap tap.* Mom. Oh my dear mom. *Tap Tap Tap. Da da da da da da da dummm.* She remembers, and whispers: *"Tequila!"* perfectly in time with the song. *Heartache. Tap tap. Heartache. Tap. Tap.* Where are all the details hiding in her brain?

Da da da da da da da dummm. Come out,

come out, wherever you are. *Da da da da da da daaaa.* Olly olly oxygen free. Olly olly income free. I never knew what it was — "oxygen" or "income." "Oxen," Google tells me. "Olly olly *oxen* free." Come out, come out, wherever you are. *Da da da da da da daaa dummm* . . . Please, come out. Hide-and-seek memory of music and maypoles.

■ ■ ■ ■

My Mother is a Crescent Moon

■ ■ ■ ■

Mom exploded into the woman I will always remember during the late hippie years of the 1960s, when we were stationed in Yokohama, Japan, where my father had been sent to help command a ship during the middle of the Vietnam War. Everything was about to change. Five children had climbed onto a Pan Am plane in Long Beach, California, and when "fasten your seatbelt" directions were given in English and Japanese (causing me to crane my eight-year-old neck around to see just who could possibly understand this garbled sound, astonished to see that there were actually real live Japanese people on board our plane) and as we looked with rapt and fearful attention at the evacuation water slide that the bottle-blond stewardess pointed out in the plastic pamphlet, and as the airbags were displayed just in terrifying case we needed oxygen, we felt for our life preservers tucked faithfully under our seats, and it finally dawned on us that we were headed thousands of miles away, flying through the night sky across a big black ocean, and that we might end up in a raft surrounded by sharks, but if we were lucky we would make it safe and sound and land in Tokyo. *Ah sō desu ka!*

Our stewardesses were dazzling in their white gloves, with their hair in full buns and sporting red, white, and blue dresses perfectly fitted to their curvaceous bodies. They smiled bright white smiles as they took our orders and quickly became our new best friends. Ahead of us, Mr. and Mrs. Lieutenant Commander Thad Harden were actually sitting in first class. Amazing! Mom and Dad in first class! It felt like *we* were in first class, too, being served a meal on little movable trays in our seats. At home we *never* went out to dinner. It was only on *very* special occasions that we were treated to *Two all-beef patties, special sauce, lettuce, cheese, pickles, onion, on a sesame seed bun* at the newly popular McDonald's — and now, here we were having water and soda brought to us whenever we wanted! When our stewardess with the shiny black hair and a name tag that read "Tamaki" (but of course we called her "mam") asked us if we wanted ice-cream sundaes for dessert, we looked across several seats with eyes raised hopefully, expecting Mom and Dad to say no. But when mom smiled and said, "Okay," we actually squealed, causing the stewardesses to laugh and say how cute we were in our cotton dresses and black-and-white saddle shoes. Free card games were given out to keep us occupied on the long flight, and free pillows and blankets were placed under our tired heads and across our cold bodies as we climbed higher and higher into the stratosphere.

We passed a crescent moon; her rays shot through the clouds and sparkled on some fish in the Pacific far below. Mom began to take shape on that flight; there, in the air, she began her transformation as we jetted toward brightly blinking Tokyo and exotic new landscapes. This hesitant young Dallas mother of five wasn't asked so much to step aside or to sit this one out, but to grow and embrace herself as an elegant woman capable of navigating a naval wife life far, far from home. Far from the safety of her parents still living in Dallas, where Aunt So-and-So had played the piano at family gatherings while Mom's mom Coco sang songs of the forties across from the china and cut glass vases, across from the sparkling ice white Waterford crystal and chalky blue Wedgewood. Farther still from our neighborhood in Long Beach and our gardenia plant in the front yard where we had lived so near to Knott's Berry Farm and Disneyland and a Ralph's grocery store.

Here on this night flight, safely strapped into a giant steel bird winging across the ocean, the moon beckoned to Mom to follow her lead and change shape in the dark of night. And Mom did. She was in fact changing right in front of our eyes. She had, after all, smiled okay to the ice cream. She had managed to tuck her sleepy brood tightly into makeshift beds hundreds of miles high while she pointed to the stars outside the cold round windows, and smiled to her sister moon. She had packed up, rented, and left behind a home with only the help of her kids, each of us packing one box *only* and one suitcase *only,* following military family rules of only so much allotted weight to transfer to their new homes. She had even let me bring my dolls: I had proof of them in my little pink carry-on bag, my favorite paper dolls and my Barbie with the three wigs!

Like a lunar hug, the crescent moon dipped her curved tip toward the Pacific on one side and the Atlantic on the other, and we flew in the center of her bosom, forward in time. Tamaki pushed her steel cart up the aisle and miraculously brought out hot eggs and sausage, which we ate at Pan Am midnight, preparing to land soon in Tokyo. We used the bathroom and screamed when it flushed loudly, but we didn't have to brush our teeth because the water wasn't "potable." That was a new word, learned between Long Beach and Tokyo. Mom rested her forehead against the cool oval window, and stared below as we lowered toward the land and the lights began to glow, first small pinpoints of light, then larger and larger as we circled over our exotic destination. She squinted at the bright neon Tokyo signs flashing, as if the city were a Japanese Las Vegas, signs written in blinking Japanese characters, and traffic zigzagging red and yellow streaks, even at midnight. Mom mimicked the lunar arms of the moon, and hugged her brood deep to her chest, saying a silent prayer of thanks that we had made the flight safely, and we were not on a raft surrounded by sharks. She told us to fasten our seatbelts but our eyes were thick with sleep, so she leaned her Chanel scent over us and secured the straps. I smelled her drift away as she went back to her seat and pulled out her new coral lipstick, which was just a little bit darker than the coral she normally wore. She coated her lips, and she smiled as her children and her husband nodded off to a last hour of blanketed sleep.

During our three-year stay in Japan, the early bloom of my mother that had begun with the night-flight crescent moon somewhere over the Pacific Ocean blossomed into a sexy, elegant, and determined woman. Even long after we returned to the States, my mother continued to grow due to her adventure in Japan. Inspired by her embrace of the city of Yokohama, she found a freedom of spirit, and she fiercely enforced open-minded transformation.

We landed and jolted awake to the wheels screeching across the runway in nighttime Tokyo. Once in the city, we were assaulted with the smells of fish and feces in the open "benjo ditch" sewers, shocked and happy to recognize the Coca-Cola sign changing its accordion lights of red and white in the inky sky of the still-bustling Tokyo. Every scent and sight and sound was new, and we were soon admonished "*Not* to judge! People did things differently here! America wasn't the only game in town!" Even the way we now had to go to the bathroom — oh my gosh! — was different. Their toilets were little holes in the ground with a small platform for each foot beside them. Mom took charge, forcing us to embrace these toilets, to embrace the hotter-than-hot baths, to embrace the seaweed breakfast, and we were not allowed to say "yuck." Mom was changing. We were changing.

When we slumped off the plane in now-wrinkled clothing, our skin shiny from unwashed sleep, Mom was thirty-one years old with five children ranging from two-year-old Stephanie to eleven-year-old Leslie. Five children, little money, no house help until she finally hired Otta-san the ancient maid, and she was soon to be left alone for long periods of time in a foreign land while her husband headed out to an unknown fate fighting on the high seas.

Fueled with her love of travel and sharp curiosity, Mom was determined to plant her homesteading seeds in education and experience, and to relish as her garden of children grew. Yes, Mom changed: she soon wore her curly short brown hair in a longer Catherine Deneuve–type French twist. She bought beautiful linens and in her soft-spoken, slightly drawled voice hired Sumiko the seamstress to sew asymmetrical dresses in oranges and yellow gilded satin, in crimson silk and woven blue. She wore the crimson silk gown with long white gloves to the New Year's Eve ball, her shawl lined with pink satin. Dad, home on leave for the holidays, wore his US Navy formal dress uniform with the medals proudly displayed on his chest and his gold cummerbund around his waist. When Mom and Dad returned home that night — in love again, tipsy, swaying — they came and peeked into our rooms to see their beloved children, flopped onto our single beds, to wake us up because it was the new year. But we kids had already banged the pots and pans outside on the porch at midnight, clanged pot tops and listened to the racket of all the other houses banging pots and pans, all the other kids from Area 1 and Area 2 whose parents were at the ball or at other parties, banging pots and pans echoing across the hills of the navy base in Yokohama, to celebrate.

Mom and Dad flopped on the bed, and she pretended his suspenders were grandfather clocks, giggling "booiiingg, boiiiing" as she pulled at the straps and they snapped back against his chest. They swayed back to their room, still giggling, he now pulling at the straps of her gown and she at his suspenders.

Years later, I wore that same gown to my first Tony nomination, for *Angels in America.* I had to widen the waist a bit because apparently Mom had a twenty-inch waist. Unbelievable.

Soon Dad was back at sea and Mom was visiting Japanese gardens, museums, and temples, where she took off her shoes to keep the tatami mats clean. She now bought woodblock prints of fishermen wearing pointy triangular straw hats who carried poles across their shoulders from which hung barrels of fish. She bought a tansu chest made of thin teak wood in which she could store clothes; it had a secret hiding place for jewels. She studied Hiroshige, and watercolors, and began a love affair with nature in art that never went away. Even now, when she can't quite remember where these beautiful things in her home came from, she traces the lines of the hand-embroidered peacocks she bought for Dad. He loved peacocks: he loved the fact that male birds were fancier than female birds, more exotic and bright; he loved to explain the mating habits of preening birds, the puffing defenses of a quail; and he especially loved the pomp of the peacock. She bought him watercolor peacocks, and cloisonné peacocks on black enamel.

She visited Hiroshima, Osaka, Thailand, Mount Fuji. She brought home chopsticks. She made friends with a woman named Tookie; she took a cruise with Tookie to Cambodia. Standing on the deck of the cruise ship, feeling the spray of the choppy sea on her face, she wiped a salt tear of longing for her husband to come home, yet nervous for her husband to come home changed by the war. Another salt tear flew into the wind — that one was for missing her children. (She never said *kids; kids* was a name for goats, she once told me.) Then she raised her salty face to the sky, gloriously free and alive with a whole world of possibilities ahead of her.

She had hired Otta-san, a seventy-year-old Japanese maid, to help us at home. There were navy wife meetings. There was garden club. There was dinner at the Officers Club with Kennedy half dollars given on your birthday. There was bingo, and there were movies at the exchange. There was the commissary for groceries, there was the New Year's Eve ball. And soon, for Mom, there was ikebana.

Ikebana is the ancient Japanese art of flower arranging. Mom took a class and fell in love with its discipline and its simplicity, with the colors and aromas and the waxy feel of the flowers and leaves. She understood that she could bring a gift home to her family, a gift of love and an expression of care and beauty and yearning. She would place the arrangements throughout the house. She would create an Ikenobo spot for the viewing of the arrangement and then wait for us to come home from a distant day of school in Negishi Heights. She met us as we hopped off the crowded yellow bus, called "Don't run" while we ran across the patchy lawn and skipped across the porch, where later we would perform a play. And she smiled as we burst through the door and gasped in unison to be greeted by such a sight as those flowers.

Pink gladiolus nestled between lime-green bamboo shoots, erupting from a long, low, olive green, square ceramic vase. The arrangements were supposed to mimic nature, to look as if the actual flowers and line materials of branches and leaves could be found in a similar scene if one wandered around a bamboo forest, or took a stroll through a park, or happened upon a pond where the snowy egret made his home. Sometimes the arrangements made me think of luxuriously clad dancers; the irises with their blue and yellow velvet gowns, the frothy tutus of the cherry blossoms, the brightly beaded red pyracantha — each was paired with its natural partner, and the arrangements swirled their way into tangos and ballets and Isadora Duncan stretches, *one-two-arabesque* and *three-four-plié* and now *five-six-reach-to-the-sky,* each standing tall on its stage of a ceramic vase. Then . . . slowly, *seven-eight-,* each shifting slightly as the days passed until they were now drooping, and *nine-somewhat-tired,* aaaaannnd *ten* — certainly faded as they took their final bow, old ladies making space for the ingénues, making space downstage center for the next flower arrangement.

Creating an ikebana arrangement, like the Japanese tea ceremony, is supposed to be a type of meditation. The rooms are quiet when the teacher is presenting the lesson — a wild contrast, by the way, to the raucous scene we experienced years later, in 1998. Mom was teaching an ikebana class to my neighbors in Venice Beach as I was preparing to give birth to my first daughter, Eulala. My friends were mostly gay, some were neighborhood beach buddies, some were actors and actresses, some old college chums, and many already knew Mom. We were a grand, loud, jovial crowd, laughing at our inability to balance the lines of the branches we were using. Wine was poured and someone hollered "HELP ME, BEVERLY." Flowers were strewn about the table at random as Mom showed how to cut the stems under water so the suction created a small vacuum. It was joyful chaos. Mom, soft-spoken, still, and delicate but not yet fragile from the losses of life and memory that were soon to come — that were at that very moment lurking like a cowardly thief just past our calendar's sight — Mom gently walked around the room grinning at our mishaps, shaking her head at these friends who had gathered with tin can vases and Mason jar vases and, thank goodness, a few ceramic bowl vases, gathered to celebrate her, to celebrate me, but mostly to celebrate the new life churning unseen in our midst. It was a fun day. The crashing Venice Beach waves could be heard under the cackle of our joy as we *oohed* and *aahed* at each other's creations. It was a time when Mom could still remember the months and the various flowers associated with each of them. She could remember that tulips bloom in the early spring. She taught us that wisteria loved vodka.

"Whaaaattt?" we crowed.

"Yes — a little vodka poured into the vase

when wisteria is cut will help preserve it."

Years later, as her memory has slowly dissipated, I ask her how she knows that wisteria love vodka. I want to see if she remembers, I want her source of information, it is a sort of test. She replies, "Well, I know wisteria love vodka because . . . I have shared some with it!" Still witty, still smart, still canny buried under this hideous disease.

But back in 1998, in Venice, Mom could remember the ikebana lessons exactly as she had been taught them in her blush of womanhood in Japan. She could remember that in Japan the students bowed low, the masters taught in a black kimono, the rooms were quiet. She could remember that *shin, soe,* and *hikae* meant heaven, earth, and man. Did she remember this — that in this peaceful state of mind, the artist in her first began to bud?

Dad was at sea for extended tours of duty — six months being the longest — fighting a war in Vietnam, stopping off in Cambodia, bringing home the chicken "gilly-gilly" or adobo pork recipes he learned from the Filipino chefs on board his ship, and murmuring with equal vehemence words like "Viet Cong" and "Mekong Valley" and

"Hippies" and "Goddamn Rock and Roll." He was visibly distressed at the unraveling of order and precision he loved so much in the navy. Long hair and beards and sideburns were now allowed, and this galled him, while on the other side of the teeter-totter mom was learning the art of precision and order through flowers.

Leaving his beautiful bride and five children tucked into their beds in the house that sat alone in the middle of the hill, he took to the waves.

We were left behind with our own system of order. We balked and grumbled at the assignments, but there was no choice in the matter. We each had chores. One person set the table, and one person made the salad, and the salad was always the same: iceberg lettuce torn up into bite-size pieces, small carrot discs, a little celery, tomatoes cut in wedges, and dressing on the table. We all cleared the table, secretly counting just how many glasses and plates each of us took from the dining room table to the kitchen, and, sure of an injustice in the making, we bickered at each other to "Heeelllpp or I'll tell Mom!"

One person did the pots and pans, and it seemed like on rice night, it was always me. It was always me so much it became a family joke, and Mom and I still laugh today when I remind her of rice night, mimicking myself scrubbing with fingernails and grimacing at the rice pan.

We drank powdered milk from the commissary. It was horrible and made me throw up, but we had to drink it anyway, and we ate chicken-fried steak because the milk and egg it was coated in made the meal seem more substantial. We bought new shoes for school, one pair only, and only once a year. We went to the library weekly and got to take out three books each. We put on plays. We did our homework and got good grades or else we would get in trouble, and we played flashlight tag on special nights. We took ten-minute showers *only,* and we were allowed five minutes on the hallway phone *only* (and my sisters and I *never* called boys). We ate breakfast and dinner together. We said our "Hallowed be thy name" prayers. We folded our clothes and helped wipe spots off the wall with Comet. We took ballet and charcoal drawing classes, we learned to sew, and there was no TV, so we read books and listened to Harry Belafonte. We waited for Dad to return from the sea, remembering how much fun we had had the last time he had come home and we were specially invited to his aircraft carrier to watch the movie *Patton.* As the executive officer, he had special privileges, and that meant we got to tag along for movie night! All the men saluted sharply when we trooped on board, and I saluted back, until Dad told me knock it off because I was a civilian and it was disrespectful to a man of service. So I just smiled and nodded awkwardly. The seven of us made our way down the steel passageways, me stepping with white lacy socks through cold gray doors and over oval hatches. We were ushered into the officers' lounge and sat on the leather couch, our feet dangling off the edge, not touching the floor, eating popcorn and swaying gently with the sea. The words *bastard* and *Goddamn* peppered the movie, and all the men loved it when Patton said, *"Americans love a winner, and will not tolerate a loser. Americans play to win."* They cheered loudly, when he said, *"I will not have cowards in my army."* "Goddamn right!" agreed my dad. Patton and my father had a lot in common. We looked forward to Dad returning from sea again, and then we used more Comet on the walls, and even though the house smelled antiseptic, it was sparkling clean with no darkness hiding even in the hallway corners. No darkness for an officer returning from the seas.

There was enough darkness in his head. Though he never spoke of it, in his deeply lined eyes we felt his sorrow for the men aboard the captured USS *Pueblo,* and his anger at the humiliation and torture they underwent. Pride and anger mingled in his manner as he walked through the door, but some of the darkness lifted from his smile as he presented "ciggi-booze" for his family. Ciggi-booze was the name given to gifts brought back from the States . . . cigarettes and booze being the most common request from officers and sailors. It felt fun, and slightly risqué, that an adult was bringing ciggi-booze home for the kids! There was scotch and cigars for Dad, Chanel No. 5 perfume for Mom, and for us the phrase meant chocolate-covered caramel, green-and-purple-striped candy sticks, blue barrettes for the hair, and pink bows, and hardcover books, and we especially loved the records. He would pull out the latest Beach Boys record and crank it up loud and we would all learn "If everybody had an ooooccceeeannnn . . ." Mom would enjoy Petula Clark singing "This Is My Song," or Peter, Paul and Mary singing "Where Have All the Flowers Gone?," or Herbie Mann piping the flute, but we never played rock and roll. Maybe, if we were lucky, the

Beatles. *Yellow Submarine.* Certainly not the Rolling Stones or Jimi Hendrix. When Dad came home, the music got louder, and Mom watched for the darkness in his smile, the sorrow in his eyes, and in her he found light — as did we all.

When we first began looking for a house in Japan, my mom wanted to live on the Japanese market, so the military realtor took us to a lovely Japanese home to discuss an arrangement with the owner. He bowed deeply to us in pants and a shirt and tie, then took a sidelong look at us five kids huddled in the middle of his rice paper home, and upon learning of our soon-to-be-adopted wiener dog, Amy, he said, *"eey-yeh,"* spelled *iie,* and meaning, *No.* Feeling somewhat embarrassed, too loud and too white, we went back to the navy base to look for housing, and we soon found the perfect spot. All the officers' housing sat on the top of a big hill known as Area 1. It was protected by a stone fence. All the enlisted housing was at the bottom of the hill, known as Area 2; it was protected by a cliff and a chain-link fence; but our house magically sat in the middle of the hill . . . all alone. Just our house. I don't know how we were so lucky to get this house. There it sat, with a rounded driveway and a koi pond in which we promptly deposited two fish and a turtle. We had sixteen lovebirds and two cats and Amy the wiener dog. We had a tetherball in the driveway, and Mom would come out and play jump rope with us on cool summer evenings. She was the only mom who did that, still jumped rope with her kids, and it made her seem cooler and younger and prettier than the other moms.

I would look down over the cliff into the backyards of Area 2, where barbecues, beer, and the football were all thrown down with equal force, and then look up the hill into the quiet officers' housing of Area 1, and I'd hope that other kids could see how cool we were in our rounded driveway jumping rope with our mom. I would sing "Miss Mary Mack Mack Mack" loudly, so that anyone driving up the hill might hear me, and might look over at us singing and playing and jumping rope by the pond with the koi fish. In our big, round backyard, there was a stone wall from which we hung a rope with a knot for a seat, and we pushed off from the wall and someone held the bottom of the rope and flung us up and dangerously down. Toward the very back of the yard there was a metal chain-link fence that blocked a bamboo forest from encroaching on the lawn, and we were warned not to go back into the thickness of it because there were caves hidden in the hills that still had the bones of warriors from World War II scattered about their dirt floors. We did go back there, of course. Wielding fake swords and stolen kitchen knives to use as machetes, we shallowly explored the caves, never daring to trespass to where it was really, really dark, but even in the dimly lit entrance we did see bones, and a spoon, and a canteen. We traipsed back through the bamboo leaves, careful not to get cut by their slicing edges, and arrived home to the safety of grilled cheese sandwiches and chicken noodle soup from the can, and paper napkins folded in triangles.

Mom planted the yard with roses. She made me help her weed. I always knew when she was in a fight with Dad because the weeding would get really vicious. She would clamp down on her jaw, with me at her side, and the blades of grass and weeds would start flying on either side of me. "Get the roots!" she would admonish. The metaphor was lost on me then, but now, I think about the roots — of pain and loneliness — and I think of those weeds in our garden in Japan.

It would be nice to pluck pain out of the

brain like a weed, to cleanse the garden of emotional toxins with the ease of weeding. It's a big deal, asking a woman to be a navy wife, to raise her children alone, to discipline with confidence but then to surrender with "Wait till your father gets home." To love and cuddle and then be separated for months, to work so hard and to be in charge and then to give up charge to the man of the house. To submit to his harsher discipline, to wonder how to mother, how to wife, and how to grow yourself with five kids to raise. To deal with the inevitable happy hours that weren't so happy. To be filled with pride at your husband's intelligence and accomplishments. To shift and change more deeply than you ever knew you would when first the crescent moon beckoned to you as you soared across the Pan Am sky. Mom shifted. The marriage shifted. Their love was still abundantly love, mostly pleasant, always present, but aged now with some cracks showing.

I think now of roots of fights, me having fought too much in my own relationships, and I know that there is a moment when hurt has gone too far and the shift has caused the load to be at crank. *At crank.* It's where the word "cranky" comes from, and it means off-kilter. It's a shipping term, and when the storms are too rough, and the weight and load and burden of a ship have shifted on the waves and rolls of the high seas, the balance of the ship is off. It is at crank. It takes work to rebalance the ship, to distribute the weight, to repair the broken items, to batten down the cargo, knowing that there are more storms to come, and the end is never in sight. In these terms, I think of both of my parents so perfectly. "Get the roots," a gardening metaphor, of course goes to Mom. And repairing the "crank" of the ship of course goes to my shipping father. I know now it's what one has to do in a relationship. Get rid of the roots of weeds, nurture and water the roots of the blooms, and always, always maintain the balance and shift of the cargo. Maintenance is work, and it's boring, and we are always wanting the calm and placid sea to enjoy, or we are drawn to the drama of the storm, but it is the balance of the load that keeps the ship afloat. Many couples aren't able to repair the hurts of their relationships at crank. Words can create unstoppable leaks in the hull, shaky finances can keep the diet too strict, the travel too lean, and war surely asks both men and women to witness valor and horror — in the same breath — and then to bring this same breath home to inhale and exhale as love during a goodnight kiss to their children. My mother and father were in this for the long haul, however, and in my mother my father was discovering an expert captain and steward of all that he, and certainly she, found precious. She would repair the hull, and in long cursive letters passing over the seas, they would rebalance the load, and redefine the journey they were on together.

She weeded and planted, and cut her lovely blooms, and her flower arrangements miraculously told stories to me of her day. The white tuberoses' full-bodied scents, with jiggling layered petals, told me of her dreams, and I was right! She had dreamed of Hawaii and hula girls dancing in the tuberose fragrance. The bamboo spikes and chrysanthemum somehow told me of a painful week when she was hurting for money, and I was right! The mail was late with a check she needed. The Stargazers, so rare that she would pay for them with their heavenly scent, told me Dad was coming home from sea and star-studded evenings, and I was right! He joined us in his Navy Blues and carved the Thanksgiving turkey, setting the carving knife next to the creamy white gravy bowl that was touching the translucent ivory-tinged edges of the speckled pink six-petaled Stargazer, dancing in a midnight blue vase that looked like the ocean.

Dad's ships had names like the USS *Henderson,* the USS *Osborne,* the USS *Kearsarge;* he commanded various destroyers and aircraft carriers, returning from Vietnam and Korea, where what he did was quite mysterious to his children. We gathered — my brother in blue shorts and a collared cotton shirt, we girls in matching dresses with white ruffled socks and patent leather Mary Janes — to welcome him home, spotting him on the top of the ship with the other officers, all lined up in uniform, their faces shadowed by their brimmed hats. On the bottom deck were the enlisted men, also lined up from one end of the ship to the other, hundreds of them, perfectly matching in navy blue bell-bottoms and navy blue sailor shirts, all of them standing at ease with hands behind their backs and legs slightly spread. Men coming to port to rejoin their families, exotic scents still lingering on their uniforms. We spotted Dad with the gruff face and half cigar, puffing a little cloud above his head, we told him we *knew* it was him because of the cigar! I could still smell it on the ride home, thick and overpowering and masculine.

His world and our world merged and collided when he came home. We were sometimes little soldiers with our "Sir, yes, sirs!," sometimes just kids showing off our latest artwork or dances, following our mother's lead in how to run a tight ship . . . at home.

One July night, when Dad was home on leave, we went to a dance that changed my sense of self forever. The Bon Odori is a traditional Japanese summertime festival honoring one's ancestors. Its songs and dances pay tribute to long dead spirits, although I didn't know that when we first went at the invitation of friends of my mom's. I thought it was a harvest festival, and pretended to hoe rice as I danced the rituals' movements with the crowd. Mom had been teaching English at a Japanese high school; she didn't speak a word of Japanese and they didn't speak a word of English, plus she had never been a teacher before, so I don't really know how she knew how to lead this class. But she did. She would travel in our little gray Volvo on the "wrong" side of the road, squeezing through the twisting, curvy streets of Yokohama, up a windy hill past open fish markets and jute stalls that sold *osembe* and *nori maki* crackers, colorful erasers, bright pink plastic purses, paper umbrellas, and children's toys, all displayed artfully on the sidewalk. She had memorized the roads because she couldn't read the signs in Japanese, and she would hold her breath as she twisted and turned through the narrow streets, finally letting it out in a long sigh of relief when she arrived at the high school. There she relaxed for a minute, enjoying bland green tea with the teachers in the rice paper lounge while she prepared her lesson, and over time she became friends with a science teacher. He introduced Mom to his family, and for the great Bon Odori festival his wife made all seven of us a yukata, the traditional cotton summer Japanese kimono. Mom and Dad's were blue and white with a bamboo design, while the rest of ours were brightly colored flowers; chrysanthemums and gerbera daisies, cherry blossoms and birds-of-paradise on a bright white background. Our obis were red, and we each had toe socks with wooden Japanese clog sandals. My dark brown hair was pulled into two pigtails, and I tied red ribbons on each one, my pigtails bouncing with the excitement of a night outing.

As the sun sets, and dusk settles the waiting crowd, the Bon Odori festival begins. I was only nine when I first sang and danced the joyful Bon Odori song under the inky black sky glittering with golden stars, yet I have never forgotten it. To this day, it is my standby song: I sing it when prodded to participate in talent shows, I sing and dance it around campfires, I embarrass my children with my yodeling Japanese voice and the studied dance movements of a rice farmer. It is in my bones, this ancient song; it fills me with the same sense of freedom I felt that hot July night when I first learned it. The night I got lost, got separated from my mom and dad, my brother and sisters, and found myself in a sea of kimonos and obis, under the floating red-, pink-, salmon-, and yellow-colored paper lanterns of the Bon Odori festival, dancing round and round the center temple stand that had been erected that day in the parking lot at the foot of the naval base, dancing crushed in among hundreds of people I didn't know, Japanese men and women and children in their brightly starched cotton yukatas, American soldiers in their starched summer whites, dancing to drums and singing this song: *"Omme omme fudee fudee kaaaasaaannngaaa."* Again and again, *"Omme omme fudee fudee . . ."* repeating each verse and motion, dancing round and round in a kind of trance, sweating in the heat that was still rising from the warm pavement, and realizing suddenly that I was alone with strangers under the speckled night sky of Japan, and I was okay. My mom and dad, my sisters, and our Japanese friends, were nowhere to be seen, and I was dancing and singing with hundreds of gracious, jet-black-haired people, celebrating their culture, and I was okay, and I belonged with them.

I knew I would probably get in trouble for getting lost and making my parents worry, I knew that I would certainly get a spanking, but I couldn't stop. Like a magnet, I was a child caught in the centrifugal force of the music and swaying crowd, going round and round and round and round, *Omme omme fudee fudee kaaaasaaannngaaa,* safe only in my exact movement and synchronized clapping and clog shoe step step step . . . making a hoeing-rice gesture, hoe hoe hoe, *Omme omme fudee fudee,* throwing the rice over my shoulder and clap! Freedom! It was my first taste of freedom! A heady feeling for a little girl. Again! *Omme omme. Fudee fudee.* Freedom. *Kaaaasaaannngaaa . . .* under the lanterns, inhaling the smell of grilled teriyaki chicken and rice and lost in the drums and shamisen guitars, *Yano men eh, Omu kaye, Huda shin ahh* . . . floating wavering flute and twanging instruments filling my ears, bouncing off my pigtails and fluttering with my red ribbons, *Peache peache kapu kapu naaa naaa naaa* . . . in perfect step to the music. Step step step. Hoe hoe hoe. Throw the bag over my shoulder and CLAP! Step step step, hoe hoe hoe, throw the bag over my shoulder, and CLAP!

Eventually, as round and round I went, over the yodeling crowd I heard a thin scared voice calling, "Marcia . . . ? Maaarrrccciiiaaa?" I looked up past the colored lanterns and I saw a familiar crescent moon bobbing through the crowd. It was Mom, pale and glowing in her yukata, approaching with her teacher friend, her brown eyes barely hiding her tears of relief, and then something strange and magical happened without words, because her teacher friend nodded his approval at my dancing with the crowd, and suddenly I wasn't in trouble and Dad would never know I had been lost and I wouldn't get a spanking. They both claimed me, Mom and the teacher, in that moment, as if I had been with them the whole time. We circled yet one more time, all step step stepping together. Then *Omme omme fudee fudee* ended and they both smiled at the child they had watched dance free. And clap!

■ ■ ■ ■

My Mother
Holds Me Like
Mary Holds Jesus

■ ■ ■ ■

"January is a time to get rid of the excesses of December, and celebrate clean lines and purity," Mom always said. New beginnings. Her arrangements for January were often white, inviting the viewer to imagine snow, or the reflective glass of a frozen lake. She hadn't really grown up with snow in her childhood home of Dallas, Texas, but in her travels around the world as a navy wife, she had seen it drift off of red Japanese temple tops, skim the backs of golden koi fish, and settle in the hushed depths of a dark Virginia wood. Snow piled high on the roof of our Volvo as it was parked in the driveway in Maryland. Dad scraped it off the windshields in the mornings, his black and gold uniform dusted with ice as he puffed and cursed, preparing to go solve problems at the Pentagon. Mom watched from the steamy frosted window, and had his coffee ready when he came inside, the fried eggs

107

and bacon already on a mat on the table. I liked that he always thanked her for his breakfast.

In Maryland, in our newly built suburban cul-de-sac that cozied up to the old woods, there were shacks that seemed to have been left over from the last century. Wandering down dirt roads into the backwoods during the early seventies, one would come across entire black communities gathered with loud laughter on their wooden porches. School busing finally introduced these porch families to the cul-de-sac families, and so I quickly made friends with a girl named Karon who often came over to our house after school to make bread. She would bring her cousin Jan, and the girls would shift from pounding basketballs in the gym to pounding dough on our cream counter. Dad loved that. He would come home in his uniform, take off his white or black cap with the black plastic brim, and begin flouring the counter and pounding and kneading the bread with the girls, his golden commander stripes bouncing with each hard pulse, teaching and learning at the same time. My sisters would join in, with Mom in the background "hoppin and choppin," as we called it. Mom provided everything for everyone, but never took center stage; instead she flitted about wiping and cleaning, sweeping flour from the floor, happy her kitchen was being used in this way.

When the bread began to rise and the wheat smell spilled through the cracks of the oven, I got the butter ready on the counter, slightly softened, slather-ready. Butter dripped off our many-colored chins around the wooden kitchen table. We were all loud and seemingly performing for each other, with our throaty laughs and our "yeaaaa gurrrrls!" Performing, and yet really feeling it, too: happiness and community and what neighborhoods and childhoods are supposed to feel like, as if we are all one and there is nothing more important in life than making bread and sharing it. The only reason it also felt like a performance was because I wondered if we would have still acted this way if the adults, or any other eyes, weren't watching. When it was just me and Karon, there was no power struggle. We were simply friends. It's not like we didn't know she was black and I was white, but without eyes watching, our friendship didn't need the teeter-totter of proving ourselves, or apologizing for the actions of our ancestors.

Mom wrapped up loaves in shiny tin foil

for the girls to take back to their families in the mysterious wood. She smoothed the foil perfectly, sliding her small hands over and over the tops of the loaves, folding the sides like hospital corners, exact and beautiful. She wrote with a Magic Marker in elegant, cursive slants on the foil: "wheat bread" or "sourdough bread," and she beamed with pride as the girls gave her a floury hug, heading back to the darkening wood path.

Mom never understood — nor did I, for that matter — why or how I got beaten up a year later in eighth grade by these same girls. Maybe it had something to do with territory and position and privilege; maybe it had to do with me flirting with the star basketball player named Mohammed; but it was a betrayal that pierced Karon's and my budding friendship, and we never quite recovered. We were all in the awkward middle school transition. My profile was something like this: *Pimply unibrow hateful hormones budding breasts sneaky cigarette puffs and eighth grade!* Friendships that meant everything one day could be entirely vanished the next. Friendships actually defined you and your group: the jocks, the nerds, the popular girls, the theater boys and backstage girls, the cheerleaders and pom-pom girls, the intellects, the freaks, the campers and the hikers, the dancers and the fighters. I was the new girl who had lived in Japan and was now going to middle school in Maryland. I was the new girl who was making friends with Karon, who liked to do drama, who hiked the Appalachians with her sisters. I was the new girl who was a volunteer JANGO (aka, candy striper, stood for Junior Army Navy Guild Organization) at Bethesda Naval Hospital. I was the girl who was making bread with her parents and Karon and Jan, and who was hoping to be in the elite group of basketball players so Mohammed would notice me.

Here's what happened: we were playing basketball during gym class, and I was adorned with a pixie haircut and scrawny hairy chicken legs that were only made more unsightly due to the white bloomers the school forced us to wear. My parents wouldn't let me shave yet, and the black hair on my legs stood out against my white skin like print on a newspaper. I was a walking unibrow with dark hairy chicken legs. To make matters worse, Mom insisted we wear skirts to school, so I used to sneak my one pair of pants, my green high-water jeans, in my satchel and scoot them on under my skirt to hide my offensive legs. But in gym class there was no escape, no cover. We had to wear short white bloomers and white socks with tennis shoes. My tennis shoes were red hand-me-downs and one size too large. I looked like a circus clown.

On this particularly fateful day, I had joined Karon and Jan and their tight group of friends on the court. It just happened to be an all-black team of excellent players, with whom I hoped to improve my game. But it was hopeless. I really wasn't very good, double dribbling and undershooting, arms flailing "I'm free. I'm free!," and then missing the one ball that was thrown my way. I was attempting a layup and missed several baskets as we were playing the game, and one of the leader bully girls bounced a basketball off my head. I held back tears and kept playing, certain that Karon or Jan would come to my rescue. We had, after all, just pounded sourdough together a week or two ago, and the taste of salted butter and boysenberry jam mixed with the tart sour of the bread still made my head spin. But a rescue didn't happen. It would have seemed like trespassing, I guess, protecting someone out of the "family," and soon several more basketballs were bounced off my head.

As the bell buzzed for class to end, I scurried into the gym locker room, where the rule was we had to strip down to our undies, and mine were of course mortifyingly high-waisted like a grandmother's. We had to grab a towel and walk around the large square shower room dabbing our under-arms, and then back out the way we had come to the lockers. As I approached the tiled exit of the shower room, with baggy underwear and my towel in hand, Karon was commanded by another girl to bounce her fist on my head like a basketball. She hesitated. We looked at each other, and her eyes seemed to freeze, her brown pupils misted over instantly. Then she did it. She hit me with her fist, bounced it on my head and said, "Boooiiiiinnnnnngggg."

"That's not funny!" I blurted. Everyone laughed.

Then Karon did the unthinkable. Of her own volition she bounced her fist on my head again. "Boooiiiinnnnngggg." More laughter. Again. "Boooiiiinnnnggg."

"Stop it!" I shouted. And I snapped my towel at her. My wet towel. I snapped it, and it popped right in her face.

She was stung, and stunned, and then her fist came up firmly under my jaw and the fight was on. I flew backward and stumbled over the bench, then landed with my feet in the air. Just me and my granny underwear, knees at a 90-degree angle on the bench, flat on my back. I jumped up and started hitting Karon and she was hitting me and there was a lot of noise. It was jumbled and slow motion and I was crying, tears streaking down my newly blooming breasts and mingling with blood. People were shouting, "Fight, fight . . ." and more rhyming ugliness, and we kept hitting each other and knocking into the blue lockers.

Before long the social studies teacher pulled us apart but not until I had sobbed to her, "I'll hit you, too!" As I was getting dressed to go to the office, the teacher discreetly waited to the side, and I noticed I had wet my pants. I would have thrown them away, but I was afraid someone would find them and tell everyone, so I wadded them up in my satchel and covered it with paper towels.

We got suspended. Waiting in the principal's office, I watched out the window as my mom pulled up in her gray Volvo. She had been doing accounting work for Sears to make the paychecks of my dad stretch a bit longer, and she had been called away from work to come and get me.

Nothing about the fight could match the pain lurching in my stomach when I saw my mother's face. She was scared and blinking rapidly, and everything about her halting movement as she staggered to hug me was full of guilt because she hadn't protected me from the slings and arrows of life. Her ladylike Dallas upbringing hadn't prepared her for the violence and struggles of my Maryland middle school. She didn't care that blood was now on her polyester bow-tied shirt, perfectly tucked into her skirt. She held me tightly, so tightly, her breast heaving against mine. She tucked me into the car like a toddler, and I had to push her away from fastening my seatbelt. Her stockings and her heeled loafers pressed firmly on the gas, and she burst into tears as we drove through the streets, past the woods, and toward home.

"I'm sorry, Marcia. I am so mad at those girls. Are you okay?"

"It was Karon, Mom. It wasn't just *those girls.* It was Karon and Jan. They were making fun of me."

That's probably the worst thing any mom wants to hear, that her child is being ridiculed and bullied by someone in their school. Mom looked baffled and asked, *"Why?"*

It was too much to try and explain basketball and how much I sucked at it, and Mohammed, and the stupid shower room. I stared glumly out the window, dreading returning to school, dreading getting home. "Am I going to get in trouble with Dad for being suspended?"

"Well, I just don't understand," she said. "Why were you suspended *too*? *They* were the ones fighting!"

"I guess 'cause I fought back," I said guiltily. I would definitely get into trouble.

"You did?" She looked at me with a mixture of confusion and admiration. She should've been mad, because fighting was wrong — that was what we had always been told. But she wasn't mad; she was more . . . hurt . . . dismayed, I guess. Bereft. She didn't know the lesson to teach. The boundaries were too blurry here — I had needed to defend myself, and so the fighting back wasn't wrong; the *rules* were wrong. "I'm glad you stood up to her," Mom finally said. Then, softly, she added, "I admire that about you, Marcia."

My eye was hurting. My jaw was bruised.

Mom made sure I didn't get in trouble, and in truth, after Dad accepted that I hadn't been acting like "a Goddamn hooligan," I could tell that he too was confused as to why the bread pounding had turned into fist pounding in the locker room. We couldn't explain it. For three days, Mom nursed my black eye, taking off work Friday, resisting the ticktock of the weekend clock, and dreading Monday's approach.

"Okay, sweetheart. Here we go." Monday morning, in a skirt with shorts hidden underneath, and my two still-hairy chicken legs, I climbed into the car. We drove to school and had to go to the principal's office for her to sign me in. The principal tried to give Mom a lecture about fighting and middle school unity, but she politely smiled and said, "I'm late for work." Her tone said "Skip it." I thought that would be the end of the conversation; it was a bit out of character for Mom to be curt, and then she really surprised me by clearing her throat and going on: "You need to do something to make this school safe. My husband and I didn't teach our children to be fighters. But we also didn't teach them to be cowards. We taught them to stand up for themselves, and what happened last week was just that — my child standing up for herself." I thought she was going to cry, but, thank God, she didn't. "I don't want to see it happen again to my daughter Marcia Gay." With that, she turned and left the office, with me in tow. We hugged good-bye, a long, tight embrace, and then I tugged my skirt down to cover my legs and walked down the hallway to class. I had hoped that at least my parents' guilt would have led to my being able to shave for school, but no. They didn't seem to understand the correlation, and though I couldn't quite articulate it, I knew there was one. Hairy legs made me more vulnerable . . . they made me a target. In my little plaid skirt, I had to walk past my crush, Mohammed, who muttered, "Is you a girl or a boy?" I pulled my skirt lower.

I was late since my mom had had to sign me back into school, and the hall was empty, except for at the very, very end, where gathered around my locker stood Karon and her small cluster of basketball friends. The hall seemed a mile long, and I could see the girls watching me as I walked the gauntlet. I slowly started to wet myself again. Thank God I was in the skirt; if I had been in pants, they would have seen the wet spot.

At my locker, Karon stood right behind me; I could feel her breath on my neck. "You the first white girl ever hit me back."

I said, "Mmmmhmmm," fumbling with my combination lock, completely forgetting the numbers. I was sure she was about to hit me again, and I held my books to my stomach to protect myself.

Karon then looked at me with misted

brown eyes and said, "I got 'specs for you."

I said nothing. It was a small victory. I would rather have made bread. I had earned her respect, but had lost the pure friendship of no eyes watching.

Our backyard stretched out across a grassy lawn, where on special evenings we built bonfires next to the vegetable garden and disco danced to Michael Jackson and slow grinded to Billy Paul's "Meeee eeee aaannnnddd Mrs. Mrs. Jones . . . we got a thaaang goin' on . . ." I could grind my way to excitement and loved my little secret, and loved our neighborhood boys for knowing just how to get into the groove and grind of a slow, sexy song. Undulating hips. The smell of Afro Sheen in the tight curls, warm necks entwined like dark swans. The firelight from the bonfire cast flickers into the thick woods, just barely outlining the edges of trees and bushes and the faint dirt path that led to my hidden fort. Sometimes we made S'mores. When Dad called brusquely for us to come in — several scotches down the pipes by now — I could just make out the eyes of my new crush, Theodore, melting smaller and smaller as he disappeared into the woods, his last-minute teeth flashing a sly smile.

In the winter, these woods filled up with snow. The trees lumbered down under the weight of the snow, the ice broke branches, and the ditch in the front yard where our family played "hit the dirt!" seemed on level with the rest of the lawn. Stepping into it, one thin tennis shoe after another, I could feel my green jeans freeze in stiff attention up to the knee. There was no sound when the flakes were fat, the silent hush whispered to my mom . . . her face relaxed without frown or smile, her chin tilted up to the sky, and the biggest flakes fell flat against her black lashes, like frozen tears melting against the heat of her serenity.

It was a cold January morning, yet the excesses of Christmas still lingered, cloud-like, in my mind. Gone now the eggnog, the shiny Santa-patterned wrapping paper, the last smelted foil ashes scooped out of the fireplace. Gone the mistletoe we had tried so hard to get caught under, screaming with fake surprise when we were kissed. Gone the Fannie May chocolates, gone Grandmother's white powdery divinity, gone the fudge, and gone the caramel-colored candied pecans. Mom's counters were now restored to their spartan sugarless display of a coffee can, a percolator, a toaster, a recipe box, and *The Joy of Cooking* cookbook.

The now-full cardboard Christmas boxes were nestled between boxes marked XMAS TREE STAND, HALLOWEEN PUMPKINS, and EASTER BASKETS on a high shelf in the garage. The once-aromatic evergreen tree, resplendent with aluminum icicles and colored balls and precious family ornaments, had been taken down and now sat unceremoniously abandoned at the curb.

A little wooden side table by the arching front window usually provided the setting for a nativity the size of a shoebox. The manger, with its glittery cardboard star balancing precariously at the peak of the thatched manger roof, sent a slightly bent ray pointing heavenward. It was a tradition for me to carefully set up the holy family with my mom — small china figures in a bed of straw. We acted as a team each Christmas to see if we could vary the relationship within the sacred grouping. Perhaps Joseph was actually talking to one of the wise men? Perhaps a shepherd and an angel shared a joke with another wise man, the one with the myrrh? What if the animals were still walking in from the desert, and only the sheep were in the manger? But Mary must always be holding Jesus, because that was what mothers did.

They held their little children, and I knew that even if I was not the Son of God, my mother held me just as tightly as Mary held Jesus.

The tape tightly closed the brown box marked NATIVITY, and the wooden side table was returned to its proper position. It was here that my mother would place her January flower arrangement.

After the mash of presents and paper and sweets and peanut brittle, after the inevitable fights and glorious laughter, after the anticipation disappeared and Barbies were dressed in their now new clothing, after Monopoly was won by those smarter with money than I was, the New Year began. And Mom arranged white flowers in clear vases filled with crumpled foil so that it looked like water reflecting on the ice, little crumpled bits of crackling water, giving rise to a burst of snow-white chrysanthemum nestled in deep green hemlock.

Shin. Soe. Hikae. Heaven. Earth. Man.

■ ■ ■ ■

SUMMER

■ ■ ■ ■

My Mother Flies with Superwoman

People often ask me, "How did you get your start?" It's an understandable question: the life of an actress is seemingly unattainable, and who wouldn't be curious? Indeed, my start had as much glamour and adventure attached to it as you can imagine: My dad was stationed in Greece, and he was the commanding officer of a small naval station named NAVCOMSTA Nea Makri, and we lived in a jasmine-surrounded home with marble floors in a little town called Mati, which meant "eye." It sat atop a hill, and a picturesque village and the sea lay at its feet.

This house! It was the first time I ever had my own bedroom, as well as my own patio in the backyard, also made of white marble and forming a little semicircle that looked out onto a lawn perfectly mowed by Yannis, our gardener. There was a fig tree right outside my bedroom window. There were lemon and orange trees, roses and night-blooming jasmine, and the enchanting, deep, and full smell of their blossoms would perfume my glistening marble room, bouncing and lobbing, drifting in slow motion off my white marble floor. I inhaled the perfume in my dreams.

But the coup d'etat was the pink bidet in the bathroom. The *what?* Yes, a bidet, where girls could sit and dip in hot water during their time of the moon.

So my "start" story often begins there, in that Eden called Mati, when I was busing down to Athens on the same road the marathon runners had traveled thousands of years before, busing down to the Herod Atticus Odeon and watching classical Greek plays beneath the gleaming white of the Acropolis. Sipping wine on the ancient stone stairs under the stars, I fell in love with the theater. Surrounded by aromatic sage and blankets of jasmine hanging like bulging laundry from the stone, we shuddered for Oedipus. His demise was no mystery; the Greeks could practically recite the words to perfection.

I'm not sure, however, that any "start" story actually has a definitive beginning, or a singular inspiration. I can trace performance — or exhibitionism at least, and certainly the love of an audience — to

Japan. There were plenty of early family stories documenting "front porch theatrics," which we kids performed in Yokohama, hanging quilts that had been sewn by my grandmother on our front porch, setting out seats for the neighbors, popping popcorn, selling tickets, and hamming up our version of *The Princess and the Pea,* no laugh too cheaply won.

A more mature appreciation of the theater occurred years later in Greece: I can trace being in awe of actors who were calling in rich voices upon the gods to the stone benches of the Parthenon, as I sat beneath the stars in Athens and watched Medea in red billowing gauze howl for her two children she had just murdered. This calling to the gods, with explosive, atomic emotion so much larger than life, howling with joy or sorrow — I could relate to this grief and giddy, surging happiness.

Mom had told all of us kids when we landed in Greece to "figure out the buses and go see Athens." And we did. We stayed at the American Hotel while we were looking for housing, and the waiters taught us enough Greek to get around (*alalti* is "salt" and *pipéri* is "pepper"), and soon we were ditching the museums in favor of the theater. Theaters where you could drop a pin in the middle, and supposedly hear it fall from anywhere in the space. The Acropolis and the ancient theater of Epidaurus were visited by thousands of tourists gathering in huddles with their tour guides, waiting to hear a pin drop to the ground. (Which, for the record, I never did hear, though it was tested several times by my sisters and me.)

But the concept of my "start" seems to me to have to do with the creative work itself. It has to do with what happened after school, after I left college. It has to do with auditions and putting myself out there to be rejected or hired. It has to do with so much more than simply loving the theater as I learned to do in Greece, or enjoying the audience cooing at the antics of an eight-year-old from the front yard peanut gallery in Japan.

And this start, the start of the actual work that I won by competing with other auditioning actors, lands solely on my mother's shoulders. After college in Greece and in Germany. After graduating from the University of Texas with a major in theater. After we closed down her parents' home in Dallas, when her father died, and we divided the antique spinning wheel and the cranberry lamps, and all the treasures of her childhood between Mom and her brother

George. After I had returned to Virginia and lived with my parents for a while, then left to be a grown-up and rented an apartment in Georgetown.

My plan was to audition for plays in the Washington, DC, area, to get my union card by doing extra work, and eventually to try to be an actor at the residential theater Arena Stage, and then maybe move to New York. But of course I had to pay the rent first, so by day I worked in a parking garage handing out parking passes to new apartment residents, and by night I served drinks in a private club called the Gaslight Club. I had an extremely ridiculous job as a Gaslight Girl, for which I wore a very sexy *Gunsmoke*-meets-*Playboy* outfit of red velvet and gold braids. It was like a fancy one-piece bathing suit with a push-up bra. I also wore fishnets, a velvet choker, high heels, and pretty hair, but more importantly, I had to *sing* during sets while I served cocktails. You heard me. Sing. I have never considered myself a talented singer, and for good reason. I'm *not.* I want to sing like a gospel singer sings! Praising God, my body shaking and notes bellowing out of the top of my head, but instead I am a tidy singer, slightly timid, careful with the notes, shy. It's like math, so black-and-white. You can either carry a note or you can't. One busy night at the Gaslight, right before I was to go up to the piano to sing "I'm gonna sit right down and write myself a letter . . . ," a bunch of billionaires at a table started laughing, and I was given a hundred-dollar bill in exchange for NOT singing — and of course I took it but later cried in the locker room while yanking off my stupid fishnets. Oh, how I wished I could sing like Aretha Franklin! I would have bellowed *R-E-S-P-E-C-T!*

On weekends, I'd drive from Georgetown down the beautiful parkway in my yellow Volkswagon convertible to visit my parents and younger siblings for breakfast — perhaps one-eyed Egyptian sandwiches or Mexican omelets, orange juice that sweated on the outside of its small glass, coffee that my parents both drank black with no sugar no cream. Their Virginia house was a mile up from George Washington's Mount Vernon, and I'd drive along the Potomac, sunshine and wind beating on my face, and arrive at their place in time to sit at the old oak table. One day, shortly after I had settled in for breakfast, my mom pulled out a newspaper article.

"Look, dear. There are auditions at the Little Theatre of Old Town Alexandria for *I*

Ought to Be in Pictures."

"It's a musical, Mom."

"No, honey, I don't think so. It says it's a play, by Neil Simon."

"Uh, yes, I know, Mom. But it's not a play, it's a musical, and I don't sing." Memories of my Gaslight Girl singing attempts still traumatized me.

Mom read the notice more closely. She described the role of Libby, an adolescent daughter who visits her unsuccessful screenwriter father in Hollywood. She wins her father's love. *Oh, boy . . .*

"Mom, it's a musical, and I'm not going to audition."

"Well, I think you should go. If it *is* a musical, just don't sing. Just leave the audition. Would that be okay?"

In the silence that ensued, I could feel, and resented, my mother's longing for me. She ran her fingers through her soft black curls and smiled, neither pushy nor disapproving. Only hopeful. It irritated me that she thought I was stronger than she was. She thought I was talented and she assumed I could withstand the hurts and rejections of Show Business. She thought I was a fighter. She wanted me to succeed, or at least to try to succeed. She wanted me to push to have a voice that she had never had, or was just now trying to build with her flower arranging. I didn't like her assumptions about me, and I didn't like her diminutive attitude toward herself. I mean, hadn't she just been recently appointed an important position in Ikebana International? Wasn't she a powerful woman in the Japanese flower-arranging world? Wasn't she a *very* important woman in Washington, DC? Why didn't she see herself this way? Once, Mom had said her strength was like a willow branch. Bendable, flexible, yet unbreakable. Yes, she was! An unbreakable willow branch! And she had tremendous poise and grace to boot! But I knew what a struggle it was for her to speak in public, to show confidence and command. Confidence and command. That was the strength that Mom thought I had, and I did, kind of sort of maybe not really. I had it on the surface — Mom never quite understood that underneath it all was a gaping hole of insecurity.

I was silent. She persisted.

"I don't think it's a musical, honey. Why do you think it is? Where do you see that?"

She was peering over her coffee, reading the audition notice.

"Mom, please? Stop" was my brilliant rejoinder.

"Well, we could call," she said. "Look,

here's a number. Should we call? Should we call and find out, honey?"

"I won't get it, anyway. Even if it's not a musical, there are probably tons of actors that the theater knows and has worked with before. They'll cast them, not me. That's how it works, Mom."

"Well, it doesn't hurt to call. Honey? Okay?"

Big, *big* sigh from me. "I *guess*. If *you* really want to."

She called. Turns out, it *wasn't* a musical. I had to prepare an audition. I wore a black beret. And I got the part.

Mom and Dad came to the opening night and cried in all the touching moments. I got good reviews, and that year I won an award from the Little Theatre of Old Town, Alexandria for my portrayal of Libby in *I Ought to Be in Pictures*. And I took those reviews and the notice of the award, and made a brag sheet out of it, and every subsequent audition I went on in Washington, DC, and later New York, I showed this brag sheet to the directors and producers. I showed it to all the casting directors so they would know that a critic had liked me. And eventually, I got another play. And more good reviews. And a union card. And that is how I got my start. All because my mother wouldn't give up on me auditioning for a play that was not a musical.

Years later, Mom would visit me in New York City, helping me move from the rat-infested Martha Washington senior and girls housing unit in midtown to the George Washington Hotel, which had several floors reserved for NYU students "at affordable prices," though they were still barely doable for me. Real estate was being bought up left, right, and center in downtown New York — which was creating quite a furor among the edgy, spikey-haired crowd on St. Mark's Place and the easy hippies of the East Village. I could understand the sadness at the loss that was occurring as corporate change became a reality, but nevertheless I was glad to find an apartment I could barely afford. Now I could start grad school at NYU Tisch School of the Arts with safety and focus. I was going there on a full scholarship thanks to Zelda Fichandler, our acting chair, and Mom made the trip up again to New York from DC to help me pack and unpack.

My room at the George Washington was 125 square feet. You could lie in bed and pull the drawers out from the dresser, which was crammed against the wall on the right, and extract your outfit for the day all without ever rolling over. Mom hollered from the bathroom, "I have to be careful not to step into the toilet when I step out of the shower!" There was just enough room on the floor to plant your feet and turn around. There was only one window. Mom liked to throw it open and hang out with her bosoms just resting on the bottom frame, mimicking all the other New York women at similar windows up and down the block on Madison Avenue, women watching people, women watching life on the streets of New York. The sunlight glancing off her left cheek, her hair damp and curly, her smile wide at the adventure we were on together. "OH, LOOOOOK!" she screamed. I ran to the window, and we saw an entire VW Beetle that had fallen into a pothole. Just the blue top poked out of the enormous chasm. No one was hurt, and we laughed and laughed that morning, at crazy New York City.

That afternoon, Mom was walking around the West Village by herself. It was the first time she had ever been on her own in the city without me by her side. I was in class, and Mom was going to talk to real estate people about other available apartments. She got scared. She felt out of place, as if everyone could just look at her and tell she wasn't from New York. She started shaking, and had her purse cemented so tightly under her arm that her knuckles were white. I had been mugged a couple of nights before, and the traces of that fear still clutched at her stomach, and made her jerk her head to the side to make sure she wasn't being followed, even in broad daylight. "Now, Beverly!" she thought. "What is it about everyone else that seems so comfortable? There are students and old women and people of all ages and walks of life! Now stop and LOOK around you!" She backed up to a glass wall and saw that almost everyone was carrying an ice-cream cone. A backpack and an ice-cream cone. A purse and an ice-cream cone. A green balloon and an ice-cream cone. Bicycles and scooters, and ice-cream cones. Hazlenut and pistachio, cones and cups, strawberry sorbet and chocolate-covered vanilla. Waffle cones drizzled with milk chocolate, and napkins already scattered on the sidewalk. She turned around to discover that her back was pressed up against a Häagen-Dazs store. Inside, a stream of cones and color and ease was emanating from the frozen sweet counter. She told herself, "Now, Beverly! You march right in there and get yourself an ice cream!" Which she did, pistachio with a small regular cone. "And then you march right outside with all those other New Yorkers, and you just decide that you belong!" And so she did.

By late fall, when Mom returned once again to help me move into a fifth-floor walk-up on Morton Street in the West Village, she was behaving like a seasoned New York veteran. We hauled boxes up those five flights, yelling at the cabbie that we'd be right back and *Please don't put our boxes on the street!* We lit a Duraflame in my illegal fireplace. We climbed out the rickety metal fire escape and up over the trees to the open rooftop so we could look at the sky together. So many times in our past, my mother and I had gazed up at the stars, at this same sky. When I was seven years old, we had traced the same Big and Little Dipper when Mom took our Bluebird troop camping in the deserts of California. We had traced this same Orion's belt in the Bon Odori sky of Japan, and the same Milky Way had hovered over the tragic actors at the Acropolis in Greece. Now, we saw a shooting star and made wishes. I knew we were both wishing for love, for ourselves and for each other. We had been without romance for too long. She wanted to rekindle her marriage with

Dad, and, for me, I had been alone for awhile — it was time to fill a void in my life. We yearned for romance. Man love. Protector love. Gentle love and sexy love. Safe. Embrace. Approve. Consistent. Nonjudgmental. Adventurous. Ours was a complicated wish, and it lasted long after the shimmer of the shooting starlight faded in the black sky. We needed a larger star. Perhaps a comet. We craned our necks up to the inky sky, on the rooftop in the West Village of Manhattan. We craned our necks up to the sky looking for God. Our hearts were bursting with the hope of being seen by more than the stars, bursting with the hope of being in the stars, the way you hope you are in the pocket of your loved one, and want to put them in your pocket, too. To be inside them, and they in you, not in a sexual way, but in their skin. To *be* them. Years later, I understood that this was called codependency, but then, even now, the utter surrender of losing yourself and meshing with another person, the odd vacancy and erasure of self that happens when first in love, it was what we wanted. It would make us feel complete. We prayed, heads dropped back and eyes wide open, and saw ourselves up inside the stars, swimming in their shimmer, wearing gold dust star capes and flying like superwomen in the cool spheres of heaven, flying in the heart of God. We closed our eyes and squinted them tight, and I felt her hold my hand. Soft skin, cool fingers. I clenched her hand tight. Then we opened our eyes again, hoping for more stars, more wishes. But there was only black night. Sated, we backed down the cold metal staircase, quietly ducking low so the creepy guy who stood naked for hours at a time in the apartment window opposite from mine wouldn't see us. We crawled awkwardly through the window, and made chamomile tea.

Several months later, we rode cabs through Central Park, and gasped when we saw the forsythia in bloom, cascading like yellow frothy waves over the rust-and-gray stone bridges traversing the cross streets from Central Park West to Fifth Avenue. And even though we were under the draping forsythia, peering up from our cab window, we could somehow also see it from above: we could fly up over the bridge and look down upon the park, tracing yellow forsythia blossoms and yellow cabs in a curving line through the damp black cross streets and white museums, around the Great Lawn, and on up into Harlem's red-brick brownstones. Mom said the forsythia branches looked like stars.

Later we bought forsythia at the local Korean Mart in the West Village. Mom reminded me that in Japanese arrangements, one made a triangle, and the different lines of the triangle were *shin, soe,* and *hikae,* or heaven, earth, and man. Forsythia was perfect for line material, and the *shin,* or heaven line, would be the first and longest line of the arrangement we would build. She bought two branches of dripping yellow forsythia. She would use it for the *shin,* and also for the second line of the triangle, the *soe,* or earth line. The final piece of the triangle, the flowers at the base, would be the *hikae,* or man line.

For the flowers, Mom bought white alstroemeria. It dawned on me that she was going to build a starry sky with the flowers, and indeed at home, she chose two flat half-circle black vases, the traditional *suiban* container — together they would make a circle, but she set them off-center so they were two black half-moons facing each other. She placed a small kenzan in each container, and carefully cut the forsythia underwater so that the cut created a bit of suction, water sucked up inside the branch. She trimmed the old petals off the branch, and caressed it into a slight bend. She measured the branch so that it was the full length of the container, then doubled the length and added two inches as that was the width of the flat moon container. She then cut the second branch to two-thirds of the length of the first. After that, she draped the forsythia back and forth, arcing from one vase to the next. They looked like stars burning and bursting forth from a dark sky. She then cut the alstroemeria underwater, and placed these flowers at the base of the forsythia in the left container. The alstroemeria were white, and appeared to be newer, fresher stars, sparkling beneath the older burning yellow stars. I stared at the yellow forsythia and the cluster of white alstroemeria arcing between the two black moon vases, and I imagined she was one vase, and I the other. The arrangement itself was in conversation, and in some abstract way, it was actually *us* in conversation, though we hadn't said a word.

Years later, Mom helped me again, with a different kind of start. She helped me plant a garden around my beautiful new raw property in upstate New York. "You must plant line material," she said, "not just flowers." So we planted dogwood trees and lush viburnum bushes. She taught me about ornamental grasses; we planted them in front of big gray boulders along the drive, and in the banks of the creek. We planted ground cover and ivy and clematis. We reminisced about our beautiful house in Greece, and I wanted to plant jasmine, but Mom said it was too cold in the Northeast and I would only be disappointed. So, we planted other flowers: daffodils in the fields, hundreds of them, hoping they would come back year after year, anthurium and lilies and tulips, lilacs and wisteria, and forsythia. Forsythia was the first bush Mom helped me plant when I bought the raw property in the Catskills. We planted forsythia because it was one of the earliest bloomers and it would greet our guests with a little pop of yellow on an otherwise drab and gray day. We planted it on top of the hill as you approached the driveway, its great droopy arms stretched out into a gesture of welcome, with the background a hundred-acre lake. We planted it to cover the electrical box at the top of the hill, and the electrical box behind the barn. It bloomed in Texas in late March, but in New York in late April/ early May. It reminded me of stargazing, yellow soft star petals on a long arching branch. Each small blossom a shooting star that would quickly open, and explode its flame of golden light down, down, down the arc, illuminating a brief moment in time, and then, snuffed out.

I think of my mom whenever and wherever I see forsythia now. It is one of those flowers that I wouldn't have really known about had it not been for her. Not like the common rose or tulip, or chrysanthemum. It's a vine, line material, and only blooms for a short burst. It's not much of a looker during the rest of the year, but in that one moment of bright yellow crescendo, it is magnificent. I make wishes on these blooms — wishes for my mom, that she might fly in the heart of God.

My Mother is
an Orange
Hibiscus in a
Brown Coffee Cup

■ ■ ■ ■

In the middle of the cold and dreary New York winter of 1991, I booked two seats on a flight for New Zealand. I had it planned perfectly: My boyfriend and I would leave just as winter was at its freezing peak in the States, which would mean summer was at its hottest peak in New Zealand! We would escape the New York cold and return with a tan! We would bask in the warm sun; I would introduce him to all the new friends I had made in New Zealand several months before when I had shot the film *Crush;* and we would hike and have picnics. He would play the bagpipes on the heath, the sound rolling across the waves, and we would hold hands as we climbed volcanoes and be one with God. We would be in love and romantic, and he would probably ask me to marry him.

The only problem was, I had just broken up with my bagpiping boyfriend, or rather, he had broken up with me, and he had timed it perfectly so that I would be deprived of a companion on this trip. It was fitting that I was supposed to be doing post-production on *Crush:* I was, indeed, crushed. Crushed, bereft, and angry. Who would I bring to New Zealand? What had gone wrong? Didn't my boyfriend appreciate that I was taking him to an exotic wonderful place? How dare he exercise this power of abandonment over me!

Trudging to the West Village several times a week, I had undergone copious therapy sessions filled with my crying and railing at the unjust outcome of my breakup. Finally, my therapist suggested I bring a friend, perhaps my best friend, on the trip.

"Arrgh! But . . . but . . . but . . . my best friend is my *mother!"* I said. "Do you hear me? *My mother!* How can I bring my *mother* instead of my boyfriend? It won't be romantic *at all.* How can I even *think* of traveling to New Zealand with my *mother* when I was supposed to hike and tramp the beaches with my *boyfriend*? What a big fat *zero* I will be!"

Mom and I sat side by side on the plane. She was looking out the window with girlish glee as the huge aircraft plunged through the clouds, suddenly exposing lush green hills and crystal blue waters, beckoning us toward the black sand beaches of Auckland. I pretended not to notice her excitement as I stared straight ahead, refusing to even glance at the looming countryside. I realized I was punishing her for replacing my boyfriend, and I realized it was small and immature of me, but I couldn't stop feeling sorry for myself. I was still angrily wiping tears away with my fists as we landed. Mom reached out and patted my wet hand, and said in her soft, understanding voice, "It's going to be really fun, honey. Thank you for bringing me." That just made it worse, her being so nice about it, and I embarrassed myself with barely disguised sobs as I thanked the flight attendants for taking such good care of us on the interminable trip.

Mom clutched her flower books and garden magazines as we went through customs, letting me lead the way. "Why is she letting me lead?" I wondered grumpily. She had traveled all over the world, hauling five kids to so many different countries, but for some reason she was now following me instead of the other way around. She seemed to think I was the strong one. Well, she was wrong. I didn't feel very strong. I felt discarded. Couldn't she see that? Fittingly, given my movie (or mood?), she wore a red "crush" skirt, the kind with wrinkles already in it and perfect for traveling because it was loose and didn't look wrongly wrinkled, just textured. She had on a red T-shirt-type top, walking shoes, and a gold necklace. I wore black. We didn't have computers or cell phones, so we lugged her big camera in my little rolling bag, and I offered to balance her heavy bag of books on top. She refused, smiling: "If I pack it, I better carry it!"

The officers did a double take as they compared my serene black-and-white passport picture to the contrasting swollen red nose and teary eyes I presented, and they seemed to smirk in disbelief when I said I was a "film actress" returning to finish my work. I left Mom in baggage claim while I snuck a cigarette behind a cement post on the curb. I pondered smoking out in the open, being just who I was, being just who I would have been with my boyfriend, but decided not to. I didn't want to see the hurt look on her face; her mother, Coco, had died of emphysema, and she hated that I smoked. I hurried back as the bags arrived so I could pull them off, I didn't want to see her struggling with the weight of them. She pretended not to notice that I stank of smoke, and she followed me with a smile, each of us rolling our own suitcases to the taxi stand.

Over the next few days, as I introduced Mom to various film friends and put in the hours at the sound studio looping the necessary sound repairs, she and I settled into a pleasant sort of balance. I didn't curse in front of her, I snuck my cigarettes, watched my p's and q's along with the number of evening drinks I consumed, and I even dressed in a slightly more conservative way than I had during the months before when I had been filming on my own in New Zealand. Mom thought everything was "marvelous," a word she used a lot, and she drawled the A sound: "Maaarvelous!" We were a bit stuck in our roles as mother/daughter. We didn't quite know how to travel as friends, so this was new and slightly formal territory for us. It was odd, and my friends felt it, as if they were seeing a watered-down version of me. ("It would have been totally different with my *boy-friend!*" I silently fumed.) We rented a car, and it was disconcerting driving on the opposite side of the road. Mom never took her foot off the imaginary brake on the passenger side, and she kept her hand on the glove compartment to brace herself, clicking her perfectly oval nails unconsciously. We drove up to the famous hot springs of

Rotorua, hoping to be educated in true Maori culture. I knew she would like the bubbling mud pools and geysers and sulphur lakes, the bizarre and barren landscape. We took sulphur baths, laughing at how our skin smelled like rotten eggs and questioning how this was supposed to be good for us.

We were honest and open with each other — sort of. It all seemed quite fun on the surface, but underneath, bubbling away in Rotorua hot springs, was a little tug-of-war of change. In small ways, she would test me, and me her. Silly things. For example, before we got to a particular tourist spot, she would ask me where the restroom was. I would respond that I didn't know, as I had *never been there before.* Or at a restaurant, she would ask if I thought they had coffee. I would respond, "Probably. *Let's look at the menu.*" It got under my skin; she could answer those questions for herself, I didn't understand why she kept deferring to me.

But for the most part, we were pretty good tourists together, Mom and I. We loved to learn, to stop and read the roadside plaques. We visited the cultural center and watched with concentration as the Maori performed for the tourists. We compared the cultures of New Zealand and Japan, and the Maori to Native Americans. She carried her little Japanese pruning shears and often cut off interesting pieces of branches or exotic flowers when no one was looking, and she arranged them in the hotel room coffee cups. She even decorated the car with a freshly cut orange hibiscus, and put it in a "borrowed" brown coffee mug set tightly in the coffee holder. We talked about the brilliant pohutukawa tree, with its red myrtle blossoms, grateful that we were there shortly after Christmastime when they were still in bloom. But it was during the drive south toward New Plymouth that New Zealand proved to be a turning point in our friendship.

I was the driver, and she was the navigator. We quickly began to discover that the spacing of signs in New Zealand was at a very different rate, or rhythm, than the spacing of signs in America. I needed a sign that read X NUMBER OF MILES [OR KILOMETERS] TO LAKE TAUPO, which we were planning to visit before heading on to Tongariro National Park, at least every half hour, especially on the winding roads — many of which had no signs at all as you passed the sheep and rural farms — and I found the markers to be very few and far between. And when there *was* a sign: it was in the native language of Maori, so we would whiz past places like Taumarunui and Kaimanawa headed to Whanganui, barely able to read, much less pronounce, the names. And to complicate matters further, the WH was pronounced F, so it would be "Fanganui." I was in a bad mood. ("If my *boyfriend* had come, *he* would be driving and *I* would be deciphering the map!") Mom seemed tense, and hesitant, and oddly fragile about navigating. She had always been the navigator in our family, so it irritated me to witness this confusion from her. Which naturally only made me gruffer, and at someplace along the road near Mangakino, we got lost. She had her reading glasses on and the sun was beating through the window as she tried to read the map, folding it back on itself and peering at the nearby town names of Whakamaru and Tirohanga. She refused to pronounce the F of Whakamaru because then it sounded like Fuckamaru. Which irritated me even more. So she said, "We are looking for Whakamaru! I think we passed it!"

We turned the car around to retrace our steps, and I said, "We already passed Fuckamaru? Fuckamaru, Mom?" I said Fuckamaru several more times, in the correct pronunciation. It was mean of me. It was intended to toughen her up. It was an effort to be myself. To curse as I liked to do. Which my boyfriend had also hated, and was one of the reasons he had broken up with me, because I cursed and it wasn't very Christian of me. He was very Christian, in a way that I wasn't. Because I cursed, for one, and for two, because I couldn't say that Jesus was the only way to God. I thought there were a lot of ways to get to know God, but in order to be a "true" Christian, I had to be able to say that the only way to God was through Jesus. Which I couldn't do, because then I would know that God would know I was lying. I certainly didn't want to lie to God, and I really didn't want to be a true Christian if it meant excluding so many others . . . which is why Mom and I ended up in a car together lost somewhere near Whakamaru. I mean Fuckamaru.

So on the road to New Plymouth, I used the Maori pronunciation to curse and make my points, and we drove back the way we had come for several miles but saw no signs, only sheep. I roughly swung the car back around and retraced our steps *again,* and then we began to really argue. All the while she was trying to read the map with the small print, and I was driving on the New Zealand side of the road, looking for signs that we were headed in the right direction. In between directions and arguing about where we were, we argued about who we were.

"There goes Whakamaru again," she said.

"You mean Fuckamaru?" I asked. She ignored me, and adjusted her glasses.

"Okay, honey, we're looking for Poihippi Road."

"Well, how far away is it, Mom? How long till I should see a friggin' sign?"

She didn't like my bullying, she told me as she squinted at the map. She could feel that my anger and irritation were controlling the mood of the car, and I felt that her timidity put me in charge all the time, which I didn't want to be. I had to be stronger for both of us the more timid she was.

"Honey, wait, we're coming up to Whaihaha."

"FAIhaha, mom! FAIhaha!"

I wanted to be myself, and I told her that now that we were traveling as friends, I wanted to be like I was with my friends. I wanted to have a beer and smoke and curse because that's who I was. I wasn't dainty like her, and I wanted her to love me anyway and not make me feel dirty because I wasn't dainty.

Meanwhile, she clutched the map, and we

passed another road with no sign. I slowed down.

"Wait — wait — Mom! Do we want the road to Turangi or Tongariro?" I barked.

"I don't know! I can't tell!" she squealed.

"*Why* can't you tell? Mom, it's on the map! Shall I pull over to read it myself?"

"No!" she yelled. "Just drive, Marcia! Drive! Tongariro! Tongariro! Go right to Tongariro!"

We continued to argue. She also didn't want to be portrayed as prissy just because she *was* dainty, she said that that wasn't fair of me, and we agreed that we should travel as friends and let each other be who we were, but she nevertheless said that she felt my anger and humor were crass, and that she had a right to that opinion.

"Left or right, Mom?"

"The car is too *bouncy,* Marcia. I can't read it."

She didn't want to disappoint me by being critical, but she also didn't want me to act like Dad. We passed a sign in a blur, and I, too, was thinking how I didn't want to act like Dad . . . "Marcia, slow down . . ." She was trying to read the map, and the curves were making it hard. We passed a national park sign. "Honey," she squinted at the map, "are we going *into* the national park? Or around it?"

"Mom! What did that sign just say?"

"Marcia! Are we going *into* the park? Are we going to see the volcano?"

"Yes! Mom, which way do I turn?!"

"There's a sign! Slow down, Marcia Gay!"

"Yes, there's a sign, but what does it say?!"

"Hold on: *Whakapapa!* It said *Whaka-papa!*" She pronounced the WH, not the F.

"Mom." I glared.

And then, she really snapped. "OKAY . . . I mean *FUCKAPAPA*, OKAY? *FUCKAPAPA!* It said *FUCKAPAAAPAAA!*"

She said it maybe ten times. With the map clutched in her hands. Jabbing at the window where the sign had just whizzed past. *"FUCKAPAAAAAPAAAAA!!!"*

We began laughing so hard that we *did* have to pull over, and we peed hiding behind the car in the middle of New Zealand's North Island on the road to Whaka-papa, with not a car in sight, only sheep, and wind, and lots and lots of green.

Later we stopped at a pub to get a beer. I wanted to smoke a Marlboro Light, but I still didn't want Mom to see it, so I quickly ran to the back of the building and lit up in the wind. It wasn't enjoyable at all. I smoked it really, really quickly, blowing the smoke straight up into the sky so that I didn't stink,

160

sucking in the air too quickly because in truth I just wanted to be in the warm pub with Mom, drinking our beer and laughing about Fuckapapa. She had brought her ikebana books with her into the pub, and some New Zealand geezer was flirting with her; Mom was bouncing her brown curls and flashing her big white teeth and describing the difficulty of driving in New Zealand. She even said "Fuckapapa" and laughed at how risqué it was. The geezer guffawed admiringly.

Mom and I were rarely spontaneous, and our travel in New Zealand had generally been well planned-out. But tonight, we threw our plans to the wind and decided to spend the night at the pub, as they had rooms upstairs. So we ate and had another beer while joking with the men, and then climbed the stairs to our queen-size bedroom. All of our anger had now dissipated in the laughter and ridiculousness of the day, scattered like the sheep on the hills. I mean, how could we have been angry when we had both had our bums hanging out in the wind while peeing behind the rental car?

We had turned a corner in our relationship, and the facades were now down. We could be ourselves, talk candidly about sex and loneliness and age and how we felt about each other, and we could be honest. Really honest. It felt warm and easy. It felt overdue, yet it was only a subtle difference. It was the difference of true acceptance, and for me it was a kind of growing up, accepting that my mother loved me and wouldn't judge me.

But that didn't necessarily mean she had to like everything that I did. It was the first time I began to understand how I unwittingly bullied my companions with my moods. And I felt deep shame that I had bullied my mom. I had always been rather proud of my transparency; if I were mad, you would know it! If I were happy, so much happier the room! But this drive with Mom made me reflect on the power of a bad mood (hadn't Dad dominated the house with his moods?), and it made me respect the ability Mom had for control and reserve. Perhaps it wasn't timidity at all . . . but simply . . . self-control?

Entirely humbled, I watched her unpack her flannel nightie and toothbrush. The toothbrush and toothpaste were in a plastic bag so the toothpaste wouldn't accidentally squeeze out into her cosmetic bag (that's how I packed, too!!!) and the nightie, as well as all her other clothes, was neatly rolled in the suitcase so it wouldn't wrinkle (I did that, too!). She set her books on one side of the bed — "Do you care which side you sleep on, honey?" — folded down her sheet in a triangle, then disappeared into the shower.

For some reason, I could only sit on the bed and stare at the door, just waiting for her to appear again. I wanted to erase any hurt I had caused for her earlier in the day, yet you can't undo the past. You can only fill the present with love and own your behavior. In that moment sitting on the white New Zealand sheets, with the orange hibiscus in the brown coffee cup staring quietly at me, I realized I had wanted her to take care of me, not for me to take care of her, and I realized that we were beginning the great migration of age, the moment when the children are suddenly stronger than the parents, when the children become the caregivers and caretakers and protectors for the parents who have loved them so well. My regret at needing her to pronounce the F in Whakapapa clutched at my stomach like a claw, and I sat on the bed watching the door, as if, by just sitting vigil and not being distracted, the full force of my love would fill and mix with the hot shower mist, and with each of her steamy inhalations, Mom would breathe in my love, and she would forgive me.

I could hear her get out of the shower, then brush her teeth for what seemed like three full minutes. Then I could hear lotions applied to face and hands, and then there she was. Damp. Clean. In a new flannel nightie of cream and lavender that she had bought specially for this trip. She sat on the bed and put on her socks, since her feet were always cold. She pulled her blue cable sweater from her suitcase and put it on, then patted my hand. "Your turn, honey."

I showered quickly, no cigarette smoke stinky skin for this queen bed couple! When I came out of the steamy bathroom, sucking air between my newly Crested teeth, Mom was propped up on her side of the bed, looking at a flower book. She had brought so many books, magazines, and photographs, and now they were surrounding her on the bed. Even though there is no such thing as a lavender tree, she looked just like one, there in the center of a garden of books, flower magazines, and Japanese flower-arranging photos. She parted a path for me in the garden, and I snuggled in, poring over the pictures with her.

She started talking about the ikebana demonstration she was planning to do when she returned to the States, and she showed me her favorite book, which was *A Guide to Japanese Flower Arrangement* by Norman Sparnon. In the introduction, I read, "Japanese flower arrangement has for several centuries provided an artistic outlet for a people sensitive to the beauty of nature." Yep — that was my mom. Sensitive to the beauty of nature. Orange hibiscus in the brown coffee cup. Sitting right there on the counter. The picture on the front of the book was a photograph of an ikebana flower arrangement; it showed a tall, thin white ceramic vase against a red backdrop. Spiraling out of the top of the vase was a spray of weeping willow, bent and swirling like a bouncing musical note. Peeking through the center of the spiral, just cresting the top of the white vase, were two small cream roses, and shooting out slightly below them were two sprigs of dark green pine. It was so simple, so elegant, and so specific. At once I could see it was a picture of the essence of my mom. Soft roses, pure white ceramic, pliable willow branches, verdant, spiky pine, and a dramatic red background. Simple. Elegant. Dramatic. Specific.

It seemed silly that in order to be true to who we each were, we had to push against each other in the ancient Mother/Daughter battle of independence. It was a battle of caretaking, and of aging. A battle of the shifting of roles — an unwillingness to accept that my mom wasn't as fast as me anymore, or couldn't see as well as I could, and that I needed to care for her. It wasn't the first time I had been in this position with her — but it was the first time we had argued about it. I felt embarrassed again at my impatience in the car earlier that day. It felt so much more right to be cuddled up on the cozy down bed, looking at flowers and talking about various line materials that existed in people's own backyards. Willow trees, bamboo, tall grasses, palm leaves, pine, pussy willow, cattails, fern, calla lily, eucalyptus, iris, bird-of-paradise, camellia, and on and on went the list.

She never mentioned the car ride. She never mentioned my angry driving and domineering temper. She simply looked at me and said softly: "You will find love, Marcia Gay. Don't worry." My throat immediately tightened, and I had to look out the window and concentrate on the moon so I wouldn't cry. It struck me that as a mom, maybe she was disappointed *for me* that my boyfriend had broken up with me. Maybe she was a little disappointed *in me,* too, because she could see how easy it was for me to argue and fight. Maybe she was worried that I would never find love and never have children. Maybe she was worried that I would never be happy, that I was too headstrong to ever find a man, that I would be alone forever. Well, I was worried, too. I didn't want to be alone! I wanted a commitment! But I was tired of being with guys who let me pay all the bills and make all the plans. I was worried that no one would ever take care of *me.* That was probably why I had been so pissed at having to take care of *her.* I was also worried that I didn't know how to surrender. That even though I wanted to be taken care of — whatever that meant — I was afraid of it. I was worried that I would never feel loved. I was worried that I wasn't loveable, which is the worst feeling. To feel unworthy of love.

I snuggled closer to her. She thumbed through the pages of the Norman Sparnon book, and I recognized so many of the same type of arrangements that she had for years placed in the center of the tansu in our home. It felt warm and lush, to be getting to know her so intimately through these flower arrangements in the book, with the sea crashing outside in New Plymouth, New Zealand, and the jovial sounds of the pub below.

She was a master of her craft, but a quiet

master, and as I was looking at the photos she had brought, I began to realize the immensity of the gifts she shared with her Dallas–Fort Worth community. There were pictures of her students arranging with her, and I regretted that I had never taken a formal class with her. I was a bit jealous in fact that I had never, and would never, know her in quite the same way as her students knew her. We looked at the photos under the bedside table lamp, and always there was Mom, dressed monochromatically, which she reminded me was because she didn't want to draw focus from the arrangement with the patterns on her clothing. Usually she was in earth tones, standing behind the arrangement, facing her class. "Oh my gosh!" I realized. "You are arranging from behind!" Now I was almost in awe of her.

"That must be hard, Mom, to arrange backwards?"

"Oh yes," she agreed humbly, "which is why I first arrange the flowers standing in front of them, and then practice replicating the arrangement from behind, so it will go smoothly for my class.

She had a notebook in which she kept her class lesson plan. It was an old black three-ring binder with the words "Battlefield

Automation Appraisal IV" written in blue, yellow, and red on the front. I couldn't believe how incongruous it was, that Mom had her lovely ikebana lesson plan in this old battlefield appraisal notebook. It must have been something of Dad's: There were sketches of tanks and helicopters, trucks and men on walkie-talkies in the battlefield, all talking to a communications person in the middle. Had she chosen to use it, years before, because she was frugal and it was a perfectly good notebook? Or had she chosen to use it because it made her feel a little bit closer to Dad?

On one of the first pages of the book, she had written "Sogetsu Basics, helpful hints by Beverly." She had jotted down easy ways to help her students remember the rules and ideas of ikebana, and she started the list with A, B, and C:

A: ANGLES: There are three angles in the ikebana triangle, 10 to 15 degrees, 45 degrees, and 75 degrees. These are repeated in all the basic arrangements, simply move the three main lines around creating an asymmetrical triangle.

I had always shut down at the math of ikebana, but now, cuddled up next to her, I forced myself to concentrate. "Okay, so, essentially, we are creating a triangle with two branches and a flower?"

"In so many words, yes." We turned the page. B.

B: BASICS: Think B — just as the capital B has both loops on the same side of the perpendicular line, the Basic upright arrangement and Basic slanting arrangement have Both main lines on the same side of the imaginary line.

I was beginning to understand. "So the *shin* and the *soe* are on the same side of the vase, Mom? If there was an imaginary line up the center, the *shin* and the *soe* are on the same side?"

"Yes, dear."

"But at different angles?"

"Yes, dear."

The "B's" went on:

B: BENDING LINE MATERIAL: Always bend in an S curve, not just a single direction curve. This gives softness to the line.

How many times had I seen her bend a branch, or a gladiola, or a pine bough? In just this same gentle caress, creating an S curve. "Like the forsythia, bending and arc-ing between the vases? Right, Mom?"

"Yes, dear."

More B's:

B: BASKETS: Grasses are good in bas-kets. Show the beauty of the artist's basket — don't let your work dominate it. Use a utility basket as a background for your ar-rangement.

"You always used baskets at Easter time, Mom, and made arrangements in them."

"Yes, but women weave baskets all over the world, and I like to use them for ar-rangements, or as a background to an ar-rangement, to acknowledge their art. I find the baskets exotic, and I like to support the women."

Then there were the C's:

C: CRITIQUE: Always say what's good first, then suggest changes.

I laughed. "*If you can't say something nice, don't say anything at all,* right, Mom?" She had said this so many times in our youth, and it was a phrase I both hated and loved. I hated it, because when certain presidents would be in office whom I particularly despised, or when policies would be put forth by Congress or the Senate denying art in the schoolrooms, or when someone said or did something that seemed mean, or when anything would happen in the world that didn't seem right, I would typically want to expound upon the problem, dissecting the injustices and "speaking truth to power." This discordant discourse made Mom uncomfortable; she would rather not engage in conflict, and with that phrase she often tried to turn the conversation to something pleasant. To me it seemed a passive way of avoiding the sometimes necessary confrontation with power and abuse. But I also loved the little phrase, because *if you can't say something nice, don't say anything at all* was of the school of positive thinking. Mom and I had spent much time at Marble Collegiate Church on Fifth Avenue in New York City in the early eighties, and had been fortunate enough to witness Dr. Norman Vincent Peale preach. We were instant acolytes of this philosophy, and we bought the books and tapes and practiced the enthusiasm and positive language and thinking that were at the core of Dr. Peale's teachings: sayings such as "You can if you THINK you can" and "To make your mind healthy, feed it powerful nourishing

172

thoughts" seemed to be of the same school as "If you can't say something nice, don't say anything at all," or another of my mother's favorites, "Pretty is as pretty does." What we say influences not just what we feel, but what others feel about us. It influences the outcome of events. It is what we put out into the world. It is the quality of light we shine on our path, and determines our happiness in the moment. We have a choice — be positive or be negative. Mom was always an advocate of the positive frame of mind, and in that way she made the world around her better.

C: COLOR: Do not always coordinate the color of flowers and line material with the container, but try contrasting surprises, like found in Japanese kimono colors.

"That's like the orange hibiscus in the brown coffee cup; right, Mom?"

"Hmmm. Yes. I hope they don't mind that I 'borrowed' it," she said, smiling. "But blue would have been a better contrast for the orange."

We pored over the lesson book, me learning so many rules about the precision and imagination of ikebana. "Oh my gosh, Mom! I didn't realize you could actually create an arrangement to depict the phases of the moon!" But there it was, described under the C's:

C: CONTAINER: Moon Containers: There are three types of arrangements depicting the phases of the moon. Waxing moon — all lines flow to the left of the container; full moon, all lines must stay within the circle of the container, and waning moon, all lines will go out of the right side.

And on and on.

As we turned the pages of the books and lesson plans, I realized that she had brought them not just so that she could prepare for the upcoming demonstration back in Texas, but also so that we could share just such a moment as this, in that New Zealand hotel room, with moonlight beaming through the window. I was proud to be her bedside student.

I was so like her, our bodies so the same, our legs the same shape, our feet always cold, our hair and eyes almost the same color, our love of adventure and travel, our need for clean rooms and no clutter, our need to feel we were making an impact on life somehow, making a difference somehow, giving back somehow. We lay under the down comforter, our chilly feet bundled in the socks we always wore to bed, two friends talking creatively about the various arts they loved.

I remembered a phrase from Shakespeare: "Thou Nature art my goddess," and I was suddenly glad my boyfriend wasn't there, telling me his thoughts about God and Jesus as if he alone sat in the lap of God and had all the answers. I was glad it would be Mom and me tramping on the beach the next day, gathering shells and driftwood to use in the various coffee cup flower arrangements she would make. I was glad to have my mother pointing out the incredible beauty of God's Kingdom, as seen in nature through the ancient eyes of the ikebana masters of Japan. I was grateful for the nightly conversations we would have throughout the week, and I was proud that Mom had lugged her flower books halfway across the world to teach me a lesson.

Much to my delight, two years later, in October 1993, Mom gave me the Norman Sparnon book and inscribed it, "To Marcia, from a proud mom." I recognized her on every page.

That was twenty-five years ago. My mom was fifty-five, one year younger than I am as

I write this. There was no sign of Alz-heimer's. No sign of forgetfulness, no sign of any weakness. Only a ladylike unwilling-ness to pronounce WH as F when referring to Maori villages.

If I am so like her, do I have Alzheimer's, too?

This week on my to-do list is "Book a test to do a brain scan."

■ ■ ■ ■

My Mother is
a Miraculous
Bamboo

■ ■ ■ ■

Even a mother with five children can be lonely. The day starts at 6:30 a.m. Breakfast is made. Five eggs, five strips of bacon, five toasts spread with jam, five glasses of orange juice. Children dress and scatter socks, toothpaste is left on sticky brushes, the remnants sliding down the porcelain sink like a mint-striped slug. Doors slam and shoelaces are broken as we run for the bus. Then the house is quiet. Except for the chatter of running water as Mom rinses the dishes, her quiet hum under the clink of china and scrape of metal pans. Chair legs brush up against the table legs and place-mats return to their darkened drawer. She hums. Now gliding down the hall, with the family pictures talking to each other across the frames, and into the bedrooms, she checks that the beds are made as they are supposed to be, opens a window, feeds the goldfish and the lovebirds, then cleans the kitty litter and grits her teeth as she picks up dog hair sitting like a forgotten dandelion fluff in the corner. She doesn't hum now. She just works and vacuums and dusts and throws T-shirts and underwear in the laundry. Hours pass. Another window is opened, and the chirp of birds reminds her to stop for a minute, to actually look outside. She stares at the pyracantha just beginning to burst into orange flame-like berries, and she makes a mental note to pick up some bright yellow chrysanthemums from the Japanese market on her way home from the commissary, which is next on her list. She hums again now, imagining the flower arrangement evocative of fireworks she will make later in the day using pyracantha and exploding yellow chrysanthemums.

Pyracantha is a winter bloomer, sometimes called firethorn. Ikebana directly translates to "the arrangement of plant materials," and its minimalist style allows my mother to work outside the Western tradition of many showy flower blooms plunked in a vase, but rather gather backyard plants and trees to create a serene arrangement. Pussy willow, palm, and pine, draping jasmine and cherry blossom, chestnut tree and candle tree, forsythia, wisteria, and evergreen — all these can be found or planted in one's own backyard, and pyracantha is an ikebana staple for line material. Its orange- and red-berry-laden branches will provide the smoldering arms of the *shin* and *soe,* and the yellow chrysanthemum will be the center of the arrangement, the *hikae.*

Monks began the tradition of ikebana, arranging flowers at the temple, and the meditation that is part of the creation is perhaps why my mother loved the process of it so much. It wasn't just the social gathering and community of ladies in the class or garden club — though those were hugely important. It wasn't just the beauty of the flowers and the small gift to the family she gave of a weekly live sculpture — though those were also important. Equally important, however, was the space of hum and meditation that filled my mother's brain as she contemplated and planned her arrangement. There would be poetry, emotion, balance, a nod to nature, a drift of peace, a fondling of hard branches and soft petals, and a hum and a hum and a hum in her head of God and of beauty. With the tools of her craft, what would emerge would be an exciting, idyllic scene, as if you were on a nature walk and, when you turned a corner, suddenly happened upon a beautiful spot in a magical garden. You would stand for a minute, admiring the coupling of lime-green fern draping over fluffy white hydrangea, with a deeper green palm arching heavenward, anchored in a dark blue vase evocative of a pond.

She begins her meditation as a hum these mornings, interspersing home care and child care with weighing the balance of two heavy arms of pyracantha. Standing at the window, her eyes resting on the bamboo across the lawn, she remembers that she has heard that you can actually see bamboo grow — right before your eyes! — for it is the fastest-growing plant on earth. But the cat meows, the dirty clothes beckon, the soured socks need to be fished from under the bed, and she doesn't allow herself to take the time to stand still for five minutes and witness this astonishing miracle.

There is a joke that goes like this: A dad and a mom are asked if they have a favorite chair in the house that they especially like to sit in. The dad responds, "Oh, yes, of course! The big leather armchair where I read the paper!" Then the mom thinks and thinks and thinks . . . what *is* her favorite chair? And she finally responds, "Well, I don't think I have ever actually sat down!" Mom doesn't stop to sit down, or to read the paper, or to watch the bamboo grow.

She doesn't stop for miracles. There is simply too much to do. She leaves the window, humming, and as she turns around past the kitty litter and drone of the dishwasher, she grabs the morning trash bag and steps outside, her dark blue Keds kicking the morning sun off the porch.

Suddenly, the bamboo chatters, its wooden reeds calling her name. A small brush warbler flies close to her head, wafting a breeze in her hair and a song to her ear, beckoning her to follow. The bird disappears in the enchanting bamboo. It's as if the warbler is guiding her, hovering for a minute in throaty song: "Beverly come see . . . come seeee . . . come seeeee the bamboo grow . . ." She turns and stares. With trash bag in hand, she stares at the moving leaves where her name lingers, and her blue Keds leave flat marks in the damp lawn as she wanders to the edge of the yard where the bamboo grows thick behind the metal chain-link fence. On the other side, the leafy wooden reeds spread for several acres along a path that is long overgrown. The path leads to caves, hidden in the mountain like sunken eyes. Hidden, like the vacant eyes that were staring out through its dark opening when the Japanese hid there during the war. We children have snuck back there, carefully bidding the light good-bye and inching into the dirt cave, slowly, slowly, one inch at a time, then screaming at the "BOO!" that inevitably comes from the sibling behind you. Once our hearts had stopped pounding and we could breathe again, we would find spoons and metal helmets, cigarette butts and joints, and bones. No *boo* then. Just imagining what war was like. What hiding in caves in the dark was like. What being bombed by the Americans was like. We had heard of torture. "For sure," we thought, "someone was tortured in this cave," we could feel it. "Maybe even an American!" We shuddered. Then we would run like lightning out of the cave, past the growing bamboo, and tumble and stumble into the backyard, laughing suddenly again with hiccups, racing for the lemonade sure to be in the fridge, racing for the perfectly cut apple on the white plate, racing for the goldfish, racing for the safety of our clean and neat home. The details of a home are usually what fill up a mother's life . . . but how often have her children stopped to consider that her sacrifices are actually gifts?

Mom clutches the trash bag, and stares past the chain-link fence, peering into the dark green shadows, not wanting to think of the mournful caves. She hears the bamboo shudder and chatter like one of those wooden hanging chimes. It's eerie, yet lovely. It makes a hollow sound as the wind beats the gentle sticks, like distant Japanese dojo drums. Standing there listening to the drum song, she is a dot of red against a lime-green backdrop. She stands still, the bamboo swaying and bending over her rose-flowered dress. She arches her curly head to the side, resembling an ikebana arrangement herself. She is the *hikae,* a dark rose in the center of lime bamboo that is now the *shin* and *soe,* and she stands still and concentrates. She stands and waits; she squints her eye, she wants to see the bamboo grow. A rose lady stands in her yard, a brown paper trash bag like a gentle thorn at her side, and she waits, and she watches. She reaches out to mark a spot in the air, her pale finger barely touches a leaf, and she stands outstretched and measuring, birds chattering in the reeds, time passes and she stands and quietly hums, she stands and measures until the spot of bamboo infinitesimally, with miniscule yet definite journey, stretches slowly upward. Ahhhh. She has seen the bamboo grow. Time. Well. Spent.

Later that day, as we run home, clattering

doors breaking the silence when we enter the cool quiet home, I stop short at the flower arrangement that dominates the stereo cabinet. "Mom," I gasp. "It looks like the Japanese fireworks we saw during the summer festival!" There is a tall, dark bamboo cylindrical vase, about four inches wide and a foot and a half tall, and it sits on a small mat of bright green bamboo leaves. Stretching out one side of the bamboo vase is a thin, flaming pyracantha arm ladened with berries. It reaches out, toward the front, and slightly dips down. Toward the back, a shorter, fatter pyracantha arm boldly rises up, its berries lightning red. In the center, three yellow large chrysanthemums explode out of the bamboo, bending forward, like huge fireworks bursting from the sky. They set off the orange of the pyracantha perfectly. I inhale her day, through the flowers.

Of all the lessons that I have learned from my mother, perhaps the most important lesson — the power of standing still — is one that I will always be learning anew. Until we stand still, we don't really notice the feelings and the essence of people around us; we are caught up in our daily routines and schedules and appointments. We miss the tilt of the earth, the hum of a bee, the ache of a heart, and all of the details that make life a miraculous treat.

I try to track Mom's journey. There are dangling threads in her tapestry I can't quite capture. So I trace a path: She started blossoming in Japan. Then when we returned by ship to the States, she seemed to be crushed for a minute as we waited out a six-month holding pattern in Austin, Texas. We were renting a cramped two-bedroom apartment behind a dilapidated 7-Eleven, a far cry from our house on the hill in Yokohama with the koi pond and the jump rope. We were waiting for my dad's new assignment in DC to be finalized. It was just Mom and us five kids, dropped in Austin in the middle of a school year. I was eleven, in sixth grade, and was shocked to witness the segregation in the Texas schools. In Japan, on the navy base, we had lived with every race and color. We had schooled with the diversity of children from all walks of life, children of Americans serving in the armed forces. Every race, color, and creed.

But my Texas school was almost entirely white. Walking out to the cafeteria tables at lunch time, I saw a lone black girl sitting, eating lunch from a brown paper bag. I sat with her. Mom had often sung the Bluebird song to me: "Make new friends, but keep the old. One is silver and the other is gold," but I didn't need the song to spur me forward that day. The girl's imposed isolation angered me. My new school endorsed spanking kids with rulers, and that angered me, too. Our ugly little home angered me. Even the Slurpees at the 7-Eleven angered me.

I don't know what Mom did with her days when we were in school. Cleaning our little apartment, I guess. I think she was angry, too. Fortunately we were near my grandparents on my dad's side, Mammau and Tattau, and we would often spend weekends out at their lake home, swimming or laying on the dock, eating pecan pie and peach cobbler, or picking bluebonnets when they were in season. My dad's brother, Uncle Don, and Aunt Linnie also lived in Austin, and they provided companionship for Mom and so much grace and fun that we didn't hurt so much thinking about our faraway house in Japan, surrounded by bamboo and caves and wooden chimes.

Finally in the summer of 1970 we moved to the Washington, DC, area because Dad would be working at the Pentagon. He had found us a home in a new cul-de-sac in Maryland, and I would enter the local middle school, which in those days started in seventh grade. As I follow this thread now, something darkens. Dad didn't like the Pentagon. He didn't like the red tape he encountered there, and he wasn't used to being at home so much. He missed the sea, and he was stressed and angry and grumpy. A lot. He was like an angry bear at times, and Mom's advice was just not to poke him: "If you can't say something nice, don't say anything at all!" So we were on our best behavior. A lot. We were glad when they discovered the opera, downtown jazz, birding, and the symphony. It took the focus off us, and made things a lot more pleasant.

But most importantly, Mom discovered a local flower club. Everything seemed to get a bit lighter then. She befriended the garden club ladies and enjoyed their camaraderie. Making friends in between the housework and schoolwork and garden work, she was mentored by Katherine Foster, and her voice began to quietly emerge.

At the time, I wasn't really paying attention to these changes in Mom. I was busy trying to be popular in school, growing my hair long and rolling it in big curlers, plucking my unibrow into two fine arches, and spreading Clearasil and foundation in equal proportions as I applied my morning makeup. But I do remember Mom taking me to meet this woman that she revered so much. She said, "Sometimes she scares me a little, but I want to be like her. Strong and independent." Katherine Foster taught an ikebana class, which Mom took. She was in her late sixties and reminded me of Katharine Hepburn — not only because her name was Katherine, but also because she was beautiful and sharp and elegant. She was a horse lady to boot, so to me she seemed tough. She had a stable and fields with wooden fences, and she actually cleaned her own horses and rode them.

Katherine had noted Mom's timidity, and she took her under wing. She seemed to be teaching Mom how to stand up for herself, how to appreciate her own worth, and how to stand up for her children. Mom, in turn, became more outspoken, and gently stood behind her own ideas. She began to build a name for herself in the ikebana clubs. She began to insist upon her own life.

Then we moved from the cul-de-sac in Sandy Spring, Maryland, to the Cheltenham Naval Base in Prince George's County. We had a big three-story house with white columns, and behind it sat the navy base tennis courts. Dad was the captain of this Cheltenham base, and we were the captain's daughters, and it was the nicest house we had ever lived in, with those columns out front and three stories of brick with windows that had shutters . . . and a yard with roses and hydrangea . . . and I felt . . . important. I felt rich. Mom helped my sisters and me set up a sewing room on the third floor, and we bought Butterick patterns and made our own dresses for prom and the cotillions at the Annapolis Naval Academy that were soon to come.

Who were Mom's friends then? I lose the thread. Did she create a new garden club? Did she like being the captain's wife on this base, with all the requisite duties that went along with the position? Was she lonely? I know we took classes together — ceramics classes. We poured vases and ashtrays, and we made a white Virgin Mary that I still bring out every Christmas. I made my boyfriend an ashtray. A navy blue one. Mom drove me to his birthday party one night. Did she know I was no longer a virgin at sixteen? I was in tears, because he had cheated on me. Did Mom know why I was in tears? I delivered the ashtray, and immediately left the party, climbing back into the car with Mom. Still in tears. But proud, with my head high, and we drove home. Did she ask me about my cheating boyfriend?

No. She just reached over and patted my hand as we drove.

Not long after that, at the end of my senior year of high school, Dad got honored with the command of a military communications base in Greece. We began the familiar routine of packing one box each to ship to our new home and one suitcase each, and my sisters and I began looking for colleges abroad. I said good-bye to my new boy-friend, Shawn, who was funny and lovely and wore red roller skates and was a fabulous dancer and a skilled actor, if not a bit of a drama queen. Mom watched us wiping our tears as we said farewell, making plans to see each other in Greece, and holding hands on the swing by the tennis courts. Her heart aching as all moms' do, in empathy for their children. Feeling her daughter's broken heart. Later I said good-bye to my good friend Ronnie, who was quiet and loyal and protected me from high school ridicule and pressure when I admitted I couldn't smoke dope because I got too paranoid. Ronnie passed by his friends skipping class in the morning, and with hands deep in his jeans pockets, walked me to my class, saying "make an A" with a lopsided grin. I said good-bye to our house with the columns, I said good-bye to the sewing machines and to the Annapolis cotillions, I said good-bye to the lovely tennis courts, to the ceramics studio, and finally, together with Mom, to Washington, DC, itself.

We drove around the Washington monuments one last time. The Smithsonian, our favorite museum, the Lincoln Memorial, our favorite president, the Jefferson Memorial, our favorite place to rent a paddleboat in the summer. We drove around Hains Point and the Tidal Basin, remembering the fat cherry blossoms of the early spring. The trees had stood like proud ballerinas en pointe, shimmering in frothy cherry blossom tutus, and Mom had explained the historic friendship between Japan and our capitol.

She told me that three thousand cherry blossom trees had been gifted to DC by the Japanese mayor Ozaki of Tokyo in 1912, and that ever since, the exchange of flowering trees was the gift of choice as our countries grew their important friendship. I remembered her speech almost word for word; I had never seen my mom so patriotic. Here in this embrace of cherry blossom trees, Mom had the meshing of three things she loved so much: America, Japan, and flowers. She wanted me to know that ikebana and flowers were more than just a beautiful ornamentation on a tansu chest. They were more than just a gathering of friends chatting about their day as they created arrangements. They were in fact a cultural bridge from one country to the other. I could tell she felt that what she was doing with ikebana was an important mission, the motto being "Friendship through Flowers!," and I could tell she was sad to leave it all behind as we prepared to move to Greece.

All around the National Mall, people were getting ready for the 1976 Bicentennial. Mom and I drove around and watched the preparations taking place. We were bereft that we were going to miss it. Dad's transfer date was at the end of May, so we would miss the two hundred–year Bicentennial. We would miss the spectacular fireworks. We would even have to miss some school.

Mom patted my hand. "Sorry you're going to miss your senior graduation, honey."

"That's okay, Mom. Sorry that you are going to miss your favorite holiday, the Fourth of July. The Bicentennial will be the largest fireworks show in America, *ever,* and we're going to miss it!"

She did not say, "That's okay, honey." She just sighed, staring out at the bustle of people, and said, "Oh . . . I do love fireworks!"

Something fierce began to flow through Mom when we moved to Greece. She became Athena, the goddess of war and wisdom. Goddess of civilization. Goddess of the arts. Goddess of crafts. Goddess of war strategy. Goddess of the city. Goddess of so many things! We had barely unpacked our bags at the American Hotel before Mom said, "I'm not going to have you swimming in the pool all day. Go explore!" She gave us a guidebook, and off we went, exploring the Parthenon, the Acropolis, and the Greek flea markets of Monastiraki. As we explored Athens, Mom got down to business. From the pay phone of the hotel, she immediately followed up on the colleges we'd researched while we were still in America: one in Rome for my oldest sister, one in Germany for my second sister, and she planned how she would get each daughter to these exciting destinations by the end of August in time for school. At seventeen I would just be entering my first year of college, and Mom and Dad both agreed I was too young to go to school away from home, so she walked me through applying to Deree College in Agia Paraskevi. (It was an American accredited college, and I was able to complete my first year there. I studied Greek language, Greek civilization, Greek philosophy, and I discovered my love for acting through the Greek theater at the Acropolis.)

We found a wonderful home with marble floors in a little town called Mati, which was just up the coast from Marathon, the town from where the soldier Pheidippides had run twenty-five miles to announce the defeat of the Persians to the Athenians. Apparently, he wasn't in the best of shape, and immediately after he delivered the message "VICTORY," he rolled over and died. "Ahh," I said to Mom, "a very good reason to avoid excessive exercise!" "Like hell!" interupted Dad. "That's a good Goddamn reason to get into shape!" Mom just smiled and encouraged Dad and me to try to jog along the same road, which we did later on in the year. Our little town of Mati was also just a few miles away from the naval base NAVCOMSTA Nea Makri, and Mom would drive past tavernas and sheep, bread shops and old men on bicycles, as she went to visit my dad at work. Mom was the wife of Captain Thad Harden. He had been sent there to maintain peace between Greece and America and Cyprus, and Mom had diplomatic duties as well. She hosted Greek high priests, and mayors, and wives of visiting ambassadors. She threw luncheons for the navy wives. She counseled homesick sailors. Because Dad was the captain of the base, and there was tension between Cyprus and Greece and Turkey, he was also a target and he often had security men surrounding him. Mom was instructed to check for car bombs hidden under the wheels of our black Lincoln. She took it all in stride. She even adopted the Mediterranean style of eating, cutting cucumbers and feta into tomato salads, and ordering baby lamb at the tavernas. Though she often depended on me to translate the Greek, she was also taking classes herself to learn the language; filling notebooks with new letters and words and paragraphs, she murmured *parakalo* and *ef haristo,* "please" and "thank you," throughout the day. She was meticulous, tenacious, and enthusiastic. The perfect student. She was also managing a household, schooling my younger brother and sister, and navigating the travel of my older sisters to Germany and Italy and then back to Greece for holidays. Without house help. Without a computer. Without a cell phone. Without the internet.

She loved her time in Greece, but it was not a time of freedom for her; she had duties, and like Athena, she would carry them out! Assisting my father in diplomatic international relations would fall into the category of "goddess of war strategies," but Athena was also the goddess of wisdom, and Mom had learned long ago to stand still for a minute, and witness nature's miracles.

She now stopped to inhale the jasmine draping over our fence, or picked an orange from the fruiting tree before she peered under the car to check for bombs, making sure it was safe to trundle her kids off to school.

She now made time to visit the islands, sitting still with me on the white stones of a Santorini hillside, drinking a shot of ouzo as the sun set on the Aegean Sea. When the outdoor lounge speakers floated "The Girl from Ipanema," Mom smiled and said, *"Kala,"* meaning "good." Athena was also the goddess of justice, and Mom made time to climb the steps of Delphi, and wonder at the oracles, wonder at the deaths of the young virgin girls, wonder at the balance, or rather imbalance, of power. Athena was also the goddess of inspiration, and when Shawn came to visit me from DC, Mom gathered my brother and sister and joined us at the beach in Marathon for a nighttime swim so we could all experience the miracles of the phosphorescent sea. We watched the waves glow as they rolled into the shore, illuminating golden starfish floating in the clear water. It was amazing. We waded in the water and stood in awe. "Look, Marcia," she said, standing still with her feet in the cool water, her head craning back to witness the vast sky. "Look, the sky is mimicked in the phosphorescent sea: sparkles and starfish and glittery blue at our feet, and midnight blue and stars above, all sparkling and glittering together. *Poli oreo!*" Meaning "very beautiful."

I knew she was imagining an arrangement evocative of the glowing waves on the bioluminescent beaches of Marathon. And because Athena was also the goddess of the arts, and of skill and of craft, I wasn't surprised when Mom found a dark blue iris whose petals rolled like the waves, its golden center glowing with light. She sprinkled sand in the bottom of a flat, square sea-blue vase. She placed several deep blue irises in a spiky kenzan, their wavy petals splashing forth, the yellow glow just peeping from the interior of the flower. She placed one pale starfish flower beneath the iris, at the lowest point of the arrangement. Above the waves of iris, she laced angel's breath, its tiny white clusters of flowers becoming a star-studded sky.

"Lampros," I said. Meaning "brilliant," "radiant," "shining." It's where we get our word for "lamp."

"Ne," said Athena. *"Poli lampros. Oreo louloudi. Efharisto."* Meaning, "Yes, very beautiful. Pretty flower. Thank you."

When Mom returned from Greece, she brought Athena with her. She settled with my father and my younger brother and sister in Vernon View, Virginia, just a mile up the Potomac from George Washington's old home. My father was working at the Pentagon again, now on the Joint Chiefs of Staff, and he was frustrated with the usual red tape. I had returned home that summer from the University of Texas in Austin where I was attending college, and was enjoying hanging with the family. One day, out of the blue, Mom said, "I want to change my birthday." Her birthday is January 11, but she never liked to celebrate it then. It was too cold. And too lonely, she said. And there wasn't any excitement; people were still sated from Christmas excesses, and no one cared about her birthday, she said. "I want to celebrate it in the summer, when people are here!" she demanded. Demanded? This was impressive! I liked this self-advocating mom! And she wasn't wrong, exactly — it was true that as we all had gotten older and gone off to college or started our own families, it was eventually just Mom and Dad at home. But in the summer, people were always visiting, or Mom was always visiting one of us kids, and it felt more like a celebration.

So . . . we changed it. We decided to celebrate her birthday in July. On July 4, to be exact. It made perfect sense: it was a built-in party! The fireworks would be for her! The gatherings and red beans, sparklers and the grill would be lit up for her! It was a celebration, and we adopted the many planned events, and put her at the center. It worked! And what better place to give birth to this idea than Washington, DC? Every Fourth of July on the great mall, between the Capitol and the Washington Monument, thousands of people would gather to watch fireworks and listen to music and honor American Independence. This particular summer 500,000 people were gathering, but to celebrate what? To celebrate my mother's birthday, of course! And the Beach Boys were going to play at her party!

One of my favorite cousins was visiting that summer — Alicat, I called her — and we all packed picnic baskets and colorful picnic quilts. Fried chicken, cheeses, grapes and apples, sodas and water, crackers and chocolates and napkins — we packed these into backpacks and woven wicker baskets, and Mom shoved in bug spray and flashlights. We kissed Dad goodnight, asking one last time was he *sure* he didn't want to go? Of course we got the answer "There is no Goddamned way in *hell* I want to go to a picnic with that many people on that Goddamned muddy mall." So we laughed and hugged him and drove the car to the Alexandria Metro station to catch the train.

It had been raining nonstop for several days, and to tell you the truth I wasn't looking forward to the muddy slog very much, either, but slog we had to: we had a birthday to celebrate, and our mall guests were already 200,000 strong. We lugged the baskets and blankets and crammed into the sleek silver Metro cars with the thousands of other revelers who had the same idea. Everyone was laughing and cheering and singing Beach Boys songs and waving flags. Mom had a small flag clutched in one hand and her purse smashed securely under her arm. She was smiling and waving the flag, holding the pole on the Metro train, laughing as it lurched forward and all the people said, "Whoooa." She was happy in this community of revelers. She was happy to be on an adventure. Happy to have a birthday that was an event, *for goodness' sakes.* At some point I shouted, "It's my mom's birthday!" and the car spontaneously erupted into what would become our theme song of the night: "Happy Biiirrrthhhdaaay dear Mommmmm/Beverlyyyyy . . ."

Hours later, under the stars, the Beach Boys played from their catalogue of songs and we all sang along. These songs were like old friends, first learned in Japan so far away across the seas, long, long ago. We felt connected to the Beach Boys, as if they were singing just for us because they knew that their records had been part of the very few we had been allowed to listen to in Yokohama. "Goood, goood, goooood, good vibrations!" rolled over the heads and off the tongues of our many guests. We ate and laughed and lolled around, muddy and somewhat cold. We patted mosquito spray on our arms, and Mom sat shining in the center of the blanket, not wanting to miss a thing. Soon after the band finished the concert, there was a pause before the fireworks would begin. In this quiet, we dug deep into a woven basket and pulled out the cake, and Alicat lit one candle. We started to sing. Other voices from nearby picnic blankets slowly joined in, and soon there were several hundred people singing those familiar strains of "Happy Birthday to You." Then we made Mom stand up and look around, and she began to cry. Spontaneous joy, welcoming community, "Happyyyy Biirrrthdaaaayyyy deeearrr Mooooommmm, Haaappy Birthday to You!" Then BOOM! A yellow chrysanthemum firework burst into the darkened sky. First one, then another starlike cluster lit up the night. Then another and another, and soon the sky was full of fireworks and colors and smoke and music. Golden chrysanthemum fireworks exploding in the night sky. Pyracantha tracers arcing over the chrysanthemums. The top of the Washington Monument became obscured by the smoke. Yet we sat with necks craned skyward, oohing and aahing at each burst, so glad that Mom had been born on the Fourth of July.

Later that year, I was back in Texas finishing college, and the continuum of daily conversation got interrupted, replaced with expensive long-distance phone calls and hurried letters, so I can't exactly trace Mom's reimmersion into the lively ikebana scene of Washington, DC.

I lose track of her thread and her growth, I lose track of her shoulders squared back and her new voice, and though they grew in plain sight of anyone looking, like the bamboo in the forests of Japan, you had to be standing still long enough to really witness it.

I wish I had been paying closer attention when she rose through the ranks of ikebana, and was finally named president of Ikebana International in 1983. She performed flawlessly during her two years of service. This prestigious Washington, DC, chapter was called Chapter 1, and it represented all of the various schools of ikebana.

There was Ikenobō school, founded by the Buddhist monk Senno in the fifteenth century, which dictated arranging flowers with reverence. There was Chiko school, which used fruits and dolls, vegetables and flowers to create an arrangement. There was Ohara school, emphasizing the seasons. There was the Saga Go-ryū school, which focused on the spiritual. The Saga Go-ryū school could trace its origins back almost twelve hundred years, to an arrangement using three chrysanthemums the Emperor Saga had created at his summer palace.

My mother's particular school was Sogetsu and she loved it because it was so inclusive. It was an "every person" art, the basic principle of Sogetsu being that ikebana "reflected the person who arranged it." Anyone, anywhere, anytime, and with any kind of material can create a Sogetsu arrangement. Mom explained that it was different from natural, raw, found beauty. Instead, it was created, crafted, sculpted by an artist, paying homage to nature. Sogetsu says one has to use natural materials, the flowers and buds and branches of trees, the driftwood and even items found in the kitchen, to create beauty with the arranger's feelings, and to express one's feelings through flowers. And so the artist is seen, the artist is known, each arrangement unique.

Athena was, finally, the goddess of the city, and of civilization. Ikebana's stated mission is to culturally bond the countries of Japan and America through the arts. Mom shone during those two years of her ikebana presidency in Washington, DC. She organized international events, she hosted Japanese dignitaries, she produced enormous demonstrations with the various schools of ikebana that were taught by Japanese masters. She hosted luncheons using her fine china and silver dishes, she placed cherry blossoms in crystal cut vases at the museum. She taught ikebana and inspired so many women and men to express themselves through flowers. She watched chrysanthemum fireworks explode over the Potomac, on the birthday she chose, the Fourth of July. She arranged flowers with a hum and a hum and a hum in her head, visibly growing like the bamboo. It happened quickly. It happened slowly. And it happened when I wasn't looking.

■ ■ ■ ■

FALL

■ ■ ■ ■

My Mother is a Driftwood Ballerina

A brown hand broke the surface of the Potomac River, then slowly disappeared beneath the debris floating in the gently swirling current. Again, fingers surfaced, chestnut brown and curved. An arm floated to the surface.

A wrist rolled over, followed by a pointed elbow, and soon a shape emerged. It appeared to be a young woman. I saw a spiny back, a flank, and the sun was glinting off a curved hip, causing the grainy brown skin to glow blood red as the shape bobbed, and seemed to float for a second, wallowing as it drifted closer to the shore. Now we could see the body emerge, a swirling dress frothing about the torso as the figure performed an arabesque through the water. Her leg was suspended straight back, and she seemed to stand on a pointed toe shoe. What *was* she?

Mom spotted her first. She had seen the hand and startled when the arm arose, she

213

turned with quivering lips, staring at the emerging body, and pointed it out to Dad, who responded with his usual booming: "Good eye, Beverly! Good eye!" *Good eye* was a birding phrase; it was a sort of shorthand validation they used on their many birding walks, and when Mom would spot, say, a small tufted titmouse perched atop a branch, almost hidden behind the verdant leaves, she would murmur, "Ssshhhh, Thad, look up! Two thirty deep in the branches, you'll see a tufted titmouse." Dad would boom, "Good eye, Beverly! Good eye!," and his voice would inadvertently scare the little bird away. This, in turn, induced a string of "Goddamn sons of bitches," and Mom would sigh, binoculars still raised to her eyes, her head tilted back. "Shh, Thad. It just flew a little deeper, one o'clock now." Dad would fumble with his Canon camera, huge lens pointing toward the wee bird so he could snap off a few shots. Satisfied with the discovery of the tufted titmouse, they would walk farther down the path, until Mom spotted another bird, perhaps a red-winged blackbird heading toward the marsh, and the Good Eye ritual would start all over again.

We stared at the wet lady, her arm curved over her brown head, her Isadora Duncan–

like scarf blowing in the wind. Her skin was dark and shiny, a lacy grain decorating her leg. She was a swirling, curving, graceful piece of driftwood. Driftwood like I have never seen before. She had sashayed her way to this particular inlet on the Potomac River, where we had seen her from the jogging path, and we wanted her. She was the dancer.

We stumbled down the incline to the inlet, our golden retrievers pulling hard at the leash, and Dad volunteered me to wade into the water and try to pull her out. I tugged at her arm, rolled her over, and pulled at her sodden toe shoe, inching her up the muddy shore. She was soaked through and heavy, impossible to move much farther, so we strategized her rescue. Fellow joggers stopped along the way, free with their advice; everyone was suddenly a paramedic, it seemed, and tow ropes and chains and pickup trucks were offered to help us bring this dancer home.

Mom stood guard over our partially submerged ballerina. She was already pulling dead leaves and slime off her tutu, and gently stroking her hair. She was in love, so soon, so quickly, with her life-size wooden doll. Dad and I left, pulled by those bad-mannered golden retrievers, and retraced our steps, heading home to formulate our rescue plan. We puffed back up the hill, enjoying the hot sun on our backs, waving at various neighbors on their riding tractors, iced tea in their little cup holders. This neighborhood was full of lovely houses — not mansions, really, but nicely built four- and five-bedroom homes, definitely not cookie-cutter, each with little structural distinctions, like shutters or gabled eaves or colonial pillars. The front lawns and gardens were beautiful, manicured, and mowed to exactly three inches. They were the kind of houses with gardens that won neighborhood pride garden contests. They had single-rope swings hanging from the oak trees where happy mothers pushed their happy children high, singing "wheeeee" as the swing touched the dangling leaves on the lower boughs. Coral and pink rose bushes and soft purple wisteria draped over the white garden gate.

It seemed like there were no arguments in these houses: windows sparkled; doorbells chimed; chimneys spouted storybook lines of smoke in the winter. Lives were on track, and children were grown or growing. No matter the age, fun could be had. Just the kind of neighborhood my mother would love. Just the kind of home she had always tried to create, and though thwarted at times by the trials and tribulations of life — by the military demands that frustrated my dad at the Pentagon, or the inevitable pot-smoking-kid discovery, or the sullen college kid returned home — she still tried to create a house where sunlight glinted off the silver kitchen faucet and little basil plantings in the kitchen window were always leaning toward the sun. For the most part in this lovely home surrounded by other lovely homes, in the soft southern breezes of Virginia, Mom's wings were spread and she was flying with her women brood: the garden club in our neighborhood, and Ikebana International, which had headquarters in Washington, DC, and a local chapter in Mount Vernon that Mom attended. She taught weekly ikebana classes at home in the garage, gathering materials from our backyard, from neighbors' gardens and roadside bushes, and of course, from the trees and plants along the Potomac. The dancer — if we could ever get her home — was soon to be part of several major ikebana installations.

Mount Vernon, George Washington's home, was a mile down the Potomac. It was our designated end point on our weekend jog

— making an easy three-mile round-trip along the dewy biking path. When guests would come visit Mom and Dad, perhaps Japanese dignitaries from Ikebana International traveling to the States to do a demonstration, or old navy buddies of my father's, or Texan relatives up to see the monuments, we would send them off to visit the stately mansion of our first president — sometimes going with them, and always marveling at the beauty of the grounds. You could walk back behind the colonial mansion, through the gardens, and down a grassy hill, and there was a dock where a boat from Georgetown delivered another bunch of tourists on their historical ventures. From our house to the bottom of the hill, if you turned right, you would get to Mount Vernon. If you turned left, you would get to Old Town Alexandria, famous for its cobblestone streets and brick-building warehouses made into artist studio spaces and living lofts, clam chowder in big bowls with chunks of bread for dipping, and several fine restaurants overlooking the water. Not to mention the Little Theatre of Alexandria, where I was soon to get my start.

The mideighties were a time of flourishing for Mom, and the cherry-blossomed outskirts of Washington, DC, provided a perfect blend of international culture from which she could launch her artistic spirit.

Somehow, rescuing the dancer was like preserving a statue of that same artistic spirit of Mom; the floating arabesque en pointe was a wooden embodiment of the reach and soar and stretch of my mother's vision. Dad sensed this, and was determined to bring the ballerina home. Perhaps because he hadn't always been the most cooperative, or the most complimentary . . . and perhaps because he regretted it; when he would walk the birding paths and gaze in remorseful recognition at the blustering quail trying to hide its eggs, or when the partridge blew up twice its size and Mom would laugh and say, "Just like you, Thad!" Perhaps in these moments he saw her anew, and realized just how lovely she was. Perhaps he had seen that again when "Good eye, Beverly" had discovered the dancer, and with oval fingernails scraped a bit of moss from the grooved eye, so gently scraped the ridged brow — perhaps he fell in love with her again in the mud of the Potomac. Though he loved Mom dearly, his gruff manner had been overpowering during much of their marriage, and often thwarted her spirit. On this day, perhaps he saw her spirit rise, and the rescue of the dancer (Was her name Giselle?) was an opportunity for his redemption. He would be the danseur in the pas de deux, and lift the sodden driftwood from the muck, pirouetting with her through the grass. Now on a mission, he packed his tools and a shovel in the Cadillac, put a big drop cloth in the backseat, sent me off to find the ropes and an old red wagon, and we loaded them in the trunk and drove back to the nearest lookout parking lot on the Potomac. Mom was sitting now on a grassy spot gazing at Giselle, her knees pulled up tight to her chest, her cheek resting sideways in the sun. She looked up with a smile as we rattled our way down the paved path, uneven black wheels bouncing behind me as I pulled the little red wagon piled high with our excavation tools.

Hours later, several *Goddamn sons of bitches* later, many grunts and plenty of laughs later, the near-drowned dancer was bundled up in a moving blanket and laid catty-corner in the Cadillac trunk, ropes still attached and ready for the home stretch. Once we arrived, she was pulled in the red wagon to the backyard, where Mom mixed concoctions of bleach and soap and with a scrub brush began to scrape the mud and gunk off of the tutu, out of her hair, and clear from her scarf. Dad set about designing a stand for her. He bought rebar from the lumber yard, and cement. He poured cement into a box, and sturdied the rebar in the middle of it so the dancer would have a place to stand. He helped Mom bleach the wood to get all the bugs out, a process that took several weeks. They worked well together, and lovingly, and it is one of my finest memories of him helping her. Finally, one weekend afternoon, they stood the dancer up on her toe, and positioned her in the perfect arabesque on the stand. Mom had discovered as she picked at the dancer's hair that what we thought was a scarf was possibly another, smaller dancer, a child in flowing gauze, arched backward over the dancer's arm. Now the important discussion was about to take place. Should she stay outside? She was driftwood, after all. Or should she come inside?

She came inside. She danced into the den and stood en pointe, hovering near the window, where the Japanese vases and old books were on display, where the Greek warrior gazed upon the brass table. She stood poised and posed, keeping the television and my dad company, observing the

221

crochet and flower books of my mom, and dreaming of the day when she would be adorned with flowers and dance her way into an ikebana demonstration my mother would perform at the Smithsonian, and again years later, at the museum in Fort Worth, Texas.

She has lived a good life, this dancer rescued from the Potomac. My mother has stood watch over her for years, and now Giselle stands watch over my mother. From a corner of the entry hall in her home on the lake in Texas, Giselle greets the neighbors as they come in to pay their respects to my mother. Danny, who helps us repair things at the house, comes to visit. He comes to "fix things that need fixin'," hands his Texan cowboy hat to Giselle . . . which she politely holds, arms curved over her head, leg pointed straight back under gauze and tutu, until he leaves.

Giselle cannot rescue my mother as she was once rescued, so she resigns herself to quietly watching over her. Some evenings, when classical music is playing, my mother's eyes settle slowly on the brown wooden grain. Mom's eyes study the bark and grainy tutu, and she tilts her head, listens, and closes her eyes. In this moment . . . does

Giselle dance? When the small speaker on the counter trills notes of Tchaikovsky and Haydn, does Mom hear those notes and dream of Giselle dancing, and dream of spiraling outward herself with the dancer? In her mind, does Mom arc backward over Giselle's arms, leap in a grand jeté over neural synapses and empty spaces, dancing in between forgotten movements and long lost memories? The music crescendos, and Mom smiles.

Where do the thoughts go? Where do the actual memories go? They surface, like the wet brown hand, bobbing through the murk, then disappear again beneath the choppy layers, disappear into the whirlpool synapse. Again a hand surfaces. A thought. A word. A spark of recognition. Lips forming words carefully. I want to rescue my mother with ropes and red wagons, red wagons filled with laughing children, as her memories should be. I want to rescue her with drives in the Cadillac, and trips to the wooden walkway in the marsh where hundreds of "Good eye, Beverly" red-winged blackbirds saucily revealed their red lingerie to our not so sneaky binoculars. I want to rescue her, to free the thoughts so they are only flying upward, only leaping higher, a grand jeté, dancers in a snowy ballet soaring through the sky, the prima ballerina landing happily in a strong lover's arms, a lover dressed in a dark blue navy uniform, his arms holding the ballerina high, and twirling, twirling, twirling, then gently setting her down again as she ends the dance in a graceful ritual of the reverence, and final swan bow.

■ ■ ■ ■

MY MOTHER IS
A BOTTLE OF EXTRA
VIRGIN OLIVE OIL

■ ■ ■ ■

Mom was about to help me welcome her eighth grandchild into the world, and I was already two days overdue. "Let's go out to the beach and pick up trash!" she suggested. "When I was pregnant, my mother always said that walking and bending were the best ways to stimulate contractions!" Mom was in her element. All of her senses were on high alert with pleasure. The sky was a bright cloudless blue, the September day warm, the salty air pungent but refreshing. The orchestra of waves and birdcalls and childrens' laughter created a lively symphony, and to top it all off, she had a maternal sense of purpose.

Like Mother Goose and her duckling, we made our way down Venice Beach. Mom paused for a moment from our sandy march, gingerly stepping over the seaweed and plastic detritus, letting her feet sink into the wet sand as she inched closer toward the sea. The sunshine was beating on the white canvas of the many sailboats peacefully navigating the wind, and we watched in silence as a pelican dove its neck-breaking descent toward a school of unseen fish.

"I've always loved the ocean," Mom breathed. "I love looking out across the vast, uncluttered water. It really lets you stretch your eyes." She glanced over her shoulder, back the way we had come, pleased to see that on either side of the long line of double footprints, the sand abutting our cool, concave steps was sparkling clean. In our hands, we each clutched white trash bags that whipped violently in the shore wind, and as I waddled to the next plastic bottle on the sand, Mom would cheerfully instruct:

"Bend!"

Waddle. Waddle.

"Bend!"

Waddle. Waddle.

"Bend!"

Waddle. Waddle.

The salt water caressed my swollen feet and chilled hers, the sound of the waves played like a noisy hum in my head. We walked past sand dollars and broken shells to the next cigarette butt or Coke can, scattering sandpipers that hurriedly returned to pecking at clam bubbles exposed by the receding waves. As seagulls dove and fluttered and cawed about us, Mom practically sang out:

"Bend!"

She had arrived three days before, stepping through the exit tunnel from the plane in her red-flowered cotton skirt. She was weighted down by a bag full of kenzan for the Japanese ikebana class that I had begged her to teach while she was visiting me in Venice Beach. The kenzan were heavy, made of steel. They were the spiky flower holders we would use in the bottoms of the vases to create the ikebana triangle, and I was impressed — jumbled up with gratitude and pride — that she had hand-lugged those twenty-odd pounds, along with her big Canon camera, *and* the usual carry-on bag full of flower magazines, garden ideas, and ikebana books, all the way from Fort Worth. As I had come to learn the hard way, you couldn't have an ikebana arrangement without a triangle, and it was *very* hard to have a triangle without the kenzan. Mom knew this, of course, so she had brought various sizes of kenzan for the class to make sure that the line material of the arrangements was accurate, placed at the correct angles, and bent to the precise degrees.

The points of the three-dimensional ikebana triangle, of course, were called *shin, soe,* and *hikae,* or heaven, earth, and man. Or, as she explained to her grandchildren, tall, medium, and small.

"Think of a ballerina in fourth position," Mom once told me. "Imagine a line from her toes right through the center of her head and going on up into the sky. Now imagine that her toes are the kenzan. The highest line of our arrangement is the arm above the head, so we will place a branch of line material like a curving arm, just ten to fifteen degrees to one side of the imaginary center line. That's her arm, reaching to the heavens. The second line is her other arm gracefully curved to the front. So we will place the second branch — which is shorter by a third than the first branch — at a forty-five-degree angle, and curved to the front of the arrangement, also on the same side of the imaginary line. That's her arm, hovering over earth. And the final point of the triangle is the head of the dancer, so we place the flower, or third and shortest line, at a seventy-five-degree angle toward the base of the arrangement." That is mankind, the *hikae.*

I didn't really understand it until I started studying the diagrams and line drawings that Mom used to accompany her teaching, but the image of the dancer's arms above her head always stayed with me.

"Mooooom!" I squealed at the airport. "Thank you for bringing all those kenzan!" She took one look at my enormous belly and grinned, "Finally!" Pointing to her skirt, she said, "I wore red because in China, it brings good luck for the baby." I hugged her hard, glad to have her with me, glad to have her quiet voice and soft smile and steady eyes fill me with comforts of the familiar, comforts of "Mother" with a capital M. She had been present at the births of each of her seven grandchildren thus far, and I was thrilled that I would finally get to go through the ritual of hand-holding and rhythmic breathing as my daughter Eulala — my very first child — pushed past my contractions and through the tunnel of my body into the hands of Life. In truth I was nervous: at thirty-nine, I felt old to be having my first child, and my paranoia was starting to get the best of me. Mom had come just in time. On my huge Staples calendar at home, a heart circled the September 9 square in red Magic Marker announcing MOM ARRIVES, and on the next day, another red heart and Magic Marker announced, EULALA DUE!

Eulala apparently hadn't gotten the memo. She was quite comfortable in the warm salt water of the womb, and grandmother's arrival or not, she had no intention of arriving at her "scheduled" time: September 10, 1998. Not a contraction in sight, not a dilation to measure, just a few well-placed kicks were the only indication that a birthing was soon to occur.

Mom was unflappable. She had given birth to five children herself, sometimes with her mother in attendance, always in a hospital, and always with my father present. I must have been just five when my brother arrived, yet I remember waiting in a hospital corridor with my father, watching him sit, head bowed, hands clasped, and thumbs circling each other. Circling, circling, me sitting next to him, mimicking the circling thumbs as a way of getting close to him, wondering what he was so worried about that he would be circling and circling his thumbs like that. For the most part, fathers weren't present in the birthing rooms in the 1950s and early 1960s; they were relegated to (or chose?) the corridors, sitting in hallway chairs lined up against the wall, invited in only after the pain and mess and blood had been cleaned up and the baby was presented fresh and rosy with a pink or a blue cap. The father would hold the baby and his wife's hand, and the mother would be stitched from the episiotomy where they had cut her to make the passage easier (and a bit itchy, as well, because her nether regions had been shaved completely, as was the practice at that time). Ice chips and lime-green hospital Jell-O were delivered on the bed tray, and soon the family was headed home, with the baby clutched in the mother's arms, no child seats and perhaps no seatbelts, either.

Five children, two miscarriages, and attendance at the births of many grandchildren, my mom was to be trusted when she said not to worry, that the firstborn was often late, and that I should get used to Eulala being the boss anyway.

Over the next few days we passed time by taking inventory of my hospital necessities: cute new travel bag holding toothbrush (check!), hairbrush (check!), clean underwear (check!), and pretty nightie (check!). Mom presented me with the short pink satin "receiving jacket" that Mammau, my grandmother on my father's side, had worn. Mammau had given it to my mother to wear when she gave birth, and Mom had carefully packed it in tissue for me to wear, as well. This jacket was something we passed down from generation to generation, connecting me like a lullaby to my heritage. I showed off my brand-new baby car seat. Mom prepared her camera in case we were in a last-minute rush. My husband, Thaddaeus, made morning coffees and double-checked the crib to make sure the sides slid down easily, and while Mom sipped her black coffee and watched the sunrise over the waves from our oceanfront apartment, he rearranged the bassinet from one spot in our room to another. We were ready.

The room where Mom slept was lovely. I had decorated it for Eulala in greens and pinks and wheat-colored curtains with English florals swirling gracefully to the ground. I had sewn them on my college graduation present — a Pfaff sewing machine that Mom had given me — and made bed skirts to match, then pillowcases with the wheat floral material and green-checkered material mixed together. Mom was impressed. She was proud that she had given me something useful years before when I had graduated from the University of Texas. I guess you're never sure if what you give your kid as a symbol of growing up and moving on at graduation will be used, but Mom had given the sewing machine to me, remembering how my sisters and I had sewn gowns for the navy cotillions we had attended when we were in high school. Using an old Singer machine, we had sewn beautiful gowns: dark purple velvet gowns, light blue eyelet lace gowns with rose ribbon trim, polyester cream satin-flowered halter dresses with peach trim, laying out the McCall's and Butterick or Simplicity patterns on the floor and cutting them out at night after our homework was done. We snuck around and sewed the hems after lights-out was called, knowing Mom could hear the hum of the machine just under the hum of my father's snoring. She had probably smiled at the thought of her daughters sewing dresses for the cotillions where they would dance with naval cadets in uniform, scratching off names on the little list that was attached to their wrist with a black ribbon. Now Mom walked around Eulala's room and admired the bed, the curtains, and the diaper bag, and she complimented me on my straight stitches. Then she pulled from her duffel bag a three-foot Raggedy Ann and Andy that a friend in her garden club had hand made just for Eulala, and placed them on the bed near the crib. Room complete!

In our little Venice Beach enclave we had established a sweet community. We were surrounded by a wonderful group of mostly gay men and some young newlywed couples. The other three apartments in our building housed author Ron, psychiatrist Chris, and activist Victor, and across the street was the fun couple Brad and David. Several streets down were Pete and Sima, then Phil and Mylin, and around the corner an old buddy of mine from New York — funny, funky, talented Nancy Hower. We played volleyball on the beach on the weekends, and we had a lively book club. I was known as "Mom-sha" even before I got pregnant.

As the news of Eulala's delay began to circulate around our little group, the excitement started to build. Mom was a bit shocked — yet tickled, too — at the group's openness.

In the mornings Brad would yell over his hedge across the alley to my open window, "HAVE YOU DILATED YET?"

"NOT YET!" I would yell back.

Mylin in her beach shorts and brown legs would yell from the volleyball net up to our porch, "ANY CONTRACTIONS?"

I hollered back, "I DON'T THINK SO . . . I THINK IT'S JUST GAS!"

Mom and Thad would shake their heads and sip their coffee. My decorum gene seemed to be missing where birthing was involved, and all this yelling and celebration and noise was so . . . public. They were somewhat alike in their gentler, more conservative natures. Both Capricorns. (Horoscope: "Known to seem melancholy and stern because they live by self-discipline and responsibility." Or as StarScope wrote: "They evaluate everything and they don't take daring chances without weighing the advantages and disadvantages first.") Regardless of her star sign, I think for Mom this fever of voices bouncing back and forth across the alley — bouncing with the volleyball on the beach, bouncing with my belly as I waddled down the apartment stairs — was simply unladylike and in danger of being "out of control." Quite unlike her quiet Dallas upbringing and, later, well-enforced military boundaries, quite unlike the hospital births that were women's and doctors' business, and certainly not the business of the entire neighborhood. She was the mom who insisted that we always wear clean underwear, because what if something terrible happened and we suddenly had to go to the hospital? We had better be in clean underwear!

And now . . . "What if something goes wrong?" she worried. "You would have to explain it to the entire neighborhood!"

Now she was making me anxious: "Well, Mom, in truth if something goes wrong I would have to explain it to the entire neighborhood anyway — I mean it's not like they don't know I'm pregnant! I will have to explain it to the entire world, for that matter! I'm the size of a small condominium!" I was starting to panic. "This is not a well-disguised pregnancy, Mom! *Do* you think something is wrong?" We were looking at the Staples calendar for the hundredth time, as if just by looking at it, by concentrating on the black lined squares, we could *will* Eulala to arrive on a given day. Mom nevertheless sipped her black coffee gingerly.

"Well, maybe it's best not to discuss the nitty-gritty quite so . . . openly."

"But it's funny. All the neighbors are my friends, and they make me laugh. Dilation is funny."

She stared at me. Dilation, or lack thereof, was definitely *not* funny to her.

"Mmmmhmmm." she said, pursing her lips slightly. Another sip of coffee.

"Mom, are you worried?" I squeaked. "Tell me! Do you think something is wrong?"

"No . . ." Her brow furrowed, her voice tightened, and for a moment we stared at each other, four brown eyes stilled by the imagination of the impossible. Just under the tips of her black lashes, swirling about her jet-black pupils, gleamed all the hopes and dreams she had for me and for this yet-to-be-discovered Eulala. In the reflection of the pooling mist on the brown surface of her eyes, I saw my own hazel eyes reflected, and like the stuttering images of an old projector, saw between us the scenes of Eulala's birth, and her first day of school, her first tutu, her first talent show, her first bicycle and skateboard, her campouts in sleeping bags and s'mores, her senior prom, her firsts, her firsts, all her firsts, which would begin with her first snuggle in my mother's arms. The stuttering images began to blur, Mom's mouth softened, she knew her presence was a gift to me — me, who was so unsure and scared.

A seagull pierced the air with its wild caw,

and Mom blinked. She couldn't bear the idea that something might go wrong, and she returned to her unflappable self, proclaiming that at least the boys and chatter were making me laugh, and there was nothing to worry about. We scheduled a doctor's appointment for Friday and walks on the beach every day in between. Picking up trash, waddling and bending, Mom felt sure this activity would get my body and Eulala moving toward the big day. And if the baby didn't come over the weekend, no problem! Mom could teach the ikebana class to the gaggle of neighbors who were wildly awaiting Eulala's arrival.

A pregnant woman's belly can be ridiculous at first sight. (Especially mine, considering I had gained seventy pounds and my belly was a bubble that entered the room at least a minute before the rest of my body.) This same ridiculous belly is also an invitation. An invitation specifically to women, to reach out and touch, to caress, to bless, to make contact with the unknown and unseen child within. I didn't mind. Some women did mind, offended at the presumption that their baby was in fact not theirs to privately carry, not theirs alone to protect and nourish, but, rather, that their baby belonged to a world of women, and harkened back to an ancient village time when women as a group birthed and cared for the baby with the mother.

My belly seemed to invite women in elevators, on the street, in restaurants, grocery stores, and gas stations, to reach out and touch it. Mom was slightly skeptical of this intimacy. She had already witnessed my new two-piece bathing suit that exposed my pregnant belly and the dark brown line running vertically straight up the middle — something that *never* would have happened in her day. I was nothing like the movie stars she had seen on the pages of *People* magazine, celebrities in skin-tight dresses with perfectly rounded basketball lumps contouring their soft jersey knits, hard little movie star bellies in which a perfectly small baby resided, actresses with single chins despite being eight months pregnant. The idea of me trying to mimic these movie stars when my lump was not at all a basketball but rather a beach ball, and I was sporting perhaps five chins in the ninth month of pregnancy — this publicness, this waddling welcoming of the women of the world and the cameras to notice me and celebrate with me was, to her, unseemly.

Her Dallas upbringing was again clashing

with the body freedoms of the modern world, the California openness, the raucous laughs of my actor friends, and though *she* was uncomfortable, I couldn't help but love the embrace of it all. I loved the warmth and the freedom. I loved it when a woman saw me on the street and smiled at my waddle, saying, "Welcome to the fold." The fold — I was in the fold! When a stranger's hand reached out to touch me, they weren't really wanting to touch *me,* but to make contact with the unknown, to make contact with "anticipation," with "potential," with *life* before it was seen and known and owned by all eyes. I was simply a conduit, a container, and as their hands felt for a lump of foot or swell of head, I thought, *The more the merrier! YES! Please do bless my belly! Bring it! Bring all the wisdom and love and healing energy you have within you. Let it stream down your long arms and through your slender fingers, into this now nine-pound baby, coiled up, sleeping in the trusting waters of the womb. Let her know it's going to be okay, that there is a web of womankind that will gather for her, that will uphold her during the trials and tribulations of growing up* Girl *in America, and let her know that no matter what life brings her, there will be a community of women, women fighting for rights and love and family in the middle of balancing corporate jobs or factory jobs — and these women will guide her along her uncharted path.* Yes. All this I felt every time I saw a woman's eyes light up as she saw my advancing belly and her arm would inadvertently begin to outstretch to touch my ridiculous mound. *BRING IT!*

Mom understood my inflated yearning. After all, she had felt the same for her daughters and son, and it was just a matter of time before she began to soften to this ritual, to relax into it and enjoy it. I wondered if she even envied it a bit. I was downright jolly, never lonely for encouragement, and in contrast, her pregnancies may have seemed a bit "stiff upper lip," something to get through, something women bore on their own until the final days of doctor's checkups and hospital check-ins. She didn't have sisters to coo and caw like dizzy seagulls at the joyous news of her pregnancy. She didn't have actor friends to scream across the phones from New York to Los Angeles, "OH, MY F-ING GOD, CONGRATULATIONS!!!" And even the valets of Beverly Hills would look at my belly and say, "God bless you, Mama." I wondered what girlfriends had been there for my mom, and soon she began to talk about Mrs. Kolarik, her next-door neighbor with the red hair in California to whom she had taught the fine art of flushing the remains of a dirty cloth diaper down the toilet, but not losing the diaper in the process. And her dear friend Bobby Morgan with her cropped brown hair who lived at the end of the cul-de-sac when we were growing up in Garden Grove, and who provided a Band-Aid when I was five and stubbed my toe on the gravel. These women had been there for Mom, in a much more understated and elegant way, but still a web of women passing on their smock tops, sewing elastic-waisted skirts, taking over childcare for my pregnant mom when morning sickness prevented her from walking her kids to the school bus, keeping home life on track and in harmony. "There is no denying community when the business of birthing is at hand," Mom said.

Waddle waddle bend Tuesday. Waddle waddle bend Wednesday and showing off playing volleyball at sunset. Waddle waddle bend Thursday and a trip to Ralph's grocery store to check out the flower supply. It was clear Eulala was going to be late, and so we would be able to have our neighborhood ikebana class over the weekend. We had noted some bright pink azaleas in the neighborhood that we could cut for our class and the green reedy bullrush planted along several beach paths that we could use for line material. Mom loved to cut from the available supply of outdoor plants and flowers. She was always teaching that you could create an ikebana arrangement from your own backyard materials, and unlike Western arrangements of twenty tulips plunked in a vase, or a perfectly rounded sea of roses, you didn't need a lot of flowers to make an ikebana arrangement. You simply needed line material for the *shin* and *soe,* and a third point — the *hikae* — was usually a flower. Simplicity and balance were the key, creating a scene in a vase as if it had been plucked from nature.

So we had made special note of what seemed to be "public property" flowers, public property trees and variegated leaves and flowing grasses. Mom carried her cutting scissors in her purse, and she brought an extra pair of scissors as a present to me; those now lived in the glove compartment of my Grand Wagoneer. As we drove through neighborhoods, we would stop while Mom gently cut a purple iris or red caladium, snipping off shapely willow branches or sharp green leaves of pampas

245

grass. As she gathered the flora she would share little secrets of the trade: "April to August is a good time to peel willow and wisteria. Try soaking it in baking soda and hot water first." Or: "Crush the bottom of long-stemmed mums to help make an angle, and to help water flow up inside the stem." Or: "Place pampas grass in vinegar and then cold water to preserve it."

She wanted to have a variety of flowers for the class; we were expecting at least ten people from the neighborhood, so we were looking to supplement with flowers like roses and lilies from Ralph's. Pointing to the fragrant Stargazers, some opened and perfuming the air, some flowers still closed ("Not yet dilated!" I thought), she said, "The buds should be highest in an arrangement. In nature they open last." She then pointed to the lovely anthurium with its white fireworks design, and showed how a simple two leaves of vibrant anthurium could combine beautifully with a single red caladium and a sprig of soft blue hydrangea to create a lively arrangement, perfect for the Fourth of July. We rummaged among the flowers. "Preserve hydrangea in liquor," she taught. "Split the stems of the calla lily and place them in cold water." "Run wire up the inside of stems of birds-of-paradise to help them bend." "Cut the tips of the palm stem and leaves for a different effect." She saw the white chrysanthemum and said: "The chrysanthemum is called *kiku* in Japanese, it is the symbol of fall. Perfect for our class!" We picked up a dozen of the chrysanthemum, swaddled tightly in their netting.

In the fruit section, she showed how pineapple leaves could be used in an arrangement.

We wandered to the condiment aisle to pick up some olive oil for dinner. There we met an elderly, soulful woman, perhaps eighty years old, wrinkled, elegant, and slender, and as she saw us approaching with the waddle and sway of a mother duck, her eyes lit up and she instinctively reached out her arm to me.

"Oh, God bleess you," she said. "May I?" She reached to touch my stomach. "Is it a girl or a boy?"

"A girl," I responded proudly.

She began stroking my belly as Mom watched patiently. "God bleeessss this little girl. Oh, she big! She big!" We agreed, and Mom shared that in her day, the pregnant mother was strongly encouraged by the doctors NOT to allow the baby to get over seven pounds. "Oh, yeeesss," the lady agreed. "It haarrrd to deliver a big baby! You have stretch marks? You gonna have stretch marks, you so big!"

I could tell Mom felt this was getting a bit personal, but I was enjoying it. I liked this old world lady who smelled like cinnamon, and I assured her I did not have stretch marks (not yet, anyway), and that I was supposed to rub cream or oil on my belly to make sure my skin stayed soft.

"Mmmmmhmmmm," she said. "Well, in my day, the doctor don't tell me to rub oil on my belly. He tell me to rub it on my vagina!"

Mom and I stared at her. She pronounced "oil" as "ol." She must've taken our silence for not understanding her meaning, so she more loudly said, "Yes sir! Your vagina!" Again she was met with silence.

"MMMMMHMMMM. You got to oooolllll your vagina so that baby can come out!" She delivered all of this extremely helpful information in the middle of the grocery store. Among the spices and exotic oils. Fellow grocers passing by and Mom frozen, staring, in the condiment aisle. I loved this lady.

"MMMHHHMMMM. Yes, SIR!" Now she demonstrated with a gesture, as our dumbstruck lack of response was a sure indication that perhaps we didn't actually know where the vagina was. So she reached over a pretend belly, and threw her head back, and gestured with a rubbing motion "MMMHMMMM. YOU got to OOooolllllllllllll your VAGINAAAAA. You got to OOooollllll your VAGINNAAA."

Mom, not to be outdone in the teachings of motherhood, grabbed a bottle of olive oil from the shelf, and said, "Extra extra virgin, perhaps?"

The old lady smiled a sparkly smile, and Mom smiled, and I imagined what this lady's birthings must have been like — surely not in a hospital but likely at home, on the supper table perhaps, just as my father had been born on his family's dining room table in the Deep South of El Paso, Texas. I wondered if my grandmothers had oiled *their* vaginas . . . ?

Friday found us at my doctor's office. Eulala was demonstrating in the womb what she would again demonstrate in her teenage years: a remarkable ability to sleep for hours at a time. The doctor was concerned. The sonogram monitor showed very little movement, and Eulala was now nine and a half pounds.

"Are you drinking enough water?" he asked.

"Probably not," I admitted guiltily.

"Are you resting? Have you slowed down?" he questioned.

"Ummm . . ." I remembered our waddle waddle bend walks on the beach and shopping at Ralph's for the ikebana class, the volleyball and flurry of friends constantly stopping by. "Probably not . . ."

He took two little flat metal things, placed them on either side of my stomach, and gently sent the sound of a buzz into the womb. It was supposed to be a wake-up call, but the monitor still showed very little movement as Eulala continued to slumber in her bubble of peace. He looked hard at me, at Thaddaeus, and at Mom. "You need to drink more water. You are dehydrated, and the baby is dehydrated, and that's why she isn't moving. And you need to slow down." We all three shrank with guilt. "I'm going to keep this monitor on your stomach, and we'll track her movement for thirty minutes. If she doesn't show more activity, I'm going to admit you to the hospital across the street and we will give you an IV with electrolytes."

The second he left, we began discussing the inconvenience of my being admitted to the hospital — we had SO MUCH TO DO! Walks on the beach! Flower classes to teach! Possibly some sightseeing for Mom! I couldn't be held up with a day of lying around getting electrolytes on an IV drip! I vowed I would drink more water . . . and began patting my belly, hoping Eulala would wake up. Thaddaeus looked at the electric pads, and announced that he knew how they worked. "Just like a door bell," he said.

I had no idea what that meant, but after fifteen minutes of waiting around, Mom and I reluctantly agreed to him putting the pads on my belly and giving it a try himself. "Be careful!" Mom pleaded.

Thaddaeus placed the silver pads near what we thought was Eulala's head, and gave the contraption a try. A loud buzz jolted through the many layers of skin and muscle and water . . . and BAM! Eulala woke right up! The lines on the monitor began to jump and wiggle, and we watched the paper feed with pride as it spat out peak after peak of activity.

"Hmmm," was all the doctor said when he came back in. He stared at the paper feed. He stared at us. "I guess she woke up . . . Well . . . good." He grinned, relieved. "Okay, Marcia. Drink more water, and slow down. I'll see you Wednesday if you haven't had any contractions, and we'll measure you for dilation."

That was Friday. Sunday, we joined my old acting friend George Newbern and his lovely family for a gospel Catholic church service somewhere down on La Brea. As the elders of the church came down the aisle during the "Peace be with you — And also with you" greeting, the lead elder woman saw the rounded tent of my lavender Sunday dress and her arm stretched out palm first and halted midair.

"Ohhhh, God bless ya!" she said. "May I?" Her hand was already caressing my stomach. "Oh, GOD BLESS this little child — is it a girl or a boy?"

"A girl," I church whispered.

She wasn't whispering. "OH, GOD BLESS THIS LITTLE GIRL! And may she come unto the LORD JESUS Christ. And may he love and bless and honor this little girl. May she come to know the WAYS of Jesus a-a-and . . . ," she stuttered, and then she held her other hand up to her ear while still holding my stomach. It was as if she were listening to a message through an earbud. She looked at me in shock. "GOD is tellin' me to tell you to drink more water! You have got toxins in your system and the Devil has put them there and you need to drink more water to get them out!" She started to move her hand from her ear, but it shot right back up as she received a second message from God. She wasn't looking at me now, but rather up to the ceiling of the church. Everyone else was looking at me, aisles and aisles of people. Murmuring "Peace be with you . . . ," but their eyes kept darting to us in our pews, wondering just what the Devil had put in my system. Someone said "Give them space," and I looked around to make sure the Devil wasn't actually there. Soon it was silent in the vast church, only the organ music playing a rich hymn, but no more murmuring.

Mom was bent over, digging the bottle of water out of her purse in a cold panic. As Mom surfaced with the water, the elder lady continued: "Aaaannnnnd GOD is tellin' me to tell you to SLOW DOWN!" She looked at me deeply; she seemed to radiate with light. "There's a time to go, and there's a time to slow, and this is your time to slow!"

Mom, Thaddaeus, and I were in shock. Verbatim — almost — what the doctor had said! Her hand hovered over her ear, waiting for any more messages, and a second later she dropped her hand and smiled. "Well, God tellin' me to tell you that!" she declared, and the "Peace be with you" resumed, while I eyed the water in the baptismal font, wanting to drink and drink and drink these toxins out of my body. Mom handed me the water from her purse, and then she rummaged around for a scented towelette to cool my fearful forehead. Then she fished out a bobby pin for my errant strand of hair, and finally presented me with a Life Saver breath mint wrapped in plastic for my now acid mouth. All that was missing was the olive oil. While the elder lady may have been receiving messages from God's shortwave radio, Mom clearly had God's first aid kit: her purse contained everything.

Despite the admonishment to "Slow down" from the doctor, the elder, and even the Being on High, we decided to hold the ikebana class. Mom told each student to bring a flat bowl or deep dish-type container, and if they didn't have that, then tin cans or coffee cans were okay. She also told each of us to bring a small piece of driftwood. We had gathered azaleas, pyracantha, and long strands of wheat grass, and we planned to combine these with brilliant white spider mums and driftwood.

Our class gathered, noisy and excited. This wasn't at all like Mom's garden club or ikebana classes in Fort Worth. Those classes were made up mostly of talented women in their forties through sixties, many of whom had been studying for quite a while, and who were all well aware of the etiquette of flower class. They sat quietly and listened to the instructor, they used the class as a sort of meditation, contemplating the beauty of the flowers and containers, contemplating nature, and in the stillness of the moment allowed their unconscious to deepen creatively and reveal itself in a balanced, harmonious, and surprising arrangement. These classes were full of Mom's friends. It was her web of women, and they supported each other's efforts and sat with hands folded while the instructor complimented and critiqued the work. They shared stories over coffee and tea only after the arrangements were made. The arranging part of the class was a quiet, almost spiritual moment.

This current class was a far different affair. Someone uncorked a bottle of white wine, which the class thought was a *great* idea, and in this noisy, loud, festive environment, Mom took on our Venice Beach enclave.

"We will start with a basic upright arrangement," she said, staring at the curious group. "Fill the container with two to three inches of water. Place the kenzan in the container, slightly off-center, Asian-style."

We did.

"Snip the ends of all the branches and flowers underwater so the suction pulls the water up inside the stem. Set them aside."

We did.

"Measure the *shin,* also known as 'heaven.' It will naturally be the highest point of the arrangement. The *shin* is the first piece of line material." She was using pyracantha. "Measure it to one and a half times the diameter and depth of the container. Snip it underwater, and place it in the kenzan leaning ten degrees away from the imaginary center line."

We did. Because math was involved, it was a bit more complicated, but Mom was patient.

"Good. Now measure the second point of the triangle, the *soe,* also known as 'earth,' to three-quarters the size of the first line."

We did.

"Place it in the kenzan at a forty-five-degree angle on the same side of the imaginary line as the first branch."

We did, with Mom gently circling the class and helping each student adjust their branch.

"*Maarvelous.* Now take your spider mum"

— and here Mom dramatically pulled off the netting holding the mum in place, and we oohed and aahed as it sprang forth its creamy butter center and bright white tips — "this is the last line of the triangle, cut the stem underwater to three-quarters or one-half — you decide using your creative eye — of the length of the second branch. This last piece is called the *hikae.* It is known as 'man,' place it at a seventy-five-degree angle on the *opposite* side of the imaginary line."

We did.

Someone hollered, "Bevverrrlyyy — HEEELLP!," and the class broke up into loud laughter as we all tried to nudge our arrangement into place.

"Finally, use your grasses or azaleas as filler. This is the designer's choice. The filler should complement the texture and color of the flowers and should help to hide the kenzan. Again, use your creative eye."

More wine was poured. The tiny room was buzzing with noise and laughter. It was definitely *not* a meditation, but it was fantastic. Mom showed how to use the driftwood in a second arrangement. She drank some wine — cold Chardonnay was her favorite — and I sat fat and pregnant and pleased as punch to see my mom so relaxed and so creative, sharing with my dear friends this art that she so deeply loved. Her talent was flawless. Her ability to caress a stiff branch into a gentle curve, her eye for balance, her knack for simplicity as she cut off the unnecessary leaves from a flower so that the form of the flower was exposed; these skills were due to years of study and craft, and it was clear to me — and clear to our group — what an incredible artist my mom was. When the class was over, she bowed, and we cheered and cheered and laughed and shouted, "Beev-verrlyy . . . Heeelllppp!" She showed us how to wrap our flowers in wet paper towels so we could re-create the arrangements at home. Each student trooped off with their bundles, and a new kenzan to boot.

When did the Alzheimer's tau weed plant itself in the fertile mind of my mother? When did this weed first begin to grow? Quietly it crept along the rows of carefully planted *shin, soe,* and *hikae.* It grew like a vine around the pyracantha and hydrangea, rising slowly with the moon-spun tide, and drowning out the years and years of lessons and knowledge and talent that had been so carefully planted, so lovingly attended, so proudly demonstrated. And why my mother? She was the poster child of what to do to keep a healthy brain. She was always active, she ate well, drank rarely, brushed her teeth, and kept her brain sharp with teaching and creating and learning new languages and travel. Why, only seven years later, was Mom showing signs of mild dementia? Why — when we gathered with her Fort Worth ikebana club just fourteen years later, in 2012, as they awarded my mother a lifetime membership for her career accomplishments — was she already foggy on the names of her dear friends? She smiled and elegantly accepted her award, sometimes forgetting what it meant, and in that moment, forgetting as well what *she* meant. At the ceremony during lunch her children were always at her elbow helping to navigate the inevitable slips and embarrassment of memory loss. We tried to pull at the vine, to tug it off the kenzan where it had tangled itself among the black steel spikes, to rip it from the roses and driftwood and flowering forsythia of her memory, and we prayed that we could stay the weed, we prayed that science would successfully pull this Alzheimer's tau weed up from the roots, and the garden would spring forth again, bees and hummingbirds landing on bottlebrush and fruited trees, butterflies in the purple allium.

What was the cause of this weed? And where, now, is the pesticide? In anger I mourn that the grandchild she helped to birth on September 23, 1998, will only briefly get to know my mother. Six years later, at the birth of my twins Hudson and Julitta, she was already murmuring, "Something is wrong." She was already forgetting where she had just put her passport, and she was dreading with a wash of fear and bile what these seemingly innocuous moments might portend.

In the brightly lit hospital room on the day of my labor, we are full of laughter. My cute travel bag lies open on the bed, stargazers arranged in a vase filling the room with heavy, pungent aroma. Mom has her camera ready, vowing to Annie Leibovitz the moment of birth, and convincing herself that she will be as stalwart as a veteran field photographer. In truth I suspect Mom will probably get squeamish and need to sit down . . . I don't quite see her as Annie Leibovitz. However, it seems Eulala is not ready for her close-up — she is still content to sleep happily in the warm womb, and as a bit of encouragement, my water is broken with help from the doctor. We celebrate and wait, but no contractions are felt, so several hours later the doctor begins to deliver Pitocin, and the contractions start to build with the beauty and fervor of a beach drum circle. They hurt, but we are laughing through it all, Mom and Thaddaeus and me, we are so excited to actually be IN the moment, and we anticipate hearing "PUSH! NOW PUSH HARDER" in just a short while.

Yoga music fills the room from my portable speakers, which later becomes the acoustic guitar of my neighbor Nancy Hower, who visits for several hours and plucks out tunes while I sweat the contractions. My doctor seems worried. I'm not dilating, and this is taking more time that he anticipated. Uncomfortable, and in pain, I sit on the edge of the bed, breathing through my mouth, with my hair now plastered on my forehead, damp and sticky. I feel Mom's gentle hands hold a wet cold rag to my forehead. My eyes are closed. I'm trying to be elegant and brave and funny, but the pain has robbed me of any humor, and I am just bearing it. Mom begins to braid my hair. As if I were still her small child, which I was and perhaps will always be, she braids my hair. It instantly calms me down. She parts the hair down the middle in the back, and brushes it again and again, and separates each side into three equal parts. Her soft hands soothe and caress my neck as she braids my hair, and she loops the elastic over the ends and asks, "There now, sweetheart, that's better, isn't it?" It was. Salty tears fall into my lap. Hours pass. Fast and steady, the contractions beat on, keeping time like the pendulum of a metronome. The entire medical team is now worried, it seems the umbilical cord is wrapped around Eulala's neck as she is trying to make her way down the passage, and the cord keeps tugging her back. Eulala is holding the cord in her hand, trying to keep it away from her throat. The doctor shows us the image, and he tells me I will have to have a C-section. I cry and cry all the way to the delivery room, because I will not get to be like my mother, I will not get to hear PUSH and PUSH, and I feel like a failure. Thaddaeus holds my hand with the rolling gurney, and Mom — true to her word — troops along the side of us, getting her camera ready.

Soon I wake up in the recovery room. Thad is there holding Eulala and gazing with adoration at her little pink face, her ruby bow lips. Mom is there, too, with wet tears on her face. They place Eulala on my breast and — I can word it no other way — she voraciously begins to slurp. I am tired, drugged, and Mom, with her camera still at her side, eventually takes her grandchild away from my drowsy arms, and coos and coos into Eulala's lovely face, and as my eyes waver shut, I smile, having just witnessed Eulala's *first* snuggle with her grandmother. But not just any grandmother. We have graphic and beautiful photos to bear witness to another first, to the first moments of my daughter's life; indeed, her first breath, her first wail, her first tear . . . all thanks to my mom.

■ ■ ■ ■

My Mother is a Silver-Wrapped Piece of Wrigley's Spearmint Chewing Gum

■ ■ ■ ■

Special occasion days.

Our school children lives were marked by special days of the month, holidays that broke up the boring sameness of classrooms. These "occasion days" provided a glimmer of color in an otherwise dull school year, and they spurred us to get through the drudgery of homework. They began with the new year, the air crisp and cold over ponytails and cowlicks as we stood in line waiting for the yellow school bus, lunch boxes clutched in our brightly mittened hands and each of us dressed in our brand-new clothes, which still smelled of pine and Christmas.

Sporting our fresh finery, we would gleefully pile off the bus into the schoolyard in January. Then, as the sameness of days began, we would trudge to our lockers and wait for the occasion days, which were like bright balloon markers along a dull biege path. First came Martin Luther King Jr. Day! Then classes classes classes Groundhog Day! Then Valentine's Day! Classes classes classes Presidents Day! St. Patrick's Day and green somewhere on your body or God Forbid you got pinched. Classes classes report cards classes Easter! Spring Break! Rich kids return with tans to school and we stare, then April Fool's Day! May Day! Mother's Day! Memorial Day! Classes classes classes and report cards again, and then . . . wait for it . . . *summer*!!!

We five kids would plan for these holiday oases in the otherwise mundane desert of monthly educational routines. On Valentine's Day, we discussed what flowers we would get for Mom, or on the night before Easter, we would try to figure out where the eggs would be hidden, and what special card we would make for our parents. On these nights, as the evening settled in and teeth were brushed, Crest squeezed like icing on different-colored plastic toothbrushes, after "Now I lay me down" prayers were said and *"LIGHTS OUT"* was hollered, the hallway that separated our rooms was still alive with the chatter of five children. The hallway always had family pictures arranged on the wall, school pictures and grandparents, and on these "occasion nights," it was as if the pictures were actually talking to each other, disembodied voices reverberating in the emptiness. Snuggled in our quilted covers and white pillow single beds we whispered from our room to the siblings' room across the hall, peering through the darkness, and it was as if our voices gathered under the hallway light, bouncing off the family picture frames, lingering on the mouths in the pictures, then drifting, floating through the hallway, into our rooms, and down to our pillows.

Saint Patrick's Day:

I whisper, "What are you wearing that's green tomorrow, Leslie?"

"Socks."

"How 'bout you, Sheryl?"

"My sweater."

"Okay, I am wearing my plaid skirt, which has a little green in the pattern."

Sheryl calls down the hall: "Mom, is green underwear fair?"

She responds delicately: "It certainly is, but you'll get in trouble for showing it!"

Leslie whispers: "Mark can wear his green shorts, and Stephanie has a green hair bow."

Stephanie peeps: "Mom, what are you wearing?"

"Quiet. It's bedtime," she says firmly, but we hear her smiling.

Thaddeus Mark calls out to Mom: "Are you wearing green?"

"Well, if I'm not, you get to pinch me. Now quiet!" Still smiling.

In the morning she would rise well ahead of us all and make green pancakes in her green blouse with the gold buttons, or fry eggs in her olive green skirt, or stir oatmeal, sporting a scarf with a paisley pattern and green accents. We would each come into the kitchen, also sporting green somewhere on our bodies, and we would gloat at our well-paid-off efforts.

A month before the green pancakes of St. Patricks Day, we had been delighted by red pancakes on Valentine's Day. February was never my mom's favorite month. Drab and gray, cold and wet, flowerless February seemed to have very little to distinguish it — other than the love and sugar festival, which occurred on February 14 every year.

Yellow roses of Texas. Those are the flowers Dad usually brought home for Mom, but on Valentine's Day he honored the rich blood-red of tradition and Mom filled vases around the house with combinations of crimson rose and deep green aromatic pine. The pine provided the line material, and it was a prize to find a perfect pine bough that still had a little pine cone on it, sitting like a wee round treasure among the roses and green needles. Red roses, and a box of rounded chocolates filled with cherries and some kind of liquor — these were the usual Valentine's gifts Dad brought home for Mom. I didn't like the liquor chocolates much, the way the sticky sweet slurped around in your mouth as it melted. I was partial to chocolate-covered caramel, sticky in my cavities. Valentine's cards and doilies, chocolates and cinnamon red-hot hearts burning my tongue.

From the grocery store Mom would buy five separate boxes of Valentine's cards. There was no SpongeBob SquarePants then, no Pokémon, but instead the images were of Tweety Bird and Sylvester the Cat. Or Casper the Friendly Ghost. Or butterflies, or trucks. On the little card with the butterfly, the butterfly would be rising off of a wildflower, and a little thought bubble would say, YOU MAKE MY HEART FLY. Or on the truck card, the truck would be looking with its headlight eyes at another more female truck with headlight eyelash eyes, and the thought bubble would say, I'D TRAVEL THE WORLD FOR YOU.

Mom would buy these boxes, and the five of us children would gather around our round table and pick the perfect cards for the perfect students and handwrite their names and lick the sticky sweet closure of each envelope. Each child in class was supposed to get a Valentine's card. So we would go through a list of names and carefully pick the boy Valentine's cards and the girl cards. We would write a note on each one, and hope that the boy we liked would know that his card had extra special attention paid to it, that we had chosen it because it was one of two cards that actually said BE MINE, VALENTINE. We hoped he would know that the only other card that said BE MINE, VALENTINE had been given to the teacher. But whereas hers had had an apple with a worm wearing glasses saying BE MINE in the thought bubble, his card had two goldfish ogling each other, the boy goldfish having the thought bubble BE MINE rising with the other sea bubbles to the surface of the water. In one of the female goldfish bubbles, we hoped he would notice the childish scrawl, a handwritten YOU'RE THE BEST. We would put the cards in a big paper bag to be distributed along with little candied hearts that also said BE MINE and YOU'RE THE TOPS and we would put the bag on our mats, waiting for us to take to school the next morning. That night from our single beds we called across the hall from our rooms again, and the hallway was full of discussions of what red or pink sweater we might wear, what boy we might like, or if we had ever held hands or even been kissed yet.

Lacy socks and red bows on Valentine's morning. A little yellow box of Whitman's chocolate holding four pieces of chocolate sat on each of our mats. Mom *never* put a plate directly on the table. That was not how it was done in her elegant Dallas home, so we had a variety of mats and tablecloths that were always used. February 14 called for red mats to highlight the yellow Whitman's chocolate boxes, white plate with red heart-shaped pancakes and orange juice and milk. A small brown paper bag with our names written in cursive held our lunches, and inside was a nickel for lunch milk. Mom didn't want to leave the nickel loose and bouncing around in the bag, so she wrapped it up tight in a white paper napkin, tied it in a knot, and let it settle between the sandwich and the snack and the secrets of our daily lunch.

She packed braunschweiger or bologna, peanut butter or egg salad sandwiches, celery sticks in plastic bags, carrots or a tangerine. On Valentine's Day, we might discover a Little Debbie Oatmeal Creme Pie with creamy icing smiling from the bottom of the bag, along with potatoes chips and the standard apple.

But deep inside the brown bag would be a red, heart-shaped construction paper card with a note from Mom, a note declaring her love for us. She loved puns, and usually would figure out how to include a small sweet treat with each one on the card. My all-time favorite Valentine from Mom was a red folded heart card, with a silver-wrapped piece of Wrigley's Spearmint chewing gum glued to the front of it. When I opened the card, Mom had written I'M STUCK ON YOU. After lunch in the schoolyard when I snuck the piece of gum in my mouth, I chewed and chewed the love of my mom, swallowing the sugary sweet saliva like a magic potion and imagining her stuck on me. I didn't spit the gum out later that night after I brushed my teeth. Because I didn't brush my teeth. I chewed and chewed the gum, and went to sleep with my dreams on my white pillow. In the morning, there was a sticky hard mass of chewing gum matted in my hair. Mom had to cut it out. Turns out, she was no longer stuck on me.

Mom was like that, always punning. Once, when my slip was showing years later, Mom said, "You're slipping, dear." Slips — no one even knows what they are today! But Mom was from a proper Dallas family, and she always wore a slip, even with her blue jean skirts. I once told her that she was completely defeating the purpose of a blue jean skirt by wearing a slip with it. She didn't seem to mind. She just smiled her demure smile, laughing somewhat at herself, and kept on wearing it.

I recently found a faded, rose-colored, silk half-slip as I was cleaning out my mom's dresser, bringing some clothing to her, editing other skirts and shirts that she can no longer fit into. The pale pink slip seemed to whisper to me of other times, times long forgotten and delicate. Times when ladies wore pearls even in the day, when families gathered to sing at the piano, times when silver was polished for Thanksgiving and Christmas, and the good china was brought out. Times that sound like my mother's voice, sweet, birdlike, demure. Slower times, before-computer times, before instant-gratification times. Elegant times, when elegance was as much an attitude and a way of life as it was a piece of antique furniture. I feel much more rugged than her good china, my jeans torn by design. I wear

Spanx, not a slip, and motorcycle boots. I am always busy, my china is thick ceramic white restaurant dishware from Bed Bath & Beyond, my daughter has a pierced nose and tattoos. We seem worlds apart, my mom and me. I wonder what she thinks as she peers across this chasm of time at our practical and bold lives. I wonder if she knows that we do uphold her values despite our surface differences, if she knows that the chocolate pot and the candelabra will be used and cherished, if she knows that we are grateful that she saved them and labeled them with little stick-on tabs saying WEDDING GIFT TO GREAT-GRANDMOTHER PAULINE STODDARD, 1832. As I watch her sharply cut crystal sit on a china cabinet shelf and collect dust, I'm saddened that we don't still lay out elaborate dinners on special occasion days. I'm saddened at the impatient rush and pace at which our lives are led. I wonder how to give my mom what she longs for. And then I wonder: Does she even long for it anymore?

Mom often visited me in New York before, during, and after I attended NYU acting school, and she would arrive with her blue Samsonite carefully packed with slips, flannel nighties, and occasionally a precious piece of her mother's silver that she had been planning to bestow upon me. A silver spoon with a note that said "from grandmother Mammy Riddler," or antique ice prongs with a tag that said "Courtney Bushfield, 1920's." Each night before we bedded down in my dorm room, or women's residence hall, or tiny fifth-floor walk-up, she would open her small blue suitcase and carefully unpack her wardrobe for the next day's adventure: corduroy maroon skirt that fell three inches below her knees, maroon cashmere sweater set, gold necklace with gold stud earrings for her newly pierced ears, stockings and of course a slip, and finally, her soft-soled walking loafers.

My schedule was always full of school or work or theater or filming, and we were always in a hurry, always walking fast and weaving through crowds to get where we needed to be, *on time*! Her steps were smaller than mine, protected, almost mincing, and I would help her through the tourists that were crammed into Times Square, guiding her with an arm around her shoulder down the street. Usually we enjoyed the city in tandem, stopping to take pictures and read the guidebooks, but on the heavily scheduled days I was sometimes impatient. I would be frustrated that I could walk the block in half the time as my mom, me with my long arrogant steps, so I would encourage her to take longer steps, too, to open up a bit, to *stride*. We would battle down the Midtown sidewalks or the angled streets of the West Village, and when it was time to cross the street, five hundred other New Yorkers and I had already edged off the curb into the street before the light flashed WALK. We Manhattanites thought nothing of crowding the turning cabs as we surged off the sidewalk in preparation to *get where we were going*! It was second nature, New York nature, and I loved it. Then I would turn and see my mom still stiffly standing on the curb, with her purse clutched hard into her hip, waiting for the light to change. My heart would lurch with a combination of love and impatience. I could see in her darting eyes that she was feeling it was far too dangerous to be in the street by even a foot or two. It was far too dangerous to break the rules. It was far too dangerous to stand in front of a turning cab. It was far too dangerous to move so fast. She wasn't necessarily wrong, but I took it personally. It was far too dangerous to be with me. So I would roll my eyes as if to say, "Come *on,* Mom . . . This is how the New Yorkers do it!" I was so proud to be ahead of the crowd, so unconscious of the constant hurry. I liked the fast pace, the espresso energy. Later in the day we would race to another destination, and if I were to insist on jaywalking, I would practically have to grab Mom by the hand with a loud "COME ONNNN, MOOMM." My not-so-subtle subtext: "KEEP UP!"

She desperately wanted to keep up. She loved being in New York! She loved the feeling of being on a mission from the second the alarm clock went off at six in the morning, she loved the constant excitement! She had conquered her fear of being attacked by New Yorkers — I think all people who have never visited but only know of New York from the movies have this fear; that they will be attacked and targeted at random by gangsters of various ethnicities. She had conquered this fear years earlier when I was still at grad school at NYU. She had conquered it with an ice-cream cone clutched in her hand so that she would blend into the crowd. But by now, she was a seasoned New York visitor, and she knew she needed not to just blend in, but to keep up with the crowd. Slowly but surely, her stride opened up a bit. Her shoulders squared off. She would often say "I'll meet you there Marcia," or "I can find it on my own Marcia," and she would arrive at whatever location we had determined to meet with a slight smile on her face, patting down her thinning hair, and giving me an "I told you so!" look. We would meet at the Metropolitan Museum of Art and gape at Monet's *Water Lilies,* or meet at the Harlem Fairway where we would don jackets hanging by the freezer room as we shopped for cheese and meat. Sometimes we took a subway to the Promenade theater on upper Broadway where we would usher together in exchange for getting to see the play for free. It was a bit dark for her to see the seat numbers on her own, and once she almost fell down the steep steps as she was trying to show a customer to their seat, so we devised a system. She would greet the theatergoer at the door, smile, and welcome them, and say "Right this way," directing them to me, as I was running back down the stairs from seating someone else. I had to work extra fast, because I was doing all the walking for two people, but I didn't mind, because there she was, trying so hard to be a part of it all. And succeeding! Stepping outside her comfort zone, and proving to herself she could do it. She loved ushering. She loved seeing the plays. Over the years, she came to love the scurry, or so she said, priding herself on hailing a cab by herself, or getting to my Harlem brownstone from the airport when she came to visit from Texas. Usually I would send a car to meet her, with the driver waiting in baggage claim holding a white board with BEVERLY HARDEN printed boldly in black. One day, however, she insisted on arriving the New York way. "No reason for you to spend the money, Marcia Gay. I can get a cab myself!" I hated thinking of her lifting her blue Samsonite suitcase off the baggage claim roundabout by herself, then rolling it behind her, with the flower books in a little bag weighing down her shoulder. I hated picturing her looking for the yellow taxi sign while holding her skirt from blowing in the breeze, the wind cold on her ankles as she joined hundreds of other New Yorkers in the taxi line at JFK, all impatient to get into the city. I hated thinking that someone might push her out of the way, and I could still sense her inbred timidity and delicacy when she would raise her hand — *inviting* the cab to stop, rather than *demanding* her ride. But I had to let her do it. She wanted to do it. She needed to do it. She rolled her suitcase to the taxi line, she got into the cab and gave her driver firm directions. "I do NOT want to be taken on a joy ride!" she said to him. "I know JUST where I am going!" And she read out the directions that I had faxed to her the day before. She stared out the window and gasped in awe when the beautiful steel and glass city loomed into view as she crossed the bridge from Astoria to Randall's Island, and she chatted with the cabbie about the "bumpah to bumpah" traffic. When she was still several blocks away from our brownstone in the heart of Harlem, she carefully tapped out my number on her cell phone. "I'm almost here, Marcia Gay! We came across 125th Street just like you said," she exclaimed, "and all the Christmas lights were on and all the activity looked so lovely!" Once out of the cab and climbing up my Harlem stoop, she patted her hair and I saw the familiar "I told you so!" look shot in my direction, and as she entered the warmth of our home, the kids hugged her hard. We all climbed the stairs three flights up to put her blue suitcase in the guest room, dogs and cats and three kids and me and Thad all trooping after her, then crowding onto her white bed while she brushed her teeth and exchanged loafers for slippers, and all of us following her back down the stairs as if she were the Pied Piper. She admired my ikebana arrangement of poinsettia and pine that I had set on the buffet to greet her. Masterfully she plucked away a lower leaf that was blurring the line, gently she bent the red of the poinsettia a speck of an inch downward, and suddenly my arrangement was perfect. We settled her with a glass of white wine in front of the fire, dogs and cats at her heels, and my throat clenched up with a mixture of pride and shame. I had to turn away so she wouldn't see the sudden tears burning my eyes.

I could sense that my not-so-gentle insistence on pace had made her feel, in the past, a burden. She needed to not be a burden. Of course in those moments, on the sidewalks hurrying to class or auditions or the theater, I had often been sorry, but it was always with a "but . . ." "Sorry we have to hurry, Mom . . . but class starts at two." "Sorry we can't stop for a coffee, Mom . . . but I have to be backstage by seven thirty at the latest." And when I had pushed her too far too fast, of course I had been quickly apologetic, awash with shame. I hadn't been unaware exactly, just righteous. As if this was the way it was supposed to be if you wanted to be a New Yorker, damnit! You HONK your horn! You WEAVE when you walk and also when you *drive*! You NEVER stop abruptly on the sidewalks of Times

Square to consult your map or *anything else*! You keep moving in the stream and sea of people or you will get *mowed down*! Watching her at that moment in my Harlem brownstone, sipping her wine and thumbing through her flower books as the kids performed somersaults for her amusement, I felt the hot red of embarrassment sliding down my face, into my heart, where it bounced around for a minute, and then melted into a heart-pounding pride. I felt so damn proud of her. Proud that she had set her mind to the task of immersion in New York City, just as she had accomplished immersion in Japan, Greece, Texas, and Maryland, and in any other place to which she had traveled or explored. Proud that she was proud of herself. Proud that she had shown me up and arrived in a taxi, New York–style, and as always, she had risen to each occasion with characteristic grace and humility. She was meant for tea parlors, for paper dolls, for sewing. She was meant for flowers. She was meant for gardenias and tuberoses and paper-thin azaleas. And now she was meant for Harlem as well.

I wear the pink half-slip to bed in lieu of a nightie. Another relic of the past, the nightie. Mom is aghast that most of her grandkids wear oversize T-shirts and bikini underwear to bed. But I wear this pink half-slip and feel it smoothly settle on my thighs as I read in bed at night, or swish past the toaster as I make breakfast for the kids in the morning, cool and silky and creamy. There is some clothing you just *can't* hurry in, and a pink half-slip is one of them.

Mom was also meant for pampering, and I loved for her to travel to fancy events with me: film junkets, charity invitationals, galas, and premieres. These events became like our adult "special occasion days," and just as they had done for us when we were kids, they would break up the sameness of whatever we were doing in our lives, providing a brightly lit balloon marker along the calendar's march through the year. It was a moment of luxury and first-class travel, champagne and massages, and I loved to share it all with her.

Packing Spanx and bras and half-slips, packing jewelry and gowns and purses, Mom and I prepared to travel again. This time we were heading to Banff Springs, Canada, to partake in a celebrity ski event and raise money for Waterkeeper Alliance, the environmental charity that was passionately headed up by Bobby Kennedy Jr. The morning began serenely enough —

Mom made breakfast for my three kids while Thaddaeus and I loaded all of our seven suitcases into the car, with my skis precariously sitting on top of the blue samsonite. We finally pulled away from the curb our typical twenty minutes behind schedule, and right on cue Mom said, "Off like a herd of turtles." At the airport we were met by the celebrity invitational representatives, so we quickly made it through the security lines and passport control, and happily settled into the first-class lounge to enjoy another cup of black coffee. Mom was on point, helpful with the kids and pleasantly chatting with Thaddaeus and me throughout the hour wait. Everything was going smoothly. Soon we were called to board the plane, and we showed our passports to the flight attendant, found our seats, dug from our carry-ons our extra socks and cashmere wraps for the long flight, and buckled up. Mom put her passport in her purse and sat back. Just minutes later, she went to double-check where it was, and couldn't find it. This happened again several times before the plane took off; she would put her passport away, and then she would panic, and look for it, not remembering where she had just put it. "I'm telling you something is *wrong*, Marcia! I shouldn't keep forgetting this!"

"Well, just let me hold onto it for you, Mom. No problem."

"*No.* I have traveled all over the world, Marcia Gay! I know how to carry a passport! I've been doing it my entire life! Stop trying to control everything!"

I really didn't think much of it; it seemed as common as misplacing the keys, but I was surprised at the vehemence with which she insisted on carrying her own passport, and surprised that she was angry that I had offered to hold onto it for her. I ignored the small prick of warning that was going off in my brain — I was just irritated that everything suddenly seemed so tense, so fraught. The rest of our trip went off without a hitch; I skied in the race for Waterkeepers and made it off the mountain alive, the kids and Thaddaeus skied and boarded with professional guides, Mom rode the gondola and then relaxed and had a massage. We all went on a blanketed sleigh ride through the freezing cold snow, and I soon forgot all about the passport incident.

That is, until our trip in 2007 to attend the premiere and press junket of *The Hoax,* a movie I had recently starred in with Richard Gere and Alfred Molina. Mom especially loved the junkets, where the actors' and director's task was to educate the press about the particular film they were hawking. Mom would watch with concentration as the cast talked to the press, or, if it was a closed room, she would explore the local museum while I did film conferences, then hurry back and meet me for lunch. In the evening, we would walk the red carpet together in our gorgeous gowns and expensive high heels.

Mom had been visiting me in New York and we were now headed to Los Angeles, just the two of us, for a lovely week of press, glam, and pampering. Soon after we settled into our first-class seats on the airplane bound for LA (boy, did I love it when the studio paid), the same passport scenario was repeated several times. Again and again she misplaced her passport, found it, and immediately "lost" it again and, just as she had done several months before, she was insistent that I not help. Again I blotted out the warning light that was now blinking in my brain, and excused Mom's forgetting with the reminder that we were all a bit stressed when we travel. Now I understand that she was trying to solve the puzzle, to prove to herself that she was okay, to test herself again and again, waiting for the string of moments to slide together where she didn't forget anything. We arrived in Los Angeles where we would attend press night, and then the following night walk the red carpet at the cinema for the LA premiere of *The Hoax.*

One of Mom's favorite forms of pampering was when a stylist would pick out clothing for her as well as me, and so our bags were packed with gorgeous dresses reminiscent of the taffetas and silks, crinolines, and velvets that she had worn in college. We had heels and evening bags and diamond jewelry and stoles. We had separate and gorgeous rooms at the Four Seasons Hotel, and our dresses were hung on cushioned hangers in our closets, with notes attached, charting which dress was for each specific event.

To my delight, we also had Richard Marin and Collier Strong, old friends by now and the most expert team of hair and makeup a girl could wish for. Richard and Collier had been my good luck Oscar charms in 2001, and we had quickly become friends as we shared our bawdy, loud, and FAAAABU-LOUS humor during our hair and makeup session. They had made up Mom, too, for the 2001 Oscars and many other events over the years, and now, as we prepared to open *The Hoax,* it was like "old family reunion time" at the Four Seasons. We were all looking forward to a few laughs and catching up as we were getting makeup applied and hair coiffed in my room while preparing for the press event.

I poured the champagne and called Mom's room. "Come on down, Mom, and bring your yellow dress for press night!"

Mom walked down the hall to my room in a white robe, her curly brown hair still wet from the shower, carrying two dresses. A yellow dress, and a black long gown. When she arrived, she explained that she was wondering which she was to wear on this particular evening. I explained (again) that tonight was the more casual "press night," and so the long yellow dress had been the choice, and that the fancy black long dress was the choice for tomorrow night, the premiere. She had her schedule in her hand, a very detailed itinerary that my assistant had made for her with the events and clothing choices highlighted in fluorescent yellow marker. She looked blank for a minute, then said, "Okay, I will come back dressed in the yellow."

"Great, Mom. Just bring the yellow gown on a hanger if you want, or better yet, leave it here. I've ordered you that club sandwich you wanted."

"No, I would rather come back dressed."

"Okay."

The boys got started on my "panel beating" — that's a New Zealand term for beautifying a dinged-up car, and it was what we called the hair and makeup sessions. As we gossiped about the business and joked about the horrors of aging, we waited for Mom. I shared with them that she was more fragile lately, and that she had been concerned about her memory. We all dismissed it as the craziness of traveling for movie festivals and premieres. Five minutes later, she came into the room, still in her white robe, with the black dress on a hanger. The itinerary was still clutched in her hand and her soft hair was now dry, except for the damp clusters around her forehead. She seemed confused, and said she couldn't remember if tonight was the press night or the premiere . . . and she wasn't sure what day it was. She was embarrassed and panicky. I realized in that instant that Mom didn't remember if we might have already gone to the press night . . . she wasn't sure if the evening before had already passed, she wasn't sure if she had missed it. I was stunned, but in truth I was still making excuses for her until I looked up at Collier and Richard. I knew from their grave faces that something was wrong.

I gently walked Mom down the hall to get the yellow dress, making jokes about all the things in our lives that keep us busy and forgetful, and when we came back to the room the boys were jovial as if nothing had happened. But Richard's nose was swollen and sniffly, and Collier's eyes were red, and there were more Kleenex in the wastebasket than had been there before. I knew then — we all knew, and they both later agreed — that something was wrong.

The next day before the premiere, Mom's eyes were slightly confused, but it only lasted for a moment or two. She hadn't remembered the yellow dress incident. She looked glorious in the long black gown, and she laughed with us as the boys flawlessly applied her makeup. Later that night, after the premiere, she comforted me when I cried with embarrassment at how much of my part had been cut out of the movie. I was devastated. Whole scenes had been cut. Entire story lines left on the editing room floor. I felt like I had seen half a character in my role, like I had told half a story. It struck me that this was what Mom's life would be like, if it were to be confirmed that she had early onset dementia, or worse, Alzheimer's. Just like an actor who, having performed a role full of emotions and lines and scenes and locations, finds that in the final edit, so much had been cut out. I couldn't bear to think of her past lying dormant on the editing room floor. I couldn't bear to think of her with Alzheimer's. She was supposed to grow old as gracefully as she had already lived. I slept with her in her hotel room that night; I didn't want her to be alone or confused when she woke up. Staring at her peacefully sleeping face, I couldn't help but shed tears again at what I feared lay ahead for her. I thought of the Valentine's Day spearmint gum, and I wanted to be a piece of gum for my mom, to stick the pieces of memory back together, to help her make sense of the events in her life, and to let her chew and chew and chew and swallow my love for her with the sticky sweet spearmint juice.

WINTER

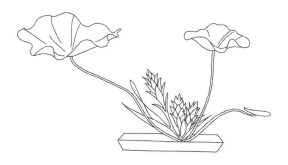

■ ■ ■ ■

My Mother is
a Harry Winston
Diamond

■ ■ ■ ■

It is human nature to attach the possibility of change to certain turning points on the calendar, gathering steam for new beginnings as the first of the week, or month, or year comes circling by. How many times have we heard, or even said, "On Monday, the beginning of the week, I'll start a new diet" or "At the beginning of the month, I'll begin my exercise program"? The first of January is famous for new resolutions and sacred oaths as a rash of bad habits are left behind. Cigarette packages are crushed and thrown away, alcohol is poured down the drain by the hands of severely hungover people, and new promises are born, new beginnings imagined. Hope is fortified like the front lines of a once-beleaguered army. No greater seismic shift may occur in a person's lifetime than the beginning of a new century, and in the year 2000, America, and indeed the world, looked to reinvent itself. So, too, did my mom. She was about to turn sixty-three. She used the rush of the millennium to reimagine her future. She knew that this was the time to tackle the goals in her life that still beckoned. This was the time to fortify her accomplishments, to achieve her full potential. Another chance to ride on the merry-go-round: reaching for the elusive brass ring.

The turn of the century began for me not just with a bang but with an explosion. I had wrapped up work on *Space Cowboys* with Clint Eastwood in the spring, and Ed Harris's biopic picture *Pollock* was in its final edit by early summer, so when fall finally rolled around, I would *hopefully* be looking forward to all the wonderful things that happened to an actor *after* a film was shot. I say hopefully, because only *some* actors, the lead actors, are invited to join the post-production release campaign, where exotic travel, awards, gift baskets, and fancy new clothes are sure to be a part of the package. Would I be invited by Clint to join the men while they promoted *Space Cowboys*? Would I be invited by Ed to help promote *Pollock*? I tried to picture myself eating bonbons by the poolside at fancy hotels, wearing sunglasses on the red carpet, and sitting with confidence, my shoulders back, as I sold the press on what was great about each movie. In truth, I was having those familiar "less than" feelings, that insecure voice in my head that told me that somehow, I was not enough. Somehow, I didn't quite measure up.

Speaking of measuring, I was also a bit nervous about the inevitable fittings with stylists who could barely hide their dismay that I was *not* a size zero as they dressed me for various publicity appearances. If I wanted to compete for the big roles, I told myself, I would have to "measure up" by quite literally measuring *down*. Fortunately, however, one of my goals for the new year was to accept myself as I was, and a size zero didn't fit into that picture. What the frig did that even mean, anyway? *A size zero?* That's a size nothing! I decided I didn't want to be a "nothing," and I would just have to work through my body dysmorphia and insist on a size 8 for my wardrobe. Of course, I would also have to make a concerted effort not to stand next to very thin actresses on the red carpet.

Then, unexpectedly in September, I was able to mark off a big goal on my bucket list: *Pollock* got accepted to the prestigious Venice International Film Festival, and I was invited to go. *Bonbons, here we come!* I felt like a rookie who had just made first pick to their favorite baseball team. Suddenly, I was in a whole new league, and I was excited — and scared.

When I was growing up, we had an old wooden ruler with little Dutch children painted on the sides of it that we hung on a wall to mark our growth. Whenever I hit a new inch line, I marked it on the wall and ran to get my mother to come and look at it. I needed to see myself through her eyes; her witness of the line somehow solidified it, validated it, made it real. "Look, Mommy, I'm changing!" I would chant as a young child, waiting for her to proudly acknowledge me. So it was no surprise that when I learned of *Pollock*'s acceptance into the film festival, the first person I telephoned was my mother. I had hit another inch on the growth line, and I needed her to know, to make it real.

"Mooooommm!! *Pollock* is being talked about for all kinds of awards, and we *just* got accepted into the Venice Film Festival, and guess what: I am invited to go, too!"

She was ecstatic. "Oh, Marcia, congratulations! Oh, my — how wonderful! Be proud, sweetheart. You deserve this!"

I paused while listening to my mom's enthusiastic compliments and motherly pride. I didn't think I *deserved* it. I didn't know that I would ever really see myself that way: as "deserving." I resisted that word. It seemed almost egotistical to think, "I deserve this or that," because the inverse thought was, of course, also true: "If I *deserve* this or that, then since *you* didn't get it, you must not have worked as hard. You must not *deserve* it." Which, of course, couldn't have been further from the truth. I feel I don't have the *right* to assume I am any more or less deserving than the next person, because over the years I've worked with hundreds of diligent, talented, brilliant actors who never get rewarded with fame. I've worked with beautiful, educated, and creative people, yet they are still overlooked when important castings occur. Didn't they deserve it? Whatever "it" is? Of course they did. They just weren't at the right place at the right time. They didn't get lucky. Luck. That great enigmatic element that carries hard work and preparation on to success.

For *Pollock,* yes, I had worked hard, I had done all my research. I had met Lee Krasner's family and practiced her sharp Brooklyn accent for hours upon end. I had even taken up painting classes in New York, hoping I would discover that deep inside Marcia Gay Harden was a real painter. But when, try as I might, I realized that I couldn't paint worth a damn, I used my disappointment to fuel Lee Krasner's own depression about her stagnant attempts to create art while she lived in the shadow of Pollock. In preparation for my role I had also studied avant-garde painters Warhol and de Kooning, and of course, Picasso. I had listened to musicians like Miles Davis and John Coltrane who had influenced the eruptive jazz scene of the 1950s. I had spent hours in the Museum of Modern Art attempting to absorb the philosophy and concepts of Modernism, trying to understand why a red dot in the middle of a white canvas was, actually, art. Yes, I had worked hard, but did that really mean I *deserved* this?

If anyone deserved it, it was Ed Harris. He had been with the project for ten years. He had set up a painting studio in his Malibu Canyon home and had actually painted *good* Pollocks. He had directed and acted in the film. Also on the hard-working, deserve-it front were Michael Barker and Tom Bernard from Sony Pictures Classics, and the bevy of producers who had given time and money and thought outside the box to get the film made, names like Fred Berner, Jon Kilik, James Francis Trezza, Barbara Turner, and Peter Brant. They deserved it. The film deserved it. But me? I got lucky. I was just lucky enough that my longtime manager Maryellen Mulcahy had insisted that I audition. I was lucky enough to get cast in a role that allowed me to transform. I was lucky enough to have a director who pushed me and trusted me, and I was lucky enough to be edited in a way that showed the spark and spunk and beauty of Lee Krasner.

It seemed to me that this good fortune was really the work of other people — that I had just shown up and done my job. I'm not saying that I didn't want to go to Venice, or that I was just "along for the ride," but for some reason it has always been hard for me to take ownership of my own contribution in moments of glory. Pride embarrasses me. I downplay my role in my own accomplishments. My therapist says it's "middle child syndrome." I call it dumbfounded gratitude.

So it was no small coincidence that recognizing myself, seeing myself through my own eyes, was also on my New Year's resolution list.

Venice has been described as the most beautiful city ever built by man. It is called the City of Love, it is artistic and palatial and romantic, and as Mom went on and on about how wonderful it was that I got to go, I could hear how much she would have loved it, too. I could hear her longing for the adventure of it all, the lush travel, the new sights, the water streets, the gleaming Rialto Bridge, the gondolas and cute Italian men, the art galleries and Chardonnay sipped from cold glasses under a sidewalk umbrella. For a moment I thought of inviting her, but then decided against it. I knew people would advise me to go to the festival alone, with just my husband, and be free and romantic. They would advise me to be sensible and leave my two-year-old daughter Eulala with my nanny in New York. And they would certainly advise me not to bring my *mother,* who surely wouldn't be able to keep up with us. In truth, all that sounded great, but this moment was a shifting of size and growth, and as with the childhood wooden ruler, I realized I needed Mom not to just witness it, but to be a *part* of the change. I wanted her to enjoy whatever ownership a mother felt at the success of her daughter. I wanted her to know that she mattered, that the endless thankless tasks of mothering she had performed over the many years were actually gifts that had not been forgotten. There are so few moments in life when we can really treat our parents to a great big "Thank you!" And this was one of them.

"Pack the blue Samsonite, Mom. You're going to Venice with us!"

Mom took to modern first class like a duck to water. Sprawling in her super-large seat, she perused the menu, deciding on the salmon and a mimosa. When the flight attendant looked at his list of names and said, "Welcome, Mrs. Harden," she smiled, and with her slight southern drawl insisted, "Oh, just call me Beverly. I'll have the salmon," she said, pronouncing the L in "salmon." Examining the little complimentary travel bag and unwrapping the extra-soft eye mask, sliding her seat up and down and up and down like a child on a carnival ride, pressing the massage button every which way, and wrapping her always cold feet in the blue airplane socks, she prepared her royal cubicle for a night of comfort. "Now this is something I could get used to!"

We raced through the distant stars, and just before bedding down for the night flight, she pressed her nose against the cold round window and stared into the charcoal sky. The crescent moon beckoned, shape-shifting just as it had done almost thirty years before when Mom first flew her family to Japan. Following the waxing moon's lead, Mom was ready to transform once again, and she decided to reach outside of the self she knew so that she could grow to her full potential. After all, this was the century to reinvent oneself, this was the year to fortify accomplishment, this was the moment to grow past every inch line on the wooden ruler, and in doing so, to seize the brass ring.

"Marcia," she began, "I have been thinking for a while about creating a show that would air on one of those home channels like HGTV."

She paused, to gauge my reaction.

"Go on," I said, truly intrigued.

"Well, we could call it *Along the Flower Path,* and in it, I would travel to different places in America, and interview famous people, maybe some of your celebrity friends if you think they would be willing . . ."

She looked at me to see if I minded that she was including my friends. I didn't.

"And I would take the audience through their gardens, and talk about what is unique about each one. We could interview actors, artists, and potters, painters, and sculptors, and talk about their art. And maybe we would end every episode with a flower lesson . . ."

I could tell that, though hopeful, she was a little bit embarrassed, waiting for me to tell her what a silly idea it was, or to question just who would want to see her, or to say that my friends would never do it. But I thought it was a brilliant idea. And I was so surprised, and so . . . proud, I guess, that she had imagined herself in this role.

"Go on, Mom," I encouraged.

We began to discuss which of my friends might be willing to be interviewed.

"Bette Midler, for sure," we decided. Bette had planted lots of trees in various parks in New York, she was all about nature and beautifying the city, and I had supported her charity, New York Restoration Project, several times. She would be a great interview.

"Camryn Manheim, definitely." Camryn was my dearest friend, she is perhaps the most spectacular and accomplished person I have ever known, a dear and loyal friend and Mom and I both just loved her. She lived on the Venice Canals in California, and I agreed with Mom that it would be interesting to discuss which plants would grow in that environment.

"Ellen Burstyn?" Mom asked.

"Absolutely!" I said. Ellen lived on the Hudson River, and had once staged *A*

Midsummer Night's Dream in her lush Nyack garden. Ellen was one of the most interesting women I had ever met; she was my mentor, and a sort of godmother to my children. We remembered fondly the name day ceremony Ellen had created for Eulala. How spectacular that day had been! Ellen had gathered at least thirty of my friends and neighbors on the beach in Venice. While the waves crashed and the sun added warmth to our sweaters, we sat in a circle, with a painted box in the middle. Each person put a treasure in the box, a button, a poem, a paperclip, or perhaps a marble, and then told the symbolic meaning of the object, which was also a wish for Eulala. Paperclip = practical. Marble = playful. Plastic sphere which changed shapes = curious, and so on. I reminded Mom that she had put in a willow branch, so that Eulala would be flexible, but also strong and unbreakable. Just like my mom. Ellen's gift was the painted wooden box, so that Eulala would gather up all the love and wisdom from the people around her, and hold onto it forever. Yes, we agreed, Ellen would be an amazing interview!

As we flew, we began to plant the seeds for her show. We talked structure and format and decided to make a rough pilot, to be shot in upstate New York on my Catskills lake. Mom wanted me to be the first interview, throwing pottery on my wheel.

"You could throw a vase!" she exclaimed. "And then show the firing of the vase in your kiln, and then finally I would use the vase at the end of the episode for a flower arrangement!"

"We should also do a calendar book, Mom. An arrangement for January, and then one for February, and so on." We were on the merry-go-round, stretching, stretching, stretching, and it felt so good.

I returned to my spacious seat and snuggled in with Thad and Eulala as the lights dimmed in first class, grateful that Thad was always so welcoming of my mom. Although many sitcoms make millions of dollars off of the "Take cover! Here comes the mother-in-law!" mentality, I have always hated it. Holding hands in the dark, I told Thad of her idea, and before I had even asked him, he said he would love to shoot it for us. Our seats slid down in tandem and we fell asleep dreaming of gardens and gondolas.

As we flew from the Atlantic Ocean to the Adriatic Sea, it was like turning a page on a whole new chapter in an enchanted fairy tale. Venice was everything that the story-books had promised. We stepped off the plane at the Marco Polo airport and onto a gleaming mahogany boat. Someone handed us a glass of Prosecco. It tasted bouncy and tickled my tongue. Never one to stint on a good glass of bubbly, I was ready for a refill before we even left the port. Mom clutched her bag with the flower books in one hand, the sparkling wine in the other, I clutched Eulala with one arm and of course the crystal glass with the other, and Thaddaeus took film of the magical ride through the glistening canals as we glided under stone bridges and made our way to our very fancy hotel. Eulala snuck a sip of my fizzy Prosecco when I pretended not to be looking. And why not? *When in Rome . . . er, Venice.* Cathedral bells chimed, an accordion played somewhere in the distance, and a handsome young tenor's beautiful voice rose to the high notes of an aria and drifted off of St. Mark's Square, floating through the air, right into our boat. We looked at each other in amazement, giddy with smiles and dizzy with our good fortune. *La dolce vita! La dolce vita! Grazie per la dolce vita!*

Over the next few days I did press, and while I squeezed into my navy blue Chanel dress or cashmere sweater with the Lee Krasner scarf in my hair, Mom squeezed into her own supply of designer dresses on loan from my stylist and accompanied me. We kept saying to each other "Just pinch me!" as we floated through the water streets. On breaks we went to the Doge's Palace, and St. Mark's Basilica. We ate thin-crust pizza with Eulala, drank champagne and ate caviar. We took a gondola ride and flirted with the handsome gondoliers. We took a tour to the three famous islands in the Venetian Lagoon, Murano, Burano, and Torcello, to see the glass blowing and lace making. We both bought swirling glass vases for future flower arrangements.

"Oh, I'll never forget this, Marcia. This is all just incredible. I've heard about Venetian glass for years, and I've always wanted to see this. And here I am."

One afternoon while I did press, Mom and Eulala joined Stephanie Seymour and her husband, producer Peter Brant, for a swim at their hotel on a private Venetian island.

"OHMYGODMOM you are swimming with probably the most famous Victoria's Secret model ever!"

"Well, I didn't know that," she said, "but just pinch me!"

Stephanie Seymour had had a small role in the film, and she crushed every stereotype of "shallow model" into the dust. She was smart, talented, funny, gracious, generous, a great mom, and of course, gorgeous. Somehow, she managed to make Eulala and my mom feel right at home while swimming in a Venetian palatial hotel. Go figure!

Part of our press tour was to go to the Peggy Guggenheim Collection. Peggy had taken on Jackson Pollock as a protégé in his early career, and she had helped usher him into the ranks of the avant-garde. To visit her museum and view a Pollock painting there was icing on the cake. Stepping back into the immaculate boat, accepting a proffered glass of ice-cold sparkling wine, I said, "This is work, Mom. This is what I actually *have* to do, for work. Just pinch me."

Later that year I won the New York Film Critics Circle Award for Best Supporting Actress for *Pollock*. It was a big deal. A really big deal. The New York critics were hugely respected, and I had just won entrance into a very elite group.

More fittings, more hair and makeup sessions, more press. I have always loved "free" anything, probably a hangover from my waitress days, and I was thrilled at all the free gift bags from various events that I could now share with my brother and sisters, nephews and nieces, and Mom. I took it all in stride. It seemed to be happening *around* me, not really *to* me. I felt like the same person inside, with the same scars from my middle school unibrow, and from being displaced in so many different schools because of my dad's navy assignments, always being outside the "in" circle. Here I was now in the "in" circle, but still feeling like an outsider. I don't think I changed much at all with the onset of fame, but the people around me seemed to change their view of me.

Mom, however, remained steadfast. She had always thought of all of her children as stars, and whenever any one of us got mentioned in any way, for any glory, she shared it with her garden club. The garden club was like her news pipeline; they began collecting articles just in case she hadn't seen them, and they often knew the lineup of what different television channels were showing my interviews, even before I did.

As the year came to an end, there began to be a buzz around the film that it would be nominated for an Oscar. I knew *nothing* about Oscars, which was odd considering that acting was my profession, but you would be surprised at all the actors who don't watch television, or haven't been to the movies in years, or know nothing about campaigning for the awards shows or Oscars, or even that they need to campaign. We gathered at my mom's for Christmas that year, and my oldest sister, Leslie, gave me a green Oscar the Grouch puppet from *Sesame Street* just in case I wasn't nominated; she didn't want me to be too disappointed. I said I probably wouldn't be nominated, and I explained to everyone what I was just learning from my new publicist Carri McClure. "Oscars are a mysterious business," I began. "I will have to go to lots of events, shake hands with lots of people, and make appearances. *Pollock* is a small film, but we have a *chance* to be nominated because Ed Harris is a legend, and the movie is good. I'm not superfamous and the odds are against me, plus there are a lot of good films in the making this year, but, fingers crossed, at least Ed will be nominated, and if so, I will get to attend." Carrie thinks I have a shot, though. Just pinch me, indeed!

Over the next few days I forgot all about awards season as I caught up with family, enjoying the excesses of Christmas at my mother's. Shopping, wrapping, divinity, fudge, popcorn garlands made with cranberries, spiked eggnog — we did it all. If you could have ripped a page out of a Norman Rockwell book, and added some Dickensian

316

description to the picture, you would have my mother's ideal — *idea* — of Christmas at her house. *Idea* because in reality, lurking in the corner of any family gathering are the ghosts of childhood past just waiting to reappear, and when they do, an argument usually ensues. Christmas is stressful, let's face it! But the idea, the ideal, is what we always shoot for. It's what we come back to year after year. It is the torch we pass down to our kids, and the ideal is what they will mimic and prepare for *their* children's Christmases, with hopefully improvements of their own.

We pursued the ideal. The Christmas tree was always live (no plastic for us!) and fully adorned with cherished ornaments that had been handed down over the years. We hauled the labeled boxes into the living room, lit the fire, put the *Christmas's Greatest Hits* album on the stereo, and as Bing Crosby crooned about a "White Christmaaass," we made the hot cocoa and began decorating. There were boxes of lights, there were boxes with antique bulbs my mom had inherited from her mother, there were boxes of childlike homemade ornaments and precious delicate ornaments from our many travels. That year Mom hung a red blown-glass ornament with a green swirl inside, purchased several months earlier in Venice. Next to this I hung the walnut ornament with an angel kneeling at a crèche that my paternal grandmother had made me when I was a girl in Japan. Just above that I hung the ceramic angel ornament that had been made by my maternal grandmother that same year. Mine was red with gold trim, and they were given a prominent position on the tree. We adorned the outermost branches with silver tinsel icicles that glistened and swished as the kids ran by, or the cat batted at a swinging birdhouse ornament that had been hung just a little bit too low. And just as she had done when we were kids, Mom waited until nighttime when all the youngsters were asleep to rearrange the balls that little hands had hung on the absolute tip of the branches, being the easiest to decorate but causing the upward reaching arms to droop solemnly toward the carpet. She burrowed deep into the green, evening out colors, her hands sap sticky, pushing sparkling lights and golden balls close to the trunk to "draw the eye in."

Mom and I picked back up on our calendar book idea, chatting in the kitchen as she made a beautiful holiday wreath.

She began: "Of course in December we

318

will use pine and red roses, white chrysan-themum and poinsettia, and arrange them into a holiday display."

I took notes. "Great idea, Mom. And you can also show people how to use the cut-off branches from the Christmas tree for their mantle," I said, "and do just what you are doing right now! Make a wreath, and show how you wind the holly and snow bells into the circle and fasten it with a big red velvet bow."

She smiled coyly at me. "I suppose I should also show them how to make the mistletoe ball, just in case there is some unexpected kissing that needs to go on."

There was always mistletoe hung in a doorframe for the unexpected kiss . . . if it could *really* be called unexpected when a child hung out under that same said door-frame for half an hour, just hoping someone would notice, and try to kiss them!

The weeks of shopping and wrapping and fudge making always ended with a Christ-mas Eve talent show.

We had two Christmas Eve traditions: One, Mom had started for purely practical rea-sons. It was the giving of *one* present on Christmas Eve. Since we always knew that this *one* present was pajamas, we ultimately got to pick out *another* present, so we could at least get *one* surprise. I loved the pajamas best, though. We were all wearing something vaguely matching and new and warm, and we were unified in our costume of sleep together. Mom started it when we lived in Japan so that we would all look cute in our Christmas photos the following morning. There is one Christmas in particular that stands out in my mind. I call it the Candy Cane Nightie Christmas, because my youngest sister Stephanie and I were both given matching flannel red-and-white candy cane nighties — I was ten, she was six — tied with a red satin bow at the bust.

That leads me to our second tradition, the Christmas Eve talent show. Rehearsals! Costumes! Programs! Popcorn! Lights out . . . and . . . lights up . . . Action! Our chosen MC announced each performance: flute playing from Leslie, guitar from both Leslie and Sheryl, a karate demonstration from Mark, and *The Nutcracker Suite* in matching candy cane nightgowns from Stephanie and me. I had been taking ballet classes with a local Japanese group, and I felt quite proud of the number I had choreographed to the "Dance of the Sugar Plum Fairy." The family sat on the couch, and applauded as we deeply curtsied, and then the

320

MC announced the big finale, a reading of *'Twas the Night Before Christmas,* by Mom.

Our talent show in the year 2000 was a real doozy! The house was full of children and parents and almost everyone performed! It was fantastic, it was the talent show that never ended! Rehearsals, popcorn, lights out — lights up! Action! I of course performed my Japanese standby *"Omme omme fudee fudee,"* dancing the rice dance with aplomb. There was harmonica, singing, dancing, comedy routines, karate demonstrations, Christmas carols, and an unintentionally funny reenactment of the *'Twas the Night Before Christmas* by the kids . . . we had already started cracking up by the time "not a creature was stirring, not even a mouse" was read. The Academy Award goes to . . . the mouse! The night ended with us gathered around the piano as my nephew Andrew serenaded us with classical music, Mom rocking in her red velvet–covered rocking chair.

This was the beginning of a new century, and it felt so good to be gathered in unity. We were indeed a Rockwellian-Dickensian group, creating an ideal communion of family. In truth, it is a very similar ideal that I have passed down to my own children, complete with labeled boxes and talent shows, an all-guests-welcome policy, and Christmas Eve "surprise" pajamas that are an expected tradition.

Thad, Eulala, and I left Texas and returned to our frozen lake in the New York Catskills to welcome in 2001. We lit fireworks over the ice, then bundled up in gloves and down jackets, and skated under the moonlight in a circling path, shouting *kooooo iiiii* and listening to it echo off the lake. Glorious last night of the old year! Glorious first dawn of the new! No matter what would unfold in the months ahead, we were grateful for what we had in that moment, under those stars.

February 13, 2001. I woke up in a hotel room in Denver, ordered coffee, and waited for my glam team and Carri to arrive so I could go do more press for *Pollock,* which was coming out on limited release. I had no idea that they had announced the Oscar nominees that morning. I didn't even know that that was a thing they did! I don't know how I thought it was done, and it never occurred to me that however it was done, it was done at the crack of dawn on national television in Los Angeles. No one told me, nobody warned me, and suddenly both my cell phone and the hotel phone started ringing off the wall. Publicist. Agents. Managers. Lawyers. Family. Friends. In one minute I had racked up fifty-two missed calls. My heart was pounding through my nightie, and I was having a hard time catching my breath, and an even harder time wiping the shit-eating grin off my face. I had never in my life experienced this level of excitement and sudden attention. I quickly learned that both Ed and I had been nominated. Unbelievable! Both of us! Me too! At some point the coffee arrived from room service, and in tears I blurted out to the waitress: "I don't have anybody to hug, but I used to be a waitress too and I just got nominated for an Academy Award and Oh My God I can't breathe and . . . and . . . and . . ."

She cut me off with, "Well, let's have a hug, then!" and we stood there hugging and bouncing up and down while the phones rang, celebrating the unexpected high of the possibility of someone coming from waitress world, to land in this moment.

It's odd how circumstances play out. In the script of my life, I would *never* have written that I would be alone on such a momentous day. I would *never* have written me, ignorant of the proceedings, groggy, while waiting for coffee in a nondescript hotel room. Instead I would have written me nervous, watching with my family and friends in Los Angeles, all cuddled up on the couch in Venice Beach, waiting impatiently and with baited breath as the nominees were announced on the living room TV.

But all I had that morning was the waitress in that hotel room, and it was a divine reminder of my steadfast journey. It was a reminder of my mother first pushing me to audition for a Little Theatre play in Alexandria, Virginia. It was a reminder of all the tables I had waited, and all the actor/waiters who had covered my shifts so that I could run down to Times Square and audition. It was a reminder of my schooling in NYC, of my teacher Ron Van Lieu, of my mother hauling boxes to help me move into the West Village. The waitress looked me in the eye and said, "Congratulations. Breakfast is on the house. You deserve it."

There was that word again. "Deserve." When she left, I actually sank to my knees to thank God and spent a moment in a prayer of gratitude. The phone continued to ring, but I ignored it. Sometimes, you just have to stop and be in the moment, and this was one of those times.

When the bustle settled down, I called Mom. She had just gotten a call from someone in her garden club, so she was already bubbling over with excitement.

"Congratulations, Marcia Gay! Hold on, here's your dad!" They put me on speaker.

"Bravo!" said Dad. FANFUCKINGTAS-TIC! Bravo!"

"OH MY GOSH!" I screamed. "PACK THE SAMSONITE! YOU AND DAD ARE COMING TO THE OSCARS!"

Over the next few weeks, Dad tried to design my dress. Unbelievable. Navy captain turned designer. He wanted me to wear a champagne pink color, soft and gauzy, and off the shoulders. I didn't want to hurt his feelings, and it made me smile — but also, a little bit irritated — that he was trying to commandeer my dress.

"Well, Goddamnit, I want you to look elegant!" he said on the phone one day.

I didn't feel skinny enough to wear champagne pink. At a size 8, I felt *fat.*

"I *will* look elegant, Dad! Trust me!" I said, clutching my stomach roll, and then I burst into tears.

My stylist Jessica Paster was there that day, pacing around deftly with her wild brown ringlets and her loud Valley-girl-accent-meets-New York attitude, and she took over the phone call. With the finesse of a woman who had dealt with many an insecure actress before, she shushed me as she complimented my dad on his ideas about a champagne pink dress. I was aghast. Was she actually going to put me in that color? Then she smiled at me and, in so many words, she told him to leave it to her. She assured him that I would look elegant, and then asked him, "Do you approve of cleavage, Captain?" He stuttered out a "Hell, yes!" and she smacked the phone back into my hand. He may have actually met his match.

I wanted him to wear his Navy Dress Whites, with his medals, but he said he couldn't fit into them anymore. "Too God-damn fat!" he said.

"Now you know how it feels!" I retorted. I told him to order a new size, cummerbund and all. I would pay for it. Mom, however, needn't worry, she too was to be taken care of by Jessica.

The famous Hollywood designer Randolph Duke and Jessica designed a sleek old-Hollywood–style scarlet dress with a long matching scarlet wrap for over my shoulders. It was a shoulderless gown, and true to her word, there was plenty of cleavage showing just above a long low curve. I had spent many long hours at the gym with my jovial but take-no-prisoners trainer Brian Gorski and was now a size 6. The waist snugly tapered in, then the dress crawled down my hips, and opened up into a long fishtail train. It was magnificent.

As the big day rolled closer, we met with the seamstress for our final fitting at a little shop on La Cienega Boulevard. The small room was crowded with bodies. There was the seamstress and her assistant, Randolph Duke and his assistant, Jessica Paster and her two assistants, my mother, my manager, and my publicist. There were also two burly VIP security guards from Harry Winston jewelers, and one equally burly security guard from Neil Lane jewelers, who between them had about ten million dollars' worth of diamonds in that tiny little sewing room.

It was time to choose the bling!

I was told that I could have up to $500,000 worth of jewels for the Oscars, and would then be able to travel with no bodyguard. If I went over that amount, I had to have a bodyguard for the evening.

"Oh, good heavens no!" I said. "No bodyguard necessary!" Other than my wedding ring, I had never worn a piece of jewelry over $200. "I am SURE five hundred thousand will be enough!" I exclaimed.

Mom concurred. "Five hundred thousand

is a *lot* of jewelry!" she said, then added sveltely, "Even if *I* get to wear a piece or two of it as well!"

Jessica unveiled the dress, we all admired it, and I went behind the curtain to slip it on. "I don't need a bodyguard," I shouted over the curtain. "I want this to be about family, you know? Private? I don't want a bodyguard hovering over us all night long."

Meantime, I heard a lot of phone calls being made, and when I peeked out to see what all the commotion was about, Jessica said, "Harry Winston got wind of how grand the dress is, and they said you can now have up to a million dollars' worth of jewels with no bodyguard." The handsome bodyguard with the blond hair smiled at me. I disappeared again, pulled up my Spanx, and stepped into the gown.

My muffled protests came again from inside the cubicle, "Oh, my goodness! That's crazy! I definitely won't need a million dollars' worth of jewels," I said. "No bodyguard — right, Mom? We just want to be free." Mom was silent. Maybe she hadn't heard me over the curtain. "Right? Mom? No bodyguard?"

"Hmm," she said.

"Yeah," I went on. "One million dollars' worth of jewels will be *plenty* for us! More

328

than enough! Right, Mom?"

"Hmm," again. "Yes. Plenty. Even if *I* borrow some, too!"

I stepped out in my magnificent gown to witness Mom running her fingers over the diamonds as the security guard stiffened next to her. "Oh, and my daughter Stephanie," she added demurely. "Stephanie will need some diamonds, too!"

Stephanie was my youngest sister who had just given birth and was heading down with her husband from San Francisco to attend Oscar night with us. I called her and asked her if she wanted to borrow some diamond earrings from Harry Winston jewelers, and she just screamed.

I posed in front of the mirror, perfecting my stance, and then Jessica said excitedly, "Diamonds! Diamonds, Marcia Gay! It's diamond time!"

I walked over to the sewing table where the velvet boxes were laid out, and as the lids were raised the table lit up with brilliant shimmers. I immediately chose a gorgeous pair of huge diamond drop earrings, and then tried on several necklaces. When I put on a big sparkling diamond necklace, the room oohed and aahed, and I felt like Elizabeth Taylor meets Cinderella on her way to the ball, but the price tag on my neck alone was over a million dollars, so I took it off again. When I did so, the room got quiet. Same thing happened with the next necklace, I put it on, the room oohed and aahed. I took it off, silence. On went the first necklace again, and again, ooh and aah. Off went the necklace, and silence. "Guys," I said firmly, "stop. It's too expensive!" I asked Mom to choose some earrings, then I chose earrings for Stephanie, and we were told that without the necklace, we were now at one million. "Okay!" I said, staunchly, "this is enough! No bodyguard!"

The room stood still again. Very still. Jessica stared.

"Oh, well, okay, let me try the necklace on again, just *one* last time." The blond bodyguard looked hopeful.

I put the necklace on again, and my entire being rose two inches. Rainbow shimmers rested on my wonderful cleavage. Even I oohed and aahed. Everyone stared, waiting breathlessly for my decision.

"Bodyguard!" I said. I had to have it.

"Oh, thank God!" Jessica shrieked. "It's gorgeous! The dress needs it!"

"Yes! Just gaargeous!" said Mom. She always pronounced "gorgeous" as *gaargeous*. "Really, really gaargeous."

Then it was like a feeding frenzy. I saw

the ring. A big, tear-shaped diamond ring. I just *had* to have that, too. "Definitely bodyguard," I said.

Then Mom saw a necklace she might like. "It's gaargeous," she said. "I won't need anything else . . . other than . . . this ring!" So we added Mom's ring to our bag of bling, then we also chose a bracelet for Stephanie since, what the hell, we were already over our mark, and before we walked out of that door, we were at four million dollars. I guess $500,000 worth of jewelry really *didn't* go that far, at least not on Oscar night in a red scarlet dress.

Oscar day, we gathered at the Shutters on the Beach hotel in Santa Monica. With the doors open we could feel the fresh ocean breeze and hear the crashing waves mingle with the screams of kids on the roller coaster at the Santa Monica Pier. I met my famous hair and makeup team Richard and Collier who were so funny and fabulous that we established an immediate bond based on loud laughter, bawdy jokes and gestures, and a smattering of fabulously catty observations. All of this, of course, covered two sentimental hearts of gold, two wise minds, and two generous souls. It was clear that we would be friends for life. First with his black bag of blow dryers was Richard Marin, famous for doing Cindy Crawford's locks, and about to glamorize mine. He was accompanied by Collier Strong, also rolling a black bag but this one full of makeup. He was famous for countless magazine covers and a celebrity clientele that stretched from Hollywood Boulevard to the runways of Milan. Just pinch me!

Dad was feeling a bit under the weather, and while he rested in his room, Mom joined us for her own panel beating. Soon all of my neighbors began to trickle in from our Venice Beach enclave just down the road. They remembered Mom from the ikebana class she had taught when I was waiting for Eulala to be born several years before and they had come to celebrate with us! "Beverly!" they cried. "You look maaarvelous!" "Well, I certainly feel just gaargeous!" she replied, as she welcomed each of them with a big hug while getting her hair and makeup applied. Jessica Pasteur had found Mom a beautiful black gown with a stunning V-neck, and when she had learned that Dad's navy uniform wouldn't arrive in time for the Oscars, she insisted on procuring him a Hugo Boss tuxedo.

His response was a flabbergasted, "Well, I'll be a Goddamned son of a bitch that anyone would care about me!" He was flattered, not used to the attention, but he loved it.

"Oh believe me," Jessica crooned, "we aalllll care about you! You are going to be one proud papa tonight! Now get out there and protect that cleavage!" Dad loved her.

We finally dressed, the bodyguard arrived with the jewels, we donned our bling, and were off!

The whole evening passes in a blur when I try to remember it. From the limousine ride with Stephanie pumping breast milk into little bottles, and me trying to write down a forty-five-second speech just in case I won. The odds in Vegas were for Kate Hudson to win. I think it was 12 to 1 against me, whatever that means. I hadn't been nominated for any other awards, not a Golden Globe or the Screen Actors Guild. And though I *had* received the Film Critics award, that wasn't a competition against others, it was more of an election. So *if* I were a gambler, I would have put the odds in Vegas at 12 to 0 against me to win, if there even is such a thing. Plus, all the other nominees had turned in wonderfully specific, beautiful perfomances in their films, and so it really seemed like it would be a very far away possibility to go home with an Oscar. Now I know this sounds like baloney when anyone says it, but it actually *is* true: *The win was in the nomination.* It is so much harder to be nominated than it is to win, if you are talking odds: 5 in over 1000 get nominated; 1 in 5 wins. I was just friggin' grateful to be there!

I loved walking the red carpet that night, I don't think I ever took my hand off my hip — that was my perfected pose. Stand slightly leaning backward, with hip thrust out and hand on the hip so that my arms looked skinnier, other hand gracefully holding the Kathrine Baumann red beaded bag, one knee bent to bring the dress in at the knees, and fishtail splayed out in back of me. With my bodyguard always nearby, I did the interviews, and kept pulling Mom into them. She loved it, she looked stunning in her black gown with the elegant sheer sleeves, sparkling Harry Winston diamonds gracing her neck and shimmering at her ears. Richard had coiffed her hair, Collier had applied her makeup, and she was proud and at ease posing with me.

Mine was the first award up. I won. I was shocked. It was so fast. I won. I wasn't prepared. I had no idea my category was first. Wait. Did I just say, I won? I won. Ed Harris, my hero, hugged me hard with Amy Madigan, his wife, pounding me on the back. Thaddaeus hugged me and up the stairs I went, wondering if Nicholas Cage, who gave me the award, was disappointed that I had won instead of Kate Hudson. These were the kind of thoughts flashing in my head in the few seconds of my walk onto that stage. One flash would be "Oh my God, I am so proud and happy," and the next would be "Oh my gosh, I hope people aren't mad at me that I won because they loved Kate Hudson more, or Fran McDormand, or Judi Dench, or Julie Walters." And then "Oh my gosh, here I am. This is amazing, I have to take it all in," then "Oh my gosh, do I even deserve to be here?"

I tried to catch my breath, and looked out to my seat to get my bearings and got hit with Ed Harris's confident blue eyes. As my husband proudly smiled, I began my thank-yous, with my eyes searching the crowd for Mom and Dad, who had been seated a few rows behind me. It wasn't hard to find them. Dad was standing straight up, his arms over his head, bellowing, "BRAVOOO! BRAVOOO!" He was crying and Mom was crying and trying to pull him down by his jacket, but he just stood there yelling "Bravoooo!"

I continued my speech, desperately hoping that Spielberg wasn't sitting behind my dad: "I want to thank my dad for teaching me how to soldier through tough times, and my mom for showing me how to do it gracefully."

Dad finally sat down, pulled by someone behind him. Thankfully, not Spielberg.

In a blur I finished my forty-five-second speech, and left the stage, and ran right into a tearful Carri waiting in the wings. When all the behind the scenes had been done and I returned to my seat, Dad was gone. Mom indicated he was up at the bar, so I snuck out of my seat to go find him. There he was in the middle of a crowd, around the Oscar bar in the upstairs lobby, ordering drinks for everyone! I squeezed in to see him, and we hugged for a long time. He said he sure was proud of me but that he wanted to go back to the hotel because he wasn't feeling very well. He had been unusually weak lately, so I was a bit concerned. He said he would like to stay to see "that Goddamned Ed Harris win, (it was a term of endearment) but that won't be till the end of the night. Are you okay if I leave, Honey?" Suddenly I could see my bodyguard jumping up over the crowd to find me. Damn! I had forgotten all about him and he was in a cold panic that he had lost me, and all those jewels!

"Of course, Dad. We'll find the limo for you." In truth, I didn't need him to stay for all the festivities. He had been there, he had seen it, and now he could go rest. We walked him down the long empty red carpet, back the way we had come, and tucked him into the limo.

My handsome lawyer Ira Schreck volunteered to take Dad's seat next to Mom for the remainder of the show, and we all glowed with happiness when Julia Roberts won, and my friend Benicio del Toro won, but I must admit I was heartbroken that Ed Harris didn't win. We all were. Nothing against Russell Crowe — a fine actor, indeed — but *Pollock* was Ed Harris's baby, and I felt like instead of him, I got to hold his baby in all the pictures. Ira stayed with Mom for the night, dancing with her at the elegant Governors Ball, and introducing her to celebrity after celebrity. She couldn't have been happier. We partied till the wee hours of the morning, and finally, slightly tipsy from champagne, we crowded into the *Vanity Fair* party, posing and hugging and toasting. At last, exhausted, we got in our limo to go back to the Shutters hotel.

That's when things got a little dangerous. The bodyguard got in the front seat with the driver, and me, Thad, Mom, Ira, and

Carri all got in the back. We drove to a nearby parking lot to drop Carri off, and we noticed we were being followed by another car. The car was still behind us ten minutes later when we dropped off Ira at his hotel, and my bodyguard alerted both the police and Harry Winston security. "Probably just paparazzi," he said, "because you won."

"OHMYGOD!" I said to Mom and Thad. "How thrilling! This is what it's going to be like now! This is what it's like to be famous!"

We entered the highway, and the car was still behind us.

"Could also be thieves," said the body-guard. "If it's not paparazzi."

Mom's heart sank. We did, after all, have four million dollars' worth of jewels in our limo. The driver began swerving and weaving on the highway, to lose the car. Thad began filming the whole thing out the back window. The car was still on us, and we were all driving a bit frantically. The bodyguard enlisted another limo to try and intercept our path and throw the car off, but it didn't work. We left the highway. The car left the highway. Mom's eyes were wide with panic. "It's thieves!" she said. "They want the jewels!"

"No — it's paparazzi, Mom! Because I

won! I'm sure of it!" I said, insistently. Hopefully.

We reentered the highway. The car reentered the highway. I heard a screech, and the chase car was right behind us now, aggressively speeding up to the side of the limo, and then tailgating us. Our mood became tense and scared; this had clearly escalated into something *not* safe. Where were those police? We needed help. In the middle of the swerving and Thad filming, with the bodyguard talking intensely on the phone, Mom eyed the sunroof and began to undo her earrings. "We could fling them out the sunroof," she said. "I want to liiiivvveee!"

"Mom!" I said, shocked. Maybe she had had more to drink than I thought. But she was dead serious, shaking and scared, with tears running down her face. She fumbled unsuccessfully with the clasp on her necklace, then she actually reached for the button to roll open the sunroof, looking at me with wild eyes, and said again, "I want to liiivvve!"

Just at that moment we careened into the Santa Monica police station and a dozen squad cars surrounded the jokers who had stupidly followed us through the gate. My bodyguard spoke to the police, while we all stood up and crammed through the hole of the sunroof, gaping at the foiled heist. As we wondered just who these jewel thieves were, I noticed that Mom had somehow managed to put her earrings back on. She still had five minutes before she lost her glass slipper and she sparkled all the way back to the hotel. We laughed uproariously the last few minutes in the limo, imitating each of us — Mom with "I want to liiivveee!," Thaddaeus acting like a National Geographic documentarian on a wild hunt, me the vain actress hoping for paparazzi, and our trusty bodyguard giving James Bond a run for his money. Getting out of the limo, we finally took off our jewelry, and slowly laid it in the blue velvet boxes. I too felt like Cinderella, about to see the limo turn into a pumpkin, with no more adornments, just the reality of swollen feet at the end of a long night.

"By the way," said my bodyguard as he was packing up the jewels. "It wasn't thieves. It *was* paparazzi."

"OH!" I said, thrilled. "So they *were* following me!" I stole a sidelong I-told-you-so look at my mother. Maybe Cinderella's reign had just begun!

"No," said the bodyguard. "They thought you were Russell Crowe."

I swear to God I heard the sound that the tuba makes in a movie when the fat man sits in a chair and it sags to the ground: *Wha Wha Whaaa!*

Mom handed me the Oscar as the limo drove away. "Here you go, honey. You were brilliant tonight. I'm so very proud of you. You have worked hard, Marcia Gay. You've earned this."

I liked the word "earn" better than "deserve." I took off my four-inch heels, and lugged my eight-and-a-half-pound Oscar proudly though the lobby, nodding to the applauding hotel staff as we wobbled into the elevator. The silver doors closed. Finally, we were alone. No bodyguard, no thieves, no fans, just we three.

"Hi," I said, "just pinch me."

Thad and I walked Mom to her hotel room, and she held me again. "Marcia, I wouldn't have missed that for the world. Thank you for letting me be a part of it. I am a proud mom!"

I wouldn't have dreamed of her *not* being a part of it. She had supported me every step of the way, from the Little Theatre of Alexandria, to lugging boxes up to my fifth-floor West Village apartment, to sending me a hundred dollars to make it through a particularly sparse week as I was trying to make it as an actress in New York. "You DID teach me how to soldier through rough times gracefully, Mom. Thank YOU for always believing in me! Now let's get going on making *your* show, Mom! *Flower Path* and *Beverly's Blooms* . . . here we come!"

"Oh, I would like that, Marcia Gay!" she said, beaming.

I had my brass ring; now it was time for Mom to grab hers. We teared up, then smiled at my snoring dad, kissed goodnight, and shut the door. Now it was just the two of us, Thad and me. *"La dolce vita,"* he said, holding my hand as we walked down the hall.

Once in the hotel room, Thad paid the babysitter and went in to check on Eulala. Now it was just me. Me and Oscar. I set my golden man on the glass coffee table, and just as I had in the hotel room in Denver when I was first nominated, I got down on my knees and prayed in gratitude. Turning out the lights, I stole one more look at him as I went to change out of my now wrinkled scarlet gown. "Good Night, Oscar! Lights out!" Minutes later, I returned, now out of my Spanx and comfy in my new pink cotton pajamas from one of the fancy gift baskets. I flipped back on the lights. Whew! Yes! He was still there! But he looked lonely standing on that coffee table, so I cuddled him up with my green *Sesame Street* Oscar who had been waiting in the bottom of my suitcase, just in case I didn't win. "I have earned you!" I whispered as I shut out the lights for the second time that night.

Perhaps the feeling of being outside the circle is a universal feeling, even for those who seem to be perpetually in it. For anyone watching that night, I was the "it" girl, the unexpected winner, the glamorous girl in the red scarlet gown. And that was true, that's who I was, I had won an Oscar, and I was grateful to all who had helped me achieve that moment. But I knew it was important *not* to see myself through others' eyes. I knew that within a week, most people would forget who won the Academy Award on Oscar night. The following year even fewer people would remember. The next day, I would wake up in my hotel room, and when I looked outside the window, the lawn would not be made of emeralds. Scorsese or Spielberg would not be standing on the sidewalk begging me to do their next movie. Yet I would still be the same person. Just a little bit taller. For me, it was an honor and an accomplishment, and it was a reminder that I needed to own my own worth as I traveled my journey. In that moment, however, I was so proud that my mom had been with me to witness, and ultimately be a part of, the new inch mark on my growth ruler. A mother's eyes will keep you real, eight-and-a-half-pound Oscar or not.

■ ■ ■ ■

My Mother is
a Star Navigator

■ ■ ■ ■

Travel, children, and a fur coat.

2011 will be a year that is cemented forever in my mind. It is a numerically positive year, a year of new beginnings and completed circles. The number 11 signifies remembrance, light, activation; 2011 is defined as a year of hope and positivity. My mom was even born on an 11, on January 11, 1937, again the repeating 11, again the reminder that 11 is a number that activates memory and light . . . or so the numerologists say. Yet it didn't seem that way to me as 2011 began the calendar tick of pages. My precious mom had recently been diagnosed with Alzheimer's, my marriage was falling apart, and I was homeschooling my kids because I was running out of money for their private school in New York. New beginnings, indeed. Visiting Mom in Texas in mid-February, having hauled my kids and math books, poetry, art material, and English books to her lovely home in Fort Worth, I was trying to understand where hope and positivity were hiding. I was trying to understand just what the "light" might be activating. I was trying to understand the cruel significance of the number 11, and I was trying to understand the synchronicity of so much disintegration.

I kept thinking of Tony Kushner's great American play *Angels in America.* I had originated the role of Harper on Broadway, and had the privilege to perform one of the most beautiful speeches ever written — Harper's last speech of the play. In this speech, Harper connects the ragged disintegration of the ozone — which is, of course, the immune system of the earth — with the equally ragged disintegration of the immune system of the human body, as made real with AIDS. She imagines the souls of dead people and hurt people, all people suffering loss, and she imagines them floating over the holes, holding hands to create a web, and repairing the ragged holes of the ozone, thus healing the earth. This speech begins "Night Flight to San Francisco . . . chase the moon across America . . . ," and as Harper begins it, she is on a plane headed to San Francisco to heal herself.

My February 2011 night flight had taken

me to Texas. I was in shock, just beginning to realize what bad shape my marriage was in, and I was feeling the quicksand terror of lost love. This terror was mixed with another terror, a sinking desperation as I watched my mother's helpless decline. I busied myself by running errands for her, teaching my kids, talking to a divorce lawyer, researching the unrelenting march of Alzheimer's, and looking silently out of a window, watching the wind blow the leaves of an oak tree to the ground.

In a daze one day, I found myself at the Apple store. I was attempting to update/repair/fix my mom's cell phone. I was trying to save her contacts from her PC computer to her iPhone (an impossible task for anyone who may want to do the same, by the way). I had been there for hours, literally hours, and I just wanted to go back to my mom's home, see my kids, teach them something about the frigging Alamo and Texas, and integrate it into their daily lessons, then lie down in bed and cover my head with a pillow. The blue-shirted Apple employee told me that there were holes in the computer's digital information. I stared at him blankly. Then when he asked me if I knew what a browser window was, I stuttered, and burst into tears, in the middle of the store.

No. I did not know what a window was. I did not understand the digital dots and dashes floating about in the atmosphere that apparently made windows on computers. I did not know why there were holes in the computer's stored information. And furthermore, I did not know why there were holes in the ozone. I did not know why there were holes in my mother's brain. I did not know why there were holes in my marriage. I did not know why her memory was ragged. I did not want to understand the day when she wouldn't know me. I did not want to get Alzheimer's myself. I did not want to be a single mother. I did not want to be alone. And I did not want to see her alone. Which, by the way, was the *only* tragic ending of the story of Alzheimer's, the fact of ultimately being devastatingly alone, without even memory for a companion. Finally, I did not know why Tony Kushner had understood that all things in the world are synchronous, and that the healing of the ozone could only happen with the healing of the immune system of the human body, and that somehow it all had to do with San Francisco and love and acceptance and tolerance, and that that was how we would repair the world.

All this I told to the shell-shocked Apple

employee. He stood very still, blinked twice, and then said with a very pronounced drawl, "Well, gee, I'm sorry, ma'am. Not real sure who Tony Kooshnyer is, but I sure am sorry about your mom. And your, ummm, well, your marriage." There was a long silence.

"My mother did my flowers," I told him. "My mother did my flowers at my wedding." He gurgled something about how purty that must've been. I paused again. I couldn't help it. The tears started rolling. I looked down and huskily said, "They were beautiful. Just beautiful."

As he stuck my credit card into his mobile device and I watched it stutter out a receipt, I thought about windows, and looked up to the ceiling to hide my tears, which were now rolling down my cheeks and filling up the holes in my ears. I imagined the holes in the ozone filling up with flowers, beautiful flowers, just as Tony had imagined them filling up with all the souls of all the people who had ever been at war, or who had ever been hurt, or who had ever suffered loss. I imagined all those same souls holding flowers, like maids of honor in a wedding, and flying up to the sparkling heavens, to the thermosphere, anointing themselves in angel dust, then shooting back down toward earth, speeding with the meteors down through the mesosphere, tumbling past lightning sprites, and then floating downward through the stratosphere until they blanketed the ozone, where they would weave a tapestry of flowers over the holes, patching up loss and sorrow, and restoring immunity.

A tear escaped the hole of my ear and slowly slid down my neck. I imagined then that some petals, too, would escape being woven into the tapestry; slipping from the angels' woven grasp, they would fall toward earth. Floating past fluttering gossamer wings, the sacred petals would drift, like snowflakes drifting through a giant window, down, down, toward the earth. Falling toward earth and toward my mother's outstretched hands. Rose petals and jonquils, anthuriums and birds-of-paradise, althea and hydrangea, petals like a bride steps on as she walks down the aisle, petals before they are crushed, sacred angel petals sprinkled with angel dust. They would fall through all the ozone holes, through these giant sky windows, and rain upon the people below. People, my mother, anyone's mother who had dementia or Alzheimer's, anyone's father or sister or brother or child, people across the earth, with arms raised high to catch the flowers and petals falling through the cloud window, people would soon be covered in petals. Then, in that moment, the holes of memory would be patched, the synapses in the brain would regrow their bridges, the plaque would disintegrate, and the brain would heal. The window would close. My mother would remember her life.

I snatched my receipt from blue shirt. Yes. I knew what a window was, motherfucker.

Later that night, sitting at the round table in Mom's Fort Worth kitchen, watching the Oscars together, we happily remembered when she had accompanied me to those awards in February 2001. I wasn't ready to dampen the spirits of our little gathering by breaking the news of my failing marriage; I was still depressed about the Apple store and the ozone. I also wanted to be strong and careful with my words in front of my kids, so I hid my sorrow and my rage, and petted Mom's wiener dog, Emmy. Emmy chinkled her irritating chains while Mom and I sipped champagne and watched the glamorous actresses in their gorgeous gowns suck it in on the red carpet. Which of course only depressed me further.

I waited till the next morning to step

across chinkling Emmy, to ease into bed with my mom, crawling into her warm crawl space, to rest my swollen face on her blue flannel nightie, and to tell her, "I don't think my marriage is going to make it, Mom."

"Oh, honey," she said softly. "You two seemed so perfect together."

She had been such a part of our lives together, throwing us an engagement party, creating the flowers at my wedding, and the stunning altarpiece, too, helping me with the birthing of all three babies, literally sleeping with me and Thaddaeus when we were so exhausted with my newborn twins and we hadn't yet hired a baby nurse. She had traveled with us, often under the guise of helping me with the kids when I was on a location shoot, but if you did the math you could see that I usually had a nanny as well on these trip, and I often hired a babysitter at the hotel. Mom had traveled with us because it was fun, and she and Thaddaeus got along, and she loved going to events with me, and she got to spend grandma time with the kids. I knew, for her, my broken marriage would also be a loss, that she would be losing a friend in Thad, too. But mostly, she would be sad, and scared, for me. She smoothed my brown hair in rhythmic strokes, and murmured,

"I'm sorry, sweetheart. I never would have dreamt that on your wedding day."

Wedding days. Does every mother dream of her children's wedding day? Does every daughter or son dream of their own wedding day? What does that look like for my children? Will millennials say, "Until death do us part," when half of them will have grown up in divorced families? Do I teach my own children to believe in the fantasy of marriage? Do I teach them that love is everlasting? Do I even need to teach them that, or does love just take over, like an unstoppable force? And is it even so much love we are talking about, as commitment? Since my divorce, I have a hard time feeling pure about wedding days. My cynicism sets in and I silently sneer, "How long will this last?" With this attitude, I worry about making my children feel jaded. What if they never believe in love or marriage?

But silly me . . . my children are way ahead of me. They are a product of the times, wise to anthropological history, aware of the influences of Victorian romance, clear about the pros and cons of the sexual revolution, pondering the seeming impossibility of monogamy, and celebrating the shifting power structures, as most homes are now two-parent working homes. After all, Santa Claus is not real. The Easter Bunny is not real. And neither, for them, is the idea of "till death do us part." And — I think? — they are okay with that. They prefer to excavate the fantasy and come to the truth underneath — just as they did for Santa Claus and the Easter Bunny. They are gender-fluid, educated, bound by neither career nor lack of it. They are excited and ready to explore themselves before they commit to marriage or family. They are clear that family will look unlike the structures of 1950s patriarchy, but instead, will look like — well, it will look like love. That's mostly what we talk about, not wedding days but family, and we've been celebrating the many alternative families that surround us in the liberal beachside community of Santa Monica and fast-paced New York.

My mother dreamed of marriage even in her early teens, and she was just nineteen years old when she tied the knot. Still a girl, really, soft olive skin, big wide smile, and a head of curly brown hair that was thrilled to imagine her new life as a navy wife. Personal exploration hadn't been part of my mother's trajectory when she graduated from high school. There had been no conversation with her parents about a Gap Year, or working for a while before heading off to college. Instead she had immediately enrolled in the University of Texas at Austin, and at some point early on she had caught the eye of Ensign Thad Harden, who was a member of the NROTC. He was dashing, and passionate, and she was quickly, deeply in love. Again, there was no talk of "Let's hold off till a few years after graduation while I go off to war and you start climbing the corporate ladder." There *was* no corporate ladder for her to climb. She was to get married, and to follow him around the world.

In the 1950s sweater-set America, marriage was a sacred union, meant to last through thick and through thin. Pearls and dishwashers and new clothes washers and dryers were promised in the magazine ads for young wives. Sparkling kitchens, cooing babies, and muddy little footprints from the inevitable jump in a puddle on a crisp rainy day. The actual "bride" was a role that lasted only a day, and whatever independence and hope the white-laced hostess enjoyed on her wedding day, she was soon to discover that they would quickly disappear, that they would just as quickly become inseparable from the role of wife and housekeeper and mother.

So a wedding day, and the white fairy-tale gown, the bride's dream, the bouquet, the church, the registry, the garter, and the cake, the tradition of that momentous day, was deeply ingrained in my mother — not yet twenty. It was certainly something my mother had imagined as she stared at her reflection first in the mirror and later in the irises of my father's blue eyes. She dreamed of her wedding day, of the bride she would be, and of the house and home she would eventually make. She was young, and she had never lived on her own but for a brief two years in her college dorm, and she was ready for change. She was ready for a Man, with a capital M.

She gulped at the exotic adventures surely awaiting her as a military wife. She sparkled as she chose her diamond wedding ring, and she vowed to make her marriage last. She imagined children, happy cozy children in red mittens spinning on a merry-go-round, and she vowed to be the best mother ever, and to teach her children that marriages lasted.

Divorce, for my mother, in her Dallas circles, was whispered about only behind closed doors, and there was a fair amount of shame attached to it, accompanied by a great deal of pity for children who came from "broken homes." Working mothers were rare (and often *blamed* for the incrementally rising divorce rates) and the Nike running shoes and business suits that women would soon wear to work were a curious fashion phenomenon not yet imagined. Indeed, ladies wore low-heeled sandals, and they knitted soft booties for the babies that were soon to come. Mom was taught by her own mother, as so many mothers taught their daughters, to believe in fairy tales and one love. The disappointments of marriage were to be kept quiet, and dealt with privately.

Yet, years later, tears on a blue flannel nightie: "Mom, my marriage isn't going to make it."

"Hush, now. Shhh. Hush, now." As if I were a baby again, she smoothed my brown hair and patted my back.

My mother got married on a Sunday — April 1, 1956. April Fool's Day, to be exact. I would have thought she would have married in June: June was brides' month after all! It was the month of flowers and blooms, rain-washed fields gently popping up Queen Anne's lace and violets. It was the month of blue iris, calla lily, hydrangea, wisteria, bright orange gerbera daisies and luscious peonies, yellow daffodil and purple roses. But no — my beautiful mother married on April Fool's Day. I have always found that slightly troublesome: hello? Isn't that bad luck? And though I know all the whys and wherefores of her decision — which mostly had to do with timing and an available Sunday at her Methodist church, and my father having to hurry off to navy flight school — still, it *does* seem to be tempting fate a bit, *if* one were superstitious.

The marriage lasted forty-six years. Punctuated with travel, jazz, learning, and love. The marriage bore five children. And the marriage bore its fair share of thick and thin, as marriages are wont to do.

My father had one best man, my mother had one maid of honor, and that was the entirety of the wedding party. Elegant, not extravagant. Traditional. Simple. It was a small church wedding, and they used the reception hall of the church for cake and Kool-Aid afterward. Mom's gown was borrowed from her cousin, satin and lace showing off her twenty-inch waist, and around her neck hung a filigreed gold pendant necklace that her mother Coco had worn, and her grandmother, too. All of my sisters wore that same necklace in their weddings, as did my brother's bride, and as did I, and that very tradition has made friends with my young nieces, and the brides of my nephews: they too have proudly worn the golden pendant.

It is wrapped in paper, and sits with a note in a jewelry box in my closet, waiting for more nieces, and of course my own daughters. The note reads, in my grandmother's loopy writing, *"This necklace goes to Beverly Ann Harden. It was given to my mother Lydia on her wedding day by my father Lyle Jackson. I wore it on my wedding day as did Beverly. Courtney Jackson Bushfield."* Then on the other side, in my mother's slanted writing: *"All of my daughters wore this on their wedding day. Beverly H."* And then she lists our names, and the dates of all of our weddings. Leslie, Sheryl, Marcia, and Stephanie.

The pendant hangs on a gold chain. It is a golden filigreed circle with a diamond in the center, surrounded by a golden four-leaf clover, each leaf in the shape of a heart, which is then surrounded by eight pearls. The pendant takes on greater importance these days, because it is one of the few ways to connect with my mother, to carry on a thread of inheritance and tradition, to say, "Your life matters, and your mother's before you, and her mother's before her. The origin of people and things and golden jewelry matters." We can't hang our hats on her knowing or remembering or even understanding the meaning of the pendant; she forgets now that she once owned it. It is enough that we know that she would have wanted for us to pass down this cherished tradition. She would be pleased that it matters to us. That we are insistent in the offering to each new bride the possibility of connecting to my mother and other women, connecting to other marriages lived and navigated by other strong women, as each bride takes her vows in her own wedding month.

Dad once told me that when they got married, Mom had made him promise her three things: travel, children, and a fur coat. Well, by the time she was thirty she had five children, and travel never stopped, and the fur coat was a gift presented to her when she stepped off a plane, having flown from Greece to Texas and back after burying her mother. Travel, children, and a fur coat.

I especially loved the travel. It shifted perceptions and came to influence how I ran my home or decorated a room. I fell in love with the concept of negative space, which I learned in Japan, and delighted in the lavender laid on our pillow cases in France. Mom was a great tourist. She loved the city bus tours, the duck tours, the walking tours, the castle tours. She read the plaques at the museum, and kept her guidebook in her purse so she could always point out the historical interests of the sites we visited. If Dad was our captain, she was our navigator.

Mom took off her shoes and we followed suit at the great temples of Japan. From the windows of a train, we waved to straw-hatted workers hoeing in the verdant rice fields, and in shiny Tokyo we bumped into kimono-garbed grandmothers in the busy street markets. We saw the flea markets of Monastiraki in Athens and learned how to bargain. We saw tragic plays at the great stone theaters of Greece; the Herod Atticus at the Parthenon, and Epidaurus, and we visited the Peloponnese and learned of the Great Peloponnesian War. Mom poured retsina at Poseidon's temple in Sounion, wetting her feet at the foot of the sea, and she cut the bread now soaked in butter that we had bought earlier in the day from the baker just down the hill. Clutching a tomato in one hand and a knife in the other, she cut chunks of feta cheese and smiled with satisfaction at the life she was sharing with her children, exposing them to mythology and language and the endless sea. We visited stunning Baroque churches and listened to Bach resounding from huge organs on Sunday recitals in Germany. We walked through death camps in Auschwitz, dumb-founded by the depravity of hatred. In France we had breakfast of croissants and strawberry jam and then climbed the steps of Montmartre Sacré-Cœur. Walking down the Champs-Élysées to the Arc de Tri-omphe, Dad grumbled something about World War II and "the Goddamned French Frogs," and "that sonofabitch Hitler," and Mom said, "Now hush, Thad," and we didn't really know what it was all about, but Paris was certainly the prettiest city I had ever seen. In London we visited the Houses of Parliament, and giggled at the John Giel-gud–like guard whom we asked to direct us to the restrooms.

"Do you mean . . . the loo?" he inquired in haughty tones.

"The what?" we chimed.

"The bathrooms," my mother whispered with dignity.

"Oh. Are you bathing?" he asked.

"The toilets," she said firmly.

When we came out of the bathroom, he asked us with his nose quite high in the air,

"Are you from the colonies?"

"Yes," my mother answered. "All thirteen of them."

In Rome, we saw Michelangelo up close, the *Pietà,* the Vatican, the Colosseum, pasta, gelato, espresso, olive oil, and old Italian women with enormous bosoms dressed in black, hanging out of windows watching the street life go by. Mom loved the bustle, the learning, the education, the art and soul of Italy. She stared wide-eyed at the Modigliani paintings, the same black hair and black eyes looking back at her.

Returning from Japan by ship, we stopped off in Hawaii, and visited the beaches and drank from freshly fallen coconuts with a straw. We drove the winding road to the Dole Plantation, and picked pineapples growing in spiky rows in the sun. We did the Pineapple Garden Maze, and we slurped on Pineapple ice cream afterward.

Dad drove our station wagon across America, Mom folding the map into large squares so she could shine as his co-pilot, five kids crunched in the back playing "I see something . . . red!" We were excited about our destinations, excited about the motels we would stay in with the nickel dropped into a machine that made the bed vibrate. We snuck sips of mint juleps at the Kentucky

Derby (we were actually there the year Secretariat won!). Driving on down to Texas through Kentucky, Mom discovered Claudia Sanders Dinner House in her guidebook. Claudia Sanders was the wife of Colonel Sanders, of Kentucky Fried Chicken fame, and he had named this southern mansion restaurant in his wife's name. Mom insisted we stop for delicious crunchy chicken and buttery corn on the cob. Driving west, she picked sand out of our peanut butter sandwiches at beach picnics along the coast of California, and she added M&Ms to our trail mix as we drove through grand sequoia trees. She was our star navigator, soaking up every minute with her guidebook, her curiosity, and her charm.

Each new sight, each new location, pops a little brain cell and makes a memory. The memory grows and connects to something else, another brain cell, a new thought, a neural synapse, and so the brain grows full and wonderfully complicated with these circuits and byways, no two brains the same even with identical experiences, and no two memories exactly the same, even with the same mirror experiences. The point is, the memories of these experiences are supposed to keep us company as we grow older. We are supposed to be able to share them again and again, and in the retelling, science has proven that even though memory changes slightly each time we recall it, our brain cells actually reexperience the original *emotion* over again. The joy of Poseidon's temple is re-felt as the story is told years later, or the memory and taste of Kentucky Fried Chicken actually stimulates specific brain cells when the story is retold. Memory becomes an adventurous companion, and is a GPS confirming our place on our life map. At some point, these stories become vessels that transcend time and space. They are handed down to our children, and our children's children, and so become the atoms that bind our past, present, and future. Our stories are the needle on a compass pointing our children North to their place in the world.

If Mom could remember, she would feel pride at what an amazing mother she is, and what a brilliant star navigator.

Once I saw an exhibit about the brain at the American Museum of Natural History in New York City. Wires and tubes were hanging on the ceiling and protruding from the walls, making a kind of tunnel, and you had to walk under and through them; it was like walking through the webbed interior of the brain. There was a complicated chaos of wires, expanding out and growing in at the same time, emitting thought like a gaseous burst from a cell. You could see the thought travel along a neuron, then jump over the synapse to another neuron, where it seemed to replicate itself and continue on through a series of neurons and synapses, and then the gaseous thought got sucked back in again, across the same synapses, and returned to its original cell where it was then stored until needed again. I had never imagined I could see the physical makeup of a thought, it was revelatory. Like a neuron, we live our life sucking in information with each breath, assimilating it, and then expelling it in an exhalation of action.

A breath: I was attending school in Germany for a year when I was eighteen, at the University of Maryland in Munich. Mom took the train from Greece across the Alps, and when she got to Munich, we set about to do a bit of touring. It was October, so naturally we attended Oktoberfest. We had beer and Wiener schnitzel at the beer halls listening to oom-pah-pah music, and of course we visited Baroque castles, greeted by Mozart concertos floating down the marble stairs, beautifully played by string quartets. Mom, in a blue skirt and matching blue cotton button-up shirt printed with small flowers on it, a sweater draped over her thin shoulders, sipped champagne and nodded her approval at the cleanliness, the organization, the beauty of Germany. It was 1977 and we were impressed with the "green" innovations of the already ecosmart country, in particular the heating systems in some of the cities. Apparently they used sewage to create fuel to heat their buildings! We were amazed, "so advanced," we agreed. We didn't have cell phones or Google to learn exactly how this innovative sewage heating was done, so we didn't turn to our gadgets and bury our heads, but instead we ordered another round of drinks and discussed energy conservation and geothermal technology between sips of German Sekt. As Mom basked in the delicate sound of violins, tilting her head toward the notes rising above the sparkling crystal chandelier, she smiled in her eyes, feeling safe when surrounded by such beauty. In bed in Munich that night, we planned our trip to Neuschwanstein Castle for the following day, and she fell asleep with that same smile in her eyes, cuddled up with me, crawling into my crawl space, both of us spooning together in flannel nighties.

Years later, life has assimilated this Bavarian experience, and now I exhale it in moments with my own children. I fill the house with Brandenburg concertos and teach my eldest daughter, Eulala, about Wagner and *Der Ring des Nibelungen,* and she wants to visit Neuschwanstein. Just like me and my mom. My daughter decides to take a language course in Berlin at sixteen years of age; she loves the metal band Rammstein, and is already learning German. Of course I go visit her in Berlin, and of course at the end of the trip, we find ourselves on an overnight train, heading to Munich. I let her have a beer on the train; my mom would have done the same. Another train to Schwangau, and we walk all the way up to the castle, and yes! *Let's take the guided tour. My mother always did! She said you learn so much more! Let's do the same!* So we do . . . and later at the beer garden we sip cold ales and talk of King Ludwig II, and laugh and laugh at his innovative elevator system that would bring up a table, fully laid out for a gourmet dinner, with a chair ready for him to occupy. We are amazed, "so advanced," we agree. We are amused that the king ate this dinner alone, with the chair facing a full-length mirror. Behind him gleamed a spectacular view of stunning mountains out of a two-story window, but narcissistic King Ludwig ate facing that mirror. We discuss the composer Wagner and his relationship to the king. We discuss the great operas he wrote, and of course we *do* Google the Valkyries descending from the heavens in various operatic presentations of *Der Ring,* and we vow to see the cycle together someday. Walking back to the train, Eulala buys an elaborate beer stein as a memoir, and of course as a future practical necessity for her college years. Mmmmmhmmm. I buy her a device that can be clamped to the top of a beer bottle so that no one can add drugs to a young college girl's drinks. An unfortunate practical necessity.

Eulala and I will one day exhale our experience in the action of seeing this great opera, *Der Ring des Nibelungen,* and we will remember King Ludwig and his table, and German beer. Our viewing of the opera will be so much more magical *because* we have this seed of memory from our past. It will give the moment resonance and dimension. This is how our lives have richness, and experience, and depth, connecting past to present.

It infuriates me that this is also how Alzheimer's becomes a robber, a stealthy thief, forcing its victims to live only in the moment. For my mother there is only the present, with no connection to her past, without the rich tapestry of her life to tell her story. No dimension, just dementia. Memory dangles like an unraveled thread, while thought seeks to connect and focus the blurred tapestry's image. I see her concentrate, I see her try to speak the right words, I see her try to connect the memory to words, and through it all, I see her eyes smile, but it seems to me, the smile is a little bit wounded these days. There is no medicine yet, no surgery yet to grasp the dangling thread of memory, to rethread the needle with thought, to weave it back into her tapestry, and connect thoughts to memory and life experience. Instead, as the patient and family wait impatiently, more threads unravel, more dangling thoughts, the tapestry of her life slowly disintegrates, the picture is blurred, and memory is lost. I think of the magnificent French Apocalypse Tapestry that depicts the story of the Apocalypse as told by Saint John the Divine, from the Book of Revelations. Only my mom's is a a different kind of Apocalypse Tapestry, with only one horseman, a thief named Alzheimer's, pulling up the threads to my mother's story.

In truth, my siblings and I despair as the tapestry unravels, and the images fade for my mother. We know she is 1 of 47 million people who suffer Alzheimer's worldwide, 47 million disintegrating tapestries. She is one of the 5.5 million people who suffer Alzheimer's in America. Red, White, and Blue tapestries, unraveling.

We are focusing on her survival, and focusing on maintaining her dignity. We are organizing caregivers and are caring for her ourselves. We sadly downsize her home so we can afford all of this, not knowing what the future is, but we do know that as of yet, there is no cure, and Alzheimer's is a progressive disease. With knots in our stomachs, we move forward, preparing for the unknown.

We have begun the painful task of sorting through some of my mother's belongings as we prepare to move her to a smaller home, my grandfather Tattau's old home on the lake. We clear off shelves and empty cabinets, packing up delicate, hand-painted china hot chocolate pots, little earthen sculptures of Japanese fishermen, a soap carving of a temple on a hill surrounded by flowers. I come across a beautiful antique china beer stein that belonged to my great-grandfather Courtney. It has a silver top that you can open and close by a small hand clasp, and eight little gnomes carved into its side. They are reading, playing the accordion, frolicking under a large red mushroom, and immediately I think of Eulala, and Germany. My sisters agree that I may pass it down to Eulala, and that Christmas I present her with that handcrafted beer stein, which is over a hundred years old. Now our journey is fully connected — Neuschwanstein to my mom, Mozart, to Rammstein, great-grandparents to Eulala. I present Julitta with the wooden carving of Saint Francis of Assisi that Mom bought from the monastery when she visited Italy. It shows Saint Francis surrounded by birds and animals, just as Julitta always is. To Hudson I present the metal bust of the Greek warrior Mom bought while we were living in the little town of Mati — when my father commanded the naval base in Greece. Hudson loves mythology, and this seems the perfect gift for him. I make a mental note to connect the circles by taking Julitta to Assisi, Hudson to Athens. I like to think these travels matter — that these collected heirlooms matter, that we come to know ourselves a little better by our shared experiences, and we love each other a little bit more by the richness and beauty of our journey. I like to think that exponentially, the world grows closer by our knowledge and love of other lifestyles. This is what my mother taught me. This is what she told me would be true. She told me that exposure was the best teacher. Star navigator.

Exposure. I take my kids to Hawaii on vacation. We are welcomed with leis to our favorite hotel in Waikiki, the Halekulani. We lay the colorful leis side by side on the white beds and take a picture with our iPhones and prepare to post them. This is our tradition, and I immediately Instagram the lovely picture — of course showing off a little, which I think is half the point of Instagram: "We are HERE! We are eating THIS! I look so good in my SELFIE!" In truth, I don't really care about the likes so much. It's the record of my life and travels and thoughts I am interested in, and Instagram seems a pretty good organizer, despite the narcissistic selfies taken from the highest angle possible so that I only have one chin.

The kids are intrigued when I insist on exposure to something other than the sun, so we leave the pool one evening and go to a symphony. They are enthralled, and bored, just as I expected. That's okay. We have Saint-Saëns, Beethoven, Haydn, Mozart.

Later we learn of Israel Kamakawiwo'ole from one of the maintenance workers at the hotel. The worker and a friend of his then serenade us, both of them with their own ukuleles. The window is open, the ocean gently sashaying up the sand in rhythm to the song, and their voices are sweet and clear. My kids sing along. The worker plays Kamakawiwo'ole's rendition of "Over the Rainbow," and I find myself thinking of my mother and how much she would have loved to be in the room with us and the leis and the ocean and the music. As he hits the high notes of "That's where you'll find me," I think of how lost Alzheimer's has made its victims. Millions of old people, wishing for a pot of gold at the end of a rainbow, not remembering where they are, but wishing to be found. Hundreds of thousands of families, yearning to find their loved ones again, knowing just exactly where they are, but not able to reach them. The next day I buy all the kids ukuleles and they practice by the pool, strumming "Over the Rainbow" in between swimming and slurping Popsicles. We later sit by the sea in the garden and watch the Hawaiian storytellers dance and sing their island songs, passing their stories down to natives and tourists alike. I take pictures, and hit SEND. We visit the

Dole Plantation; we excitedly do the Pineapple Garden Maze and eat pineapple ice cream in the warm sun. I take pictures and hit SEND. We all surf, gliding with the boards toward the shore. I take pictures, and hit SEND.

Back in Los Angeles, we see an opera. It's unfortunately not very good, so I stick to playing the odd aria in the car, simply to expose my children to fine music. Jazz drifts through the home, only to be joined, when my eldest is home from college, by Metallica, Graham Nash, Crosby, Stills, Nash & Young, or Bob Marley. When my boy Hudson is here with his friends, show tunes resound through the kitchen, as well as the sounds of kids singing and tapping and dancing. My youngest girl Julitta listens to it all, absorbs it all, Green Day, Nirvana, *Frozen,* Janis Joplin. Harry Belafonte. Marty Robbins.

For me, growing up in a mostly quiet home, music was a way the household had of holding hands. We were all brought together for a moment by the universal song of the home. We delighted when Mom put on a record, and Gary Puckett & the Union Gap bellowed "Young Girl, get outta my mind" or Harry Belafonte sang "Matilda," or jazz, always jazz, Wes Montgomery

"Bumpin' on Sunset." For my children, however, music is often a personal expression, a singular experience. They have earbuds and headphones, and with headphones on they occasionally wander around in what appears to be a silent room but is loud in their ears, swaying their heads and bobbing their shoulders, wiggling butts that once were in diapers, and my heart aches a little, but I understand: music isn't *always* to be shared. But then later in the car, Eulala will say, "Mom, do you know this band?" And she'll introduce me to some heavy metal, or punk bagpipes, or a forlorn folksinger, and it always seems to be — unexpectedly — the music of my heart at that particular moment. My boy will say, "Mom, can I play . . . ?," and he will put on the latest trending musical — *Hamilton* or *Falsettos* or *Dear Evan Hansen* — again and again and again, and I begin to learn the words. My young girl will sense my mood, and put on classical or introduce me to an AC/DC song, for which I am sure I have absolutely no interest, but she cranks "Highway to Hell" anyway and we blast down the road with the music loud in our ears, and it seems perfect. They are exposing me to what they love, educating me as I am educating them.

"Do you know Joni Mitchell?" I say. And while Joni trills, I tell stories of Crete and when I camped there, and the little town of Matala, and I say, "Listen closely now to Joni Mitchell sing 'Carey, get out your cane.' Yes, that was in Matala, where I camped one Grecian summer." They know me, a little, by the music I play and share. Just as I knew my mother by her music. Our households holding hands for a moment.

I begin to understand the synchronicity of dissolution. It makes perfect sense to me, as I lie on my mom's big bed in Texas, that we are both going through loss. Tony Kushner was right: all pain, and all healing, is related. The world *is* connected. Divorce, like Alzheimer's, creates holes in history, and leaves each person — parents and children — with an unknown future. We define ourselves by our relationships, by our "things": homes and cars and clothes, by our work, by our health, by our memory. But in the face of loss, we often have to redefine ourselves. Without my husband, who was I? Without her memory, who was my mother? Without their father, what was our family? Defining the self without any attachments or anchors would prove to be our most difficult task. "The uncertainty of tomorrow" was causing me to hold even tighter to traditions and values that I wanted to pass down to my kids. I worried that much would dissipate as I began to accept divorce. Would the kids still want to pick blueberries on our country property in the Catskills and make blueberry jam? Would we still take our annual Christmas picture? Would they rather spend time with me or with their dad, or would it be a — God forbid — competition? Would they still clock the seasons by the loud honk of Canadian geese flying north and south over the lake? Or would those experiences just be holes, empty memories of a time now past?

Inhale: Mom and Dad loved birding. Assimilate: they passed that on to their children together. Exhale: at the lake home we built, Thaddaeus and I passed on to our kids the love of birds. I worried that the breath of exhalation would become ragged with divorce, that these gifts of how to observe nature, this love of birding and identifying the birdcalls, would be lost. When we had first settled into our stone cottage, we had bought birding books. On nature walks with the children, we had pulled them out and identified the winged creatures. With binoculars focused to the sky, we pointed out the soaring red hawk, the diving osprey, and the great horned owl sitting still in the trees. We had seen swans on the lake, and the common loon, the scarlet tanager and black cormorant. We had watched the eagle build its nest and raise eaglets each spring. I feared that I wouldn't be strong enough or diligent enough to uphold these customs alone. But I was wrong. Eulala insisted, "You are a warrior, Mom. A warrior." Me? A warrior?

And a warrior I became. I still gather my children on the porch during a storm, and we watch the sheets of rain blanket the lake. We pull out the bird books to identify the mallards. We delight in the Canadian geese as they loudly honk and honk in their gliding V preparing to go south for the winter. Tradition is not lost, even when I am a single mom. I am relieved when my children marvel at the great blue heron as he glides in dusky grace across my lake. I laugh that we still shout "eagle" as we see the mother bird, capped in white, soar high above the trees, and on our walks heading to blueberry hill, I smile with pride when I hear my kids point out, "That's a red-winged blackbird, Mom!" as we pass the marsh and see a glimpse of shocking red and black lift off a cattail and flit to a new spot. Now, I wish my mom could connect this thread to herself. I wish she could connect the fact of her canvas bag filled with flower books, her binoculars and camera to the small values that my children have inherited, ones that enrich their lives. And I wish she could see what a woman *can* do alone. I wish she could know that I could only have made it alone because of her warrior example. But I felt like no warrior as I was lying on her bed in Texas that cold February in 2011. In the trenches of her covers, I felt embarrassed, and a failure, and somehow stunned that life hadn't turned out as I had expected it to.

"Hush, Marcia Gay. Hush, now." She stroked my brown hair, with no smile in her eyes.

I had expected my marriage to surmount the rising statistic of the divorce rate. It went from a low 23 percent in the late fifties to almost 50 percent in the eighties and nineties. It has supposedly tilted to over 50 percent today. Whatever. It is high. And as divorce rates rose due to societal changes and attitudes, so rose my certainty that I would not be part of this new statistic. This statistic did not change my thinking on "the wedding day" and vows. Taught by my parents, who stayed together till death did them part, through thick and through thin, through sickness and in health, I knew the same would be true for me. No April Fools were they — a vow was a vow, a promise was a promise, and they made their choices and lived their lives. Travel, children, and a fur coat. For me it would be: travel, children, possibly a fake fur coat, and my work. I believed in the fairy tale, and I believed that marriages would last forever and that there was such a thing as one love. At least I believed that mine would last. No, I wouldn't be a part of the declining marriage statistic. I would wear virginal white and throw the bouquet; I would even wear the lacy garter at the insistence of my girlfriends, and I would proudly wear the golden pendant, handed down from my great-grandmother.

When Thaddaeus popped the question on New Year's Eve in New York one frozen wintery night, we knew we would have a Texas ceremony. My parents and two sisters lived there, and much of my extended family as well, but most importantly, my ninety-year-old grandfather, Tattau, lived in Texas. Tattau was one of my favorite people in the world, and he and Thaddaeus were like two peas in a pod. When I first introduced Thad to the family, Mom had of course loved him. His name was Thaddaeus, after all, the same name as her husband and her son — what were the chances? My typically skeptical dad softened after Thad presented him with a signed Cowboys football at Christmas. And Tattau sized him up positively due to Thad's mechanical ability that Tattau said was a lost art. They spent hours in Tattau's "fix it shop," building things, repairing things, and talking about history.

I didn't want a church wedding, I told my mom. I certainly didn't want anything too traditional. I had waited too many tables at The Pierre hotel in New York City and had seen too many banquet-type weddings and I did *not* want a banquet-type wedding. I had also catered many events at museums and private homes, and I wanted something simpler, something rustic. Also, I wanted Tattau to attend, and he refused to fly on a plane. And he wasn't getting any younger, so I knew I had to do it sooner than later. When suddenly I booked two movies that would be shooting back-to-back starting in the summer and well into the fall, that decided our place and timing. We needed to have a wedding no more than two hours from my grandpa's home in Texas, and it needed to be before I began shooting the movies!

Mom, my aunt Lynnie, and I began to location scout, and it didn't take long before we found a Christian ranch in Hunt County that catered to large youth groups at the same time as hosting private events. It was wonderful and rustic and enormous. There was an exterior golden stone amphitheater overlooking a valley and the Pecos River below. Red-tailed hawks soared at sunset. Just above the amphitheater sat a hunting lodge that could sleep the wedding party; it had a rounded bell tower topping the sky, and I could already envision the bell deeply ringing when I would walk down the dusty road in my bridal gown from the hunting lodge to the amphitheater. "Perfect," my mother murmured. There was a bunkhouse for all twenty of my college chums. They were my second family — the small group of NYU graduate actors with whom I had spent three wonderful, tortuous years of acting prep. There were several other lodges and buildings, perfect to accommodate my extended family, and Thaddaeus's extended family. Maybe about 150 people were to be invited — and many of them I planned to put up at the ranch. "It's just perfect, Marcia Gay," Mom said. "I will do your flowers!"

We planned a three-day weekend, except that it wasn't a weekend, really. All dates before July 4 were taken, so we took the next Monday and Tuesday. I wasn't aware at the time how inconsiderate I was, asking my friends and family to take off work and travel to Texas on a hot Sunday, in the middle of a drought, to attend my wedding on a Tuesday in July. The fact that I wasn't aware meant that everyone had been amazingly understanding, because I also wasn't aware of any gossiping or grumbling, either, and my mother didn't admonish me to pick another date and my sisters didn't fuss about missing work — all of which would have been perfectly understandable! I think everyone understood the ticking clock involved in my decision: Tattau's age and health, coupled with the fact that the movie I had booked, *Desperate Measures* with Andy Garcia, was now set to begin filming the day after the wedding! I literally had to fly to Los Angeles the next morning. (Of course I was hungover and of course I missed my flight, but that's another story.) I would be shooting *Desperate Measures* in tandem with *Flubber* with the late, great Robin Williams, so things were moving really quickly and I was racing to keep up.

It was a fast time, a heady time, and my friends and family completely supported this magical moment: me starring in two movies, and *finally* getting married.

My mother was ecstatic. She had, in truth, been worried about me. She wanted love and family and home very badly for me, because she knew how much I wanted them, too. I had wanted children since I was four, and here I was now, thirty-six years old with eggs surely in the "soon-to-be-overripe" category. I wanted a husband — no, I wanted a knight. But he had to be a hippie, a hippie knight. And I wanted children. Beautiful hippie children who were kind and talented and artists.

My desires seemed simple enough — I mean, weren't there hordes of hippie knights roaming the cities? But my lack of being in any kind of an enduring relationship was troubling to my mom. She had seen how I picked on my boyfriends; my standards were high and surrender did I *not.* "You are not the boss of me" was a silent mantra in my head. I was outspoken and loyal and capable, a little wild and often mean, and demanding and critical, to boot. I had gotten into the pattern of picking rather unformed men, men who couldn't possibly be the boss of me. And I would naturally try to change them, yet be angry at the parts of them that were still undeveloped, and of course such a man couldn't possibly also be a knight for me. I picked poets, who enjoyed my apartments and my credit cards. I picked other actors who resented my limelight. I picked champagne drinkers with hidden lipstick stains on their collars. I picked hippies in colorful vans who couldn't settle down, and through it all, Mom watched, and waited. Though happy that I was pursuing my lifelong dreams and on my own journey, she wished I was softer, she was concerned that my no bullshit nature wouldn't make room for a husband, and thus I would never achieve my other dream, that of domestic bliss.

Several years after I graduated from NYU and was well into building my film career, my mother visited me in Santa Fe while I was shooting *Late for Dinner.* I was playing a woman who welcomes back her cryogenically frozen husband, and on the day Mom visited the set, I was in old-age makeup, which I had forgotten to tell her about. My trailer was parked near a little stream, with a view of pine and birch trees, and pine needles covering the ground. Mom was picked up from the airport by our film transpo guys and delivered to base camp, where I could now see her out the window of my trailer as she picked her way across the parking lot, drinking in the crisp mountain air. She was carrying her camera across her shoulder, and in her cloth bag I could see the familiar binoculars and flower books.

I burst out of my trailer to welcome her, and she gasped when she saw me, then stood still. She stuttered, "Coco . . . you look so much like my mother Coco." Then she burst into tears. It had been years since her mom had passed away, and she hadn't really gotten to say good-bye to her. Suddenly, unexpectedly, she had seen her in me. I held her in the parking lot as we both stood on crushed pine needles, her bag limp at her side, and it was odd, me the daughter playing a woman my mother's age, but looking like her mother, holding her as her mother would have done, while she cried.

The PA blithely interrupted with "You're wanted on the set, Ms. Harden," and we walked arm in arm across the stream, Mom in her rust-colored sweater and Indian print skirt, and flat loafers tapping across the bridge. Once on set, the crew arranged a director's chair right behind the monitor, and someone brought her a plate of food from craft service. Everyone treated her like a queen! I was so proud. Mom's visit to set was going exactly as I had imagined.

I was finding my marks, rehearsing the moment just before my supposedly dead husband reappears after having been frozen for nearly thirty years. My character (Joy) was worried: she was now old and he was much younger coming back to her, and the scene was about how love defied age and how my husband loved me now just as he did thirty years ago when he had been frozen (*ummmhmmm*). So I was rehearsing this scene, and was imagining Joy's fear as she was about to reunite with her long lost husband. In the final moments before action was called the set buzzed with last-minute adjustments. I could see Mom was thrilled as she watched intently from the sides, staring raptly into the monitor. As I concentrated on my character Joy, a tear came to my eye, and I looked understand-ably perplexed and worried while waiting for my husband — played by Brian Wim-mer, my super-handsome costar — to knock on the door of my house. Creating my moment before . . . a frown, a tear, anticipation . . . I was now ready!

They called for quiet on the set. I heard the clapper board clap and sound speed confirmed, and seconds before "Aaannnnd Action!" was called, in the blackened silent room, I heard a soft *"Psssst. PSSTTT."* It was coming from somewhere behind the monitors. *"Pssst"* again, and I looked up to discover my mother hissing at me. She gave me the gesture of "Smile," moving her two hands into a large grin at her mouth.

"What?" I whispered, completely flummoxed. "What?" I repeated, a little louder, irritated a bit that Mom was now directing me.

"Smile," she whispered back from the dark. "Smile, honey. You look so much prettier when you smile!"

Oh, my, did I love that lady . . . though at that moment I wanted to say, "Get her OFF the set!" Instead I tried the scene with a little smile, just for her.

I knew *why* my mom wanted me to smile so much. I had fallen in love with a local boy in Santa Fe, a coffee-serving, bagpiping poet, and already my mother could sense the teary and tumultuous separation that took two years to come, at the end of which she held me while I sobbed, "What is WRONG with MEEEE? Why won't anybody love MEEE?"

Though she soothed me with "Nothing, darling — nothing is wrong with you," resting my head in her corduroy lap, my tears falling on the brown couch, she did wish I had a softer tongue, a more willing smile, and a greater sense of surrender. She liked that I was bold, but did I have to jaywalk? Did I have to be so tough? She didn't quite know how to tell me how to hold on to my power and yet be a partner at the same time. Perhaps because she had relinquished her own power so much of the time — though she never relinquished her dignity. So in that moment, in Santa Fe in that scene with my returning husband, Mom needed to see me smile in order to validate the possibility of love in my future.

She was to be rewarded, as was I, because years later, again on another movie set, I fell in love with a crew guy, a remarkable man named Thaddaeus. A week before Mother's Day weekend, Mom arrived in Peacham, Vermont, where we were shooting the film *The Spitfire Grill.* Mom loved to visit me while I was filming on location; it was her way of continuing to travel and explore. Travel, children, and a fur coat. Dad was busy working at an important air communications company in Texas, and he liked for her to get away and have fun — as long as she didn't expect him to join her.

The film was a small independent feature starring the phenomenal, mystical Ellen

Burstyn, and I was renting an old stone house in the middle of the woods and biking to set along a dusty country road, mooing back at the cows that cheered me up the hill. The house was perhaps four hundred years old, with an enormous walk-in fireplace, and rooms with no closets, just pegs on the wall for hanging clothes. It smelled of lavender that I boiled in little pans on the stove, and wood, and earth, and fresh laundry.

So this Mother's Day visit in the beautiful Vermont woods was precious girl time, precious mother-daughter time, and we had planned to drive up to Montreal in my Grand Wagoneer over the weekend. Mom had barely arrived and put down her bag with the flower books and camera before I burst out with my news that I had fallen in love with a prop boy named Thaddaeus. Of course, she was shocked that he had the same name as my father and my brother. We joked that there would be many long hours on a psychiatrist's couch to figure that one out! (And we were right . . . as it turns out.)

Thaddaeus was living nearby with the prop boys — they soon rewarded me with the nickname, "Prop-tart" — and we were in the first flush of love, so Mom's arrival was a kind of intrusion into our very fresh and new affair. But it *was* Mom, after all. From her point of view, perhaps Thad was an intrusion on her trip? She never said as much, of course, as we had long ago decided on that mother-daughter trip to New Zealand that when we traveled together, we would give each other the freedom to be ourselves, to be adults! I could curse and smoke and have sex if I wanted to, I didn't have to be her "little girl," and she didn't have to be "Mom," or even "the mom of Marcia Gay," she could just be Beverly. I could be myself, and she could be herself. So I wasn't about to ignore Thaddaeus or pretend he didn't exist, but it was a bit of a balancing act to give my best to both of them. She was so generous, though, as usual. She just wanted to be a part of it all, and she was hopeful and joyful that finally, I was in love. Thaddaeus in kind was very welcoming to Mom, he could see that she was my best friend, and whoever would be with me would have to learn how to share me with her.

I cooed to Mom how perfect it was, my budding relationship. Thaddaeus came over, he chopped wood, and I made stew, using the *Moosewood Cookbook.* You would think I was describing *Little House on the Prairie,* and looking back now I cringe at my earnestness, but in fact it was an ideal time. Living in the Vermont woods, shooting a movie, doing pottery on the side, taking long walks with Ellen Burstyn while we discussed poetry and dug up wild asparagus, serving my new love dinner and breakfast, and on top of it all welcoming my mother to this rustic setting — it filled me with such happiness and grace that I thought I was about to burst. Mom and I walked the wooded path, stepping over mushrooms and bees, and I told her all about Thad. As she spent time with him on set, he was kind and charming, and I could see the hope arise in her eyes that I just *might* have a husband, and children, and I would not die an old maid.

They were very similar, both born in January and both Capricorns, and they shared a wry sense of humor as they discussed events of the day, film, politics, life, or me. They got along superbly! It was funny though, I noted that Mom often took Thad's side in a discussion. This wasn't unusual — she did like to flirt with young men, but somehow it always seemed she could see her daughters through the eyes of their beaus especially during a disagreement. I had found she often took the "other" side, in an argument, and she would laugh and tease me and admonish "Now, Marcia . . . that wasn't very nice!" Or she would roll her eyes at Thad and say, "Oh, my, I don't know how you take it!" It was her way of dissipating the conflict, of keeping us together, of enforcing "if you can't say something nice, don't say anything at all."

In truth, she was deeply invested in me having a softer smile, a gentler touch, a lasting relationship, and this is where her judgment of me really came from. I think I reminded her of Dad at times, impatient and demanding on a bad day, and she didn't want me to sully my relationships with the attributes that had caused her pain in her own marriage. She wanted me to be happy, and married, and she didn't know what that looked like if the woman was in power. Yet she wanted me to be an actress, too. Not that they were mutually exclusive, but I could see her hope churning that perhaps in Thaddaeus, I had found the perfect balance, the hippie knight, the man with whom I could be a wife, mother, lover, actress, and powerful woman. With whom I could just be me.

Sitting on the lawn of my stone cottage, surrounded by dandelions, Mom and I talked of love and marriage. Walking through the woods with long Vermont walking sticks, we talked of nature and flower arranging, and she carried her pruning shears and cut long dogwood branches to pair with small magnolia flowers. Throwing pots with the local potter with whom I was studying in my off time, we hand-built vases, and we talked of art and self-fulfillment. I made clay teapots for which Thaddaeus wove hemp handles. Mom never seemed to stop smiling, and I never wanted her to leave. I liked my happy threesome — Mom, Thaddaeus, and me.

The day before we left for our trip to Montreal, Mom came to the set with me and sat next to the script supervisor, a job she always said would suit her if she were ever on a film crew. She huddled near the heater in her cashmere brown cardigan, and beamed with pride when the director told her he would love to use her as an extra in the church scene. I watched her as she chatted with all the extras, and I watched her as she gazed happily through the church window, following the dogwood petals floating to the ground outside the stained glass. I watched her as she ate chicken in the church basement with the crew. I wondered if she perhaps imagined herself an actress, or a member of the crew. She loved learning about each and every job. They all knew her and called her Beverly. They talked to her of their own lives and she talked to them about ikebana and the courses she taught. I watched her shine, delighted to educate a new audience. She explained her flower lessons, mostly pointing out the triangles of heaven, earth, and man in the classic ikebana arrangement. Our vases had just been fired up the road in my pottery teacher's kiln, and Mom took her vase and decided to give a little demonstration at the end of lunch to some of the crew, using a kenzan she always had tucked in her suitcase and had for some reason brought to set that day, and the ikebana scissors she always had tucked into her purse. She cut crabapple branches for pink line material, and paired them with several wild yellow jonquils that were growing in the ditches, and placed them at proper angles in the burnished brown vase, creating a cloud of pink and yellow softness. Thaddaeus took her arrangement and placed it as a centerpiece on the crew buffet table, and we all admired it as we took snacks off the table. At the end of the day Mom and I hugged Thaddaeus good-bye, and we went back to our stone cottage, lit a fire, packed for our trip, then bedded down together snuggling and giggling under the big down comforter.

The next morning, I peeked out the window at sunrise, and across the glistening dew saw my white and wood Grand Wagoneer covered with jonquils, bright yellow jonquils, hundreds of them. Thaddaeus had worked late on the film, and he had gotten off much later than I had, and on his way to his home he had very romantically picked bunches and bunches of jonquils growing wild in a field, and had strewn them about on my car as a kind of "Good-bye, I will miss you, and have a great weekend" gesture. Over her black coffee, Mom cooed with delight at his charm. "Well, he obviously left them for me," she said. "It is, after all, Mother's Day." She was sold.

For our wedding, my mother did, indeed, do the flowers. As my friends and family swam in the river, she lugged white plastic buckets full of sunflowers to her lodge. As nieces and nephews jumped off the enormous plastic blob in the river, or slid down the huge slide in their bathing suits and landed with a cannonball in the Pecos, Mom cut birds-of-paradise and calla lilies underwater to suck up the water into the stem, and she placed them in huge vases in her lodge's kitchen. She gathered Mason jars and vases and carried them from her car with Dad's help, and she hefted many kenzan pieces to make sure the main arrangements stood upright and with respect for the lines and values of ikebana. In each and every room, Mom put a little flower arrangement welcoming the guests, and I laid a note on the bed doing the same. They were greeted with mostly sunflowers, Indian paintbrush, blue delphinium, some Queen Anne's lace, and daisies. She must've made over a hundred arrangements, cutting the sprigs underwater, placing them in vases, then placing the vases in boxes, and driving around the ranch and decorating the rooms. She saved about fifteen arrangements for the actual wedding party dinner, and placed them on the rounded tables covered in white linen that were scattered around the exterior of the hunting ranch. The main arrangement of the day however was the altarpiece, and Mom devoted her entire spirit to it.

There was an altar made of stone; it was a dark golden hue — and it sat in the semicircle at the bottom of the outdoor amphitheater, upon which Mom designed a beautiful natural, driftwood flower arrangement. She simply saw the altar and knew what she needed to do. She didn't even ask me what

I thought about it. She didn't need to ask. Her designs were sublime, and I was eager to witness her vision, and grateful that that was her gift to me, flowers at my wedding. "There is no need for you to pay for these, Marcia Gay. I can do this!" She had brought a beautiful piece of undulating driftwood, about two feet high and three feet wide, from Fort Worth. It was in the shape of an open hand, its pointed branch fingers cupping the air. Inside the hand, using the perfect alignment principles of ikebana, Mom nestled calla lily and fern among long rust-colored velvet cattails.

"Marcia," she began, "I want to tell you about your wedding flowers. I have made white rose boutonnieres. Roses are a symbol of passion. I pray you have lots and lots of that in your marriage! It's good for a couple. It keeps them strong.

"And in your altar arrangement, I've used flowers with very special meaning. Calla lilies are a symbol of holiness, of faith, and of purity. They signify humility — which I think you need in a marriage, and, Marcia, also in your life. Especially in your life as an actress. They also signify devotion. Devotion to your husband, to your marriage, and to the family that I am so hopeful you will create. I have been devoted to my family, especially my children, and Marcia, I am, I think, the proudest of that of anything. When we lived in Greece you learned the word *kalá.* Meaning 'good,' or 'beautiful.' Well, that's what these flowers stand for. Calla Lily.

"And the fern, the fern is a remarkable plant, it is medicinal and used for healing and in many cultures it represents peace, tranquility, and spirituality, as well as new growth or new beginnings. Marriage is a new beginning for you, Marcia, and I wish you great success. But in Japan, the fern is also the symbol of hope and posterity, with the thought that as it branches, so may the family increase and multiply through the generations. I want lots of grandchildren, Marcia! I wish your marriage great posterity!

"And finally, cattails are a symbol of peace. When you are fighting, giving a cattail to each other promotes your friendship. It's important to be friends with your husband, Marcia. I don't want to see you fighting too much. It's not good for a relationship. Be friends."

I wrote her words down. I remember them always. When we bought our Catskill property several years later, I was thrilled to see acres of fern in the fields, and hundreds of velvet cattails surrounding the lake, as if a gift from my mom. Maybe I should have used the cattails more often.

Emmy the wiener dog chinkles her chain and tries to lick me, and I want to fling her out of the room. Lying on my mother's bed that wintery Texas morning, hot tears melting into her downy scented flannel nightie, I hate that I am feeling sorry for myself, but I am. I'm feeling sorry for myself and for my children, for my mother and for all people who are suffering loss. But mostly for myself. Emmy chinkles onto the bed. I shove her off. I'm not sharing my mom. I push my body into her body, into her space, where comfort lives warm and generously. Just past her shoulder, I can see out the front window into her lovely yard. Staring blankly, I finally focus on the stone bench her garden club gave her, years before. A stone bench, dedicated to the memory of my brother's children who died in a fire. Audrey and Sander.

My brain splits. Shuddering sobs now. For my brother and for his children. For my marriage. For my mom. For everyone, for all of us. *Stop!* I tell myself. *Loss is everywhere. Be strong, and humble.* I think of my brother, and how he has with such nobility created a new life for himself. *Oh, God, I miss my niece and nephew.*

My vision blurs ugly red saltwater tears. My brain splits again. The room gets blurry, it's as if clouds of hope and sorrow come pouring through the distorted little screen squares outside the window, and the room is suddenly full of cloud squares, and floating windows, and flowers and weeds, and memory and lost threads and blurred tapestries, hot tears and Apple workers in blue and windows of despair, and all that I cherished, all that I loved, is lost, melting into flannel nighties, disappearing like tear stains, with only damp remains on the skin. Mom hugs me tighter, and then the clouds all begin to swirl and disconnect in the room. It's not like Tony Kushner's play at all, nor is it one giant ozone cloud in the middle of the sky as in my vision. It's not clean and white and operatic and smelling of lavender. The future is ugly and splitting, and the clouds come pouring through the screen like poison gas, dropping weeds and flowers together. They are all bumping into each other, and they are getting all mixed up, and they are changing shape, some ominous and dark, some cirrus and wispy, and I feel they are the universe, the universe gathered in my mother's room, presiding in her ceiling, clouds raining down flowers and weeds upon the bed. Weeds of loss. For the second time in my life, I'm not sure how to go forward. Why me? Why loss? What is the message here? What am I supposed to learn? What am I supposed to do? How can I face tomorrow? I can hear the children in my mom's living room, playing around on the piano. I think of Eulala and say to myself: *GET UP, WARRIOR!* The room fills with war cries, General Patton yelling *NO COWARDS* and Churchill crying *NEVER GIVE UP!* and my dad's command *PULL YOURSELF UP BY THE BOOTSTRAPS, GODDAMNIT!* And Norman Vincent Peale preaching *"It's not a problem, it's a challenge!";* these all blend together, with my mother's voice saying *"devotion to your children, devotion to your children"* as a kind of background murmur. My mother strokes my hair, and as she hears me cry out raw and loud and ugly, I feel her stomach heave in a sob. So that's what we do for a while, cry together. Time passes. Then I hear her stomach growl, in hunger, and just like that she has brought me back to the moment. *"Don't take tomorrow to bed with you,"* I remember Dr. Peale preaching. *Or yesterday, either,* I think.

I find her hunger comforting. It's a necessary jolt back to reality. Chinkling Emmy. The tinkling piano. My children, flattened by my grief, trying to find laughter and meaning for their own lives, sit in the living room waiting for me to come back to them. Mom's room is dark, no cloud windows, it is just dark inside, with a stone bench outside under a tree. *Warrior.* My mother strokes my hair. *Weave the holes yourself . . .* as my brother did. I hear my dad's voice more clearly now: *Pick yourself up and carry on!* As each of my sisters did, whenever they suffered distress. My own critical voice says, *Don't lick your wounds! Be strong!* And my kinder voice says, *Show your kids that there is joy!* And Patton: *Americans play to win!* And Dr. Peale again and again: *"Any fact facing us isn't as important as our attitude toward it, for that determines it's success or failure," "learn to like yourself," "take action!," "formulate a mental picture of succeeding."* And still my mother's gentle voice: *"Cattails and calla lilies and devotion."* Maybe I need to give myself a cattail? Take action. Get up off the bed. Maybe I need to devote myself to myself first. Travel, children, and a fur coat. I silently vow to take my kids to Yosemite. For some reason, it seems that Yosemite is the place where we will find joy.

I will buy down coats, no fur for us. I am of a different generation from my mom's, but I will devote myself to healing, and to children, and to light, just as she has done her entire life. I will take them in the spring, when my head isn't dark. Right now, it's too dark.

"What is wrong with me, Mom? Why doesn't anyone love me?"

And my mom strokes my hair. "Nothing, darling. Nothing is wrong with you."

That night was perhaps the loneliest night I have ever spent. I had a punch-in-the-gut realization that though Mom would remember this story for a while, perhaps for a few years, eventually she would forget it, and for the first time in my life I would be truly alone as I patched up the holes in my ozone, watching with despair while my mother's own tapestry was unraveling.

And she did forget. And I did repeat the story of the demise of my marriage for a while, until I got bored of it. Then I would just bullet the story, and finally I skipped it altogether. Not important, really. Not anymore. The calendar had ticked on, light had changed, and my numerologist had been right. Much had been activated in 2011. I was ready for 2012. I was ready for the end of the Mayan calendar, or really, the end of life as I knew it, and the beginning of a new life. I was ready.

My kids and I *had* taken that trip to Yosemite, and as I was camping under the star-studded sky, I was shocked to find that I was healing, and strong, and single, and using the best parts of my mother to inspire me. As we biked to Vernal Falls past the towering granite rock formations, we sang an old favorite camp song at the top of our lungs. I had learned it years before from my mother at a Bluebird campout around a bonfire: "I love to go . . . awandering along a mountain paaaaath . . . and as I go I love to sing, my knapsack on my back!" We shouted, "Faldereeeeeee, Falderaaaaaaah," until it echoed through the valley. Of course I was healing! Hadn't my mom first shown me the way? Hadn't she been so often alone while we were growing up and Dad was off to sea? Yes. And she had flourished, embacing her children in her crescent moon hug. She had long ago shown me how to be strong, purposeful, and happy. I just needed to follow the example she had set as she traveled the world and exposed her children to sights and wonders unknown to them. Of course. This was a torch she had passed along to me, and now I was to run the marathon, and pass it on to my own beautiful children. She was a woman wearing a gold filigree pendant passing down to her kids and grandkids her strength and tenacity, her ferocity and devotion. She was the original warrior. What a fool I would be to wallow in windowless rooms, when there were angels sitting on the stone bench.

Rain down upon me, beautiful calla lilies! Rain down upon me through God's window in the sky, and blanket me and my children and my mom and even old Emmy in healing! My mother is a star navigator, and I will take up her torch. I will fly with her up through the troposphere, through the stratosphere, through the mesosphere, through the thermosphere, and into the exosphere, where we will grasp the cure for her illness by its starlight mystery, and bring it home for all who suffer loss.

■ ■ ■ ■

My Mother is an Easter Bunny in a White Confectioner's Egg

■ ■ ■ ■

Jesus rises. Easter is coming. Anxiety over-whelms me. I'm hoping for a kind of second rising *within* me, a rebirthing of hope.

I expected this moment would come. My mother doesn't remember me. It was a simple conversation — we were on the phone discussing spring break and whether I would be able to make it to Texas or if I would take the kids to Hawaii — and her reply, "I'm sorry, but *who* are you?," was surely harder for her than for me. It was just a fleeting moment; I was prepared for it, it'd actually been coming on gradually, slowly, so there wasn't really a shock, just my verbal reaffirmation: "It's okay if you don't remember me, I will always remember you." These moments come and go, clarity comes and goes, words come and go, recog-nition comes and goes, and time passes. I listen carefully; one minute she is struggling for a word, and the next minute she is giving Deepak Chopra a run for his money. Her teachings come unexpectedly, and surprisingly. Once, we were discussing parenting and my kids. "Use the word 'child,' Marcia Gay; kids are for goats," and how each *child* is special. She didn't search or stumble for a word. This sentence came out quite succinctly. I wrote it down, word for word. Mom had said how important it was that I was impartial with my children. I said, "You've showed me how, Mom; you've always loved all your children the same."

"Not exactly so. That's a hard one. Because they are each different. I love all of my children, because they're mine. But they are each different, each individual, and I want it that way. I love them for what they want to be, and for what they struggle to be, and for their disappointments. I sometimes feel disappointment. But I love each one because of the way they treat me, and how they are with me, and what they bring to me. And they are each different in that. I don't want them all to be the same. I am happy with how it is. I want them to be individual, because I love them individually."

Words of wisdom come, and go. Several months later, she said to me, "I know there is something important about you, but I can't remember what it is," and then later, "When you walked in the room, I felt something happy, like there was something about your face that was special to me." Happiness too comes, and goes. I want the cure to come, and not go.

I've walked about in a dark cloud lately: taking the kids to school, traveling to Vancouver for *Fifty Shades of Grey*, performing the various tasks of mother/actress/worker/sister — but not daughter. As a daughter, I feel I am lost in some tunnel where there is no light pointing toward the end, no exit sign or glow-in-the-dark rails to illuminate the path, and I'm stumbling about in ignorance and fear, trying to make sense of what is happening to my mom and praying that it doesn't happen to me.

I keep imagining my head has a lid on it, and when I open the lid, inside are dead leaves and debris. It is quite dark, and musty. There is no light, there are no green buds springing forth, nothing affirming a hopeful meaning, or a raison d'être. Instead there is only black water pooled at the bottom of the cavity known as my head, rising to the top, threatening to drown me. I want to siphon and dispel the toxic waters. I want to take a leaf blower and blast out all the clutter and mulch and decaying wood and erase anxiety and fear. Once clear, in the blank rows of fertile change, I will plant hope. I will sear my head with warm light, invite in spring and youth, roses, a ladybug, an earthworm perhaps, a sliver of sunshine dancing on a dragonfly's gossamer wings. And then, I want to do the same for my mother. For her, I will siphon away the fog, siphon away the amyloid plaque on her neural synapses, and with my leaf blower blow the damn wheels off of her wheelchair! Then, I will plant bright healing orbs in her brain, and soon, she will remember me. She will remember her life. She will remember herself. I want to see my mother walk straight up and tall, flashing her beautiful teeth, delighted with her children.

We have sold my mother's lovely home in anticipation of the mounting costs of caretaking. It is one of the hardest decisions we have had to make so far; the loss of her home is something that all of my siblings feel, indeed felt, with such a dread and sense of helplessness that it has somewhat devastated us. I keep reminding myself that we're doing the best we can, with the tools and knowledge that we have. This is uncharted territory, and most people, certainly my siblings and I, are unprepared for it.

She now lives in a smaller, comfortable ranch-style house that my grandfather built in the sixties. It doesn't have her plants and her ficus, her pyracantha or American beautyberry. It doesn't have her ikebana friends or the museums of Fort Worth. Not that she remembers these things exactly, but she feels them. We feel them for her, too. We want things to be "as they were before," but Alzheimer's is a progressive disease, and it only marches forward. So we adjust, preparing for the unknown, calculating all possibilities and subsequent actions, and most importantly ensuring her comfort, care, and safety. Where she lives now is lovely. It is a family home. On a lake. Full of birds and old neighbors, near medical needs and a church, near sisters who shower Mom with love and visits, and near caretakers who take wonderful, dutiful, and exacting care of all the various indignities of aging and Alzheimer's. But the change has depressed us, and the inability to do much, to do more, to set her up like a queen, has darkened my spirit. A second rising is called for, and I've sat on my cat-clawed linen couch, meditating with Deepak Chopra and Oprah. (By the way, why has no one coined "Deepak Choprah Winfrey?") I've said the serenity prayer again and again:

God grant me the Serenity to accept the
things I cannot change,
Courage to change the things I can,
And the Wisdom to know the difference.

I've thought about lightness. And beauty.
And the home. I've bought daffodils and
berry branches and hydrangea, and tried to
do an ikebana arrangement, to bring a spot
of bright Easter loveliness into my third-
floor walk-up on Venice Beach. It droops,
poking fun at all that I haven't yet learned
from my mother.

These days, I think about memory, a lot.
Every time I fumble for a name, or forget a
supposedly familiar face, I worry. So I read
constantly about Alzheimer's and have
introduced coconut and vitamin B supple-
ments, gingko and pomegranates into my
diet. I've cut way back on sugar — some
doctors have called Alzheimer's "Diabetes
3," and they have linked too much sugar in
the brain to mental dysfunction! If I forget
where I put my cell phone, I jump on the
treadmill right after I find it. Exercise is supposed to put off the possibility of memory
loss! I do campaigns to make others aware

of the early signs of dementia and Alzheimer's, and I am flummoxed that the line
is so vague between forgetting where one
put their keys and true concern for having
the disease. I watch the news; the numbers
are climbing. Now, it is estimated that 5.5
million Americans suffer from Alzheimer's
or related dementia. Five-point-five million
in America, and nearly 47 million people
worldwide! Forty-seven million? I am
dumbfounded. This is the crime of the
century. Why is there not more money and
effort and research to discover the cause of
Alzheimer's? Where is the cure? I don't want
to be another statistic, so I compare myself
with other people my age, and I test myself,
starting by trying to remember my past.

I *vaguely* remember my childhood. I
remember holidays, and certainly I remember our home. But I don't remember specif-
ics, like the childhood couch. Should I? Do
you? Do most people? I wrack my brain for
remembered artifacts of youth. I remember
a table, and occasionally remember a
dresser. I want to remember more: I want
to know the stories of the marble dresser,
the antique curved china cabinet, the picture
that used to hang above the bed in my
mother's guest room — handmade by her
when we lived in Japan. It was a colorful

scene showing three little Japanese girls, their three-dimensional shapes constructed out of silk kimonos and cotton obis, and they are playing — could it be? — "London Bridge Is Falling Down."

Much of the furniture that is meaningful to my mother came from Coco, her mom. There are lovely antique wooden carved beds, a pink velvet love chair on which my father proposed to her, a rounded glass china cabinet, writing desks and secretaries. Then there is another style of furniture . . . sleeker, more contemporary. This is the furniture that she acquired — when exactly? I don't remember — much of it came, I think, from Japan. There is a tansu chest with a secret compartment for hiding treasures. A matching teak china cabinet and buffet, a teak stereo console. A rounded brass table. Childhood stories, a different kind of treasure, is hidden in the furniture.

I will always remember the intricately carved Chinese coffee table with matching wooden nesting tables. It was here that silver-wrapped kisses were hidden on Easter morning. Little fingers would search for presents left by a Bunny, hidden in the tiny rectangles of the innermost stacked table, wedged between carved temples and carved roses. Colorful foil chocolate eggs of pink and green and light blue were tucked among the wooden rectangle squares, hidden so well that a certain three-year-old couldn't see them. Hidden so well that a certain three-year-old burst into tears as the older girls gathered eggs, jelly beans, and chocolate dreams, and my father bellowed, "Look *there,* Goddamnit! *There!*"

I laugh about it today, how unseemly, how un-Easter-like, to roar like that. He was a big man, and could be rather scary to a three-year-old. Yet now I also muse at how frustrated he must have been, to have hidden the eggs so carefully with my mom in the dawning morning, black coffee percolating, hoping each child would find their pre-planned eggs in their defined area of the living room. Yet I didn't. How frustrating, to point so many times: "It's *there,* Marcia Gay. Right *there.*" And still I didn't see it. My sisters desperately wanted to help me, their eyes popping in the direction of the brown coffee table. Me not understanding, not even imagining that an egg could be hidden in someplace so hard to see, but to them, it was as if the egg were sitting right out in the open, with blinkers on, screaming, "I'm here! I'm here!" My mom: "Look again, Marcia." My dad, pointing again, until the point and instruction became a bellow, a roar, using God's name loudly and in vain on Easter morning, but all under-standable because for him to actually pick up the egg and put it in the plastic green grass of my basket would have forfeited the game . . . the game of the Bunny. The game of finding. The game of basket-filling and chocolate melting on little pursed lips. I will always remember that table with whimsy, with love even — because it has a story of me woven into its carving.

Which stories of my mom are lacquered onto her furniture? What whispers are stored in the carved woodworks of her Japanese screen? What childhood coos murmur under the marble of her dresser? What teenage squirms has the mirror of her vanity witnessed? As she prepared to walk to church each Sunday, and ran next door to her Grandmother Mammy's house, did she steal a glance of reflected admiration in the oak-framed oval mirror? Jet-black hair and perfectly arched brows, milky pearls hovering over her collarbone, shimmering above softly emerging breasts, staring at herself in the oval looking glass that hung in Mammy's foyer. A child, delighted in her blossoming. And now, generations later, this same oval hangs in a small bedroom in Mom's own home. Does the oval mirror long to speak for my mother? To help my mother remember herself? To reflect with her, *for* her, her life?

Two years ago, Mom caught sight of herself in the small square mirror of the visor in the passenger seat of my car. "Who is that old lady?" she asked, astonished. She didn't recognize herself. She didn't remember her face. When her brain caught up to her a second later, she made it a joke, as if to apologize for forgetting that she wasn't still young. "Ha-ha. You can't go backwards in time!" But she does. She does go backward in time even as she is moving forward. Like a hummingbird flies. Minutes later she says, "I never thought I would lose my mind. I was always quicker to the punch of a joke than someone else."

I wish the oval mirror could speak. I wish the bowls and the plates and the china could speak. I wish the boxes and boxes of old magazines, old checkbooks, saved lessons of Greek and Spanish, the spoons and chimes and knickknacks, the silver stapler and the star paperweight with the flag inside it, I wish they could speak, and tell me of my mother's life. And the vases! Oh, how I wish the vases could spill stories of arrangements and ladies' chatter at the flower-arranging table. My mother teaching, holding bamboo and shears in her hand, teaching, entwining the philosophy of art and flowers and home while she entwined bright yellow snapdragons with lime-green bamboo.

I think of a second rising "The home should feel peaceful," she taught, "and the flower arrangements can be reflective of the seasons, or even the holidays and celebrations." She always somehow honored the holidays with her arrangements. For Easter, Mom often chose a basket for her "container," or vase. She would tell me, "A new idea is ikebana's hidden strength," and then she would combine the basket with an unusual texture, or an unexpected flower. When we were younger, colorful eggs were often used in the bottom of an Easter arrangement, and sometimes moss. Each arrangement had to have a main point of focus. Sometimes it was the color, sometimes the shape, sometimes the container. If Mom had an especially lovely basket of golden woven reeds, she would usually determine that she wanted the container to be the main point of focus. At which point she would study the color, the shape, the depth, and angle of the basket.

Pursing her lips, she would explain that she wanted her Easter arrangement to look like spring. Hope rising. Sun rising. New beginnings, and growth. Scanning the purple iris, the butter-colored daffodil, the ivory lily, she would then choose the material for the arrangement, studying the shape, thickness, and flexibility of the lines she planned to use, and weighing their compatibility with the basket. She breathed in the possibilities, meditating on the placement and balance and space she was creating. "The lines must harmonize or contrast, depending upon your feelings and thoughts," she would say. "Each line should be placed in a determined fashion — and this is how the arrangement reflects the character and feeling of the creator." Sometimes the line above the basket rim would be arcing (pussy willow), sometimes spiky (cactus plant). It was as if it were telling a story, understanding what she wanted to express. She would use the shapes and colors, the sharpness or gentle softness of the plants and flowers as an extension of herself. She wasn't a demonstrative woman. She wasn't one to wear her emotions and feelings on her sleeve (unlike me), and it was often from these weekly creations that I could discern what she was actually feeling. For Easter, she liked to create arrangements evocative of hope and life bursting forth from darkness. Second risings.

Mom's hands were small, and her fingers quite delicate, her nails slightly pointed ovals. Her palms were pale. Perhaps I first really noticed her hands when we would dye the Easter eggs, glass bowls arranged on a plastic tablecloth, the cardboard egg holders carefully punched out of the little kits bought at the grocery store. We dropped the colorful tablets carefully into the glass bowls of warm water and watched mesmerized as the colors formed. Mom pricked each end of the raw eggs with a small ice pick. Then she lowered them carefully in the not-yet-boiling water on the stove. And though a little bit of gelatinous white hardened on the end of each egg, they didn't crack. Our dyed water darkened, the eggs hardened, and then they were set out to cool. Paper towels were laid out, as were crayons, and when the dozen eggs were delivered to the table, we each got to pick three or four. We'd draw stripes or polka dots or swirls with the crayons, then lower first one half of the egg into orange, then the other half into purple, or green or blue or red, and watch with delight as the eggs bejeweled the table.

On Easter Sunday the next morning, each child had their own basket adorned with a colorful silk bow waiting on their mat at the breakfast table. Inside was a large chocolate bunny nestled in the lime-green grass, and the grass was dimpled with the crayon-striped eggs dyed the night before, as well as a smattering of jelly beans.

Once, when my father had returned home from the sea, he brought us those white confectioners' eggs made of sugar that were carved out in the middle. You could peer through an oval window and peek into a secret scene sculpted in miniature detail inside. My favorite egg had a cozy scene of a bunny in a white apron with red strawberries falling from the sash, sitting at a pink table set for tea. Another had a bunny in a garden, hoeing a green crop. Yet another had two little bunnies in purple bonnets, heading through a white picket fence. All the bunnies were so safe in their confectioner's eggs, and I loved gazing inside the little ovals and imagining myself in the domestic scene.

On Easter morning, in the center of our dining room table, Mom always made a flower arrangement in a basket — daffodils hidden behind a driftwood curve, fern covering the extra blue eggs she had dyed and would later mash to make an aqua-tinged egg salad sandwich. (Embarrassed at school the next day, my white Wonder Bread now splotched with blue from the leaking dye, gooey blue and green-yellow egg salad oozing about the sides, I would slump slightly forward at the long cafeteria table so others couldn't see the sickly looking sandwich — yet I ate it with pleasure since it was so delicious. This was before I learned to look around and actually see the rest of the cafeteria, and when I did, I noted that there were other splotchy sandwiches from other mothers. There were orange and blue and green sandwiches, pink and red and purple. Followed by chocolates waiting loose in the bottom of brown paper lunch bags, and jelly beans stored in sticky pockets.)

But at home, on Easter morning, before we sat down to pancakes and Aunt Jemima syrup, the hunt had to take place, and every year it was exactly the same. We liked tradition. We didn't need variety. Just your basic egg and candy hunt, which vaguely had to do with Jesus and second chances. We were let go in a *1 — 2 — 3!* and began to search under pillows and in picture frames, on lamp-tops and in plant holders. We popped open plastic eggs and sucked on candies as we crawled on hands and knees and searched under the couch. In a frenzy, baskets were filled, some faster than others, and sometimes tears were shed, chocolate was always smeared on cotton nighties, jelly beans stuck in not-yet-brushed teeth, all culminating with a proud basket of Easter goodies. Only then would Mom make pancakes on an old griddle. Did she actually wear an apron? In my mind she did. A white apron with red strawberries, just like the bunny in my confectioners' egg. We ate, we put the dishes in the dishwasher, and we washed sticky hands and faces as we prepared to go to church on Easter Sunday. On went the hats! Straw bonnets with pink velvet ribbons circling the center. Little cotton dresses my grandmother had sewn, and patent leather shoes. My mom in perhaps a matching cotton dress. We showed off: We knew we were cute and clean and my mother's daughters. We knew we smelled of powder and new socks with lace on the edges, and holding black Bibles clutched tightly in our white gloved hands, we knew we were loved by Jesus. *Jesus loves me this I know, for the Bible tells me so.* Well, there it was, a black Bible with my name inscribed on the front page! It must have been living proof of Jesus's love.

Jesus rises. Easter is coming. Anxiety overwhelms me. I want my own personal second coming. A second rising. Church songs and

Sunday school and cookies, tea and apple juice. On a lake in Texas, a pink table is set for tea. My mother, the Easter Bunny no more, will smile and drink her cupful. My sister will visit, and take her to the Zilker Botanical Garden in Austin. No Easter eggs there. Instead, blooming birds-of-paradise peek from emerald leaves, maroon roses, striped iris. The garden basket is full and waiting to be picked.

Mother/daughter/sister/worker/actress/boss. Daughter? Racked with guilt about not visiting my mom over Easter, I justify my spring vacation trip with "It's my since-my-divorce-tradition to take my kids to Waikiki in Hawaii, and stay at the beautiful Halekulani hotel." (Forever named "Hock of Salami Hotel" by my daughter Julitta when she was seven.) I can sense the kids need to spend time alone with me; I've been busy with travel and work, I've been depressed and worried, and they miss me. "Please Mommy, let's go to Hawaii. Pleeeaaaasssseeee?" says Julitta. Hudson logically adds, "It's our tradition, Mom. We should go." Eulala offers helpfully, "And I can work in Ty Gurney's surf shop over the break, and pay for my own lessons." "I don't know," I say. "I miss my mom too." Again I debate going to Texas, again I ponder

Hawaii, and — creaking open the lid on my head — decide in favor of surfing. A glimmer of light leaks in. I pack colorful, foil-wrapped chocolate eggs, three Easter Bunnies, and jelly beans. I cram them into suitcases that are already packed with bathing suits and cotton dresses and colorful hats with no ribbons. I will hide them around our hotel room, in picture frames and under beds, in the slanted shutters and hotel slippers on Easter morning, just as I have done for the past few years. After the giant plane lands in Honolulu, I breathe in the damp air, and let the lush hush of the breeze waft across my cheek as I stand for a moment on the pavement, watching the kids count the bags as I have taught them to do. Colorful leis greet us as we arrive, the aroma of tuberose wafts across the starched white sheets of our suite, and on the balconies we search for dolphins or sea turtles. Leaning out over the rail, we watch the surfers, tanned and poised, skim the long, long breaks of Waikiki, and we drink in the sweet, pineapple-light Hawaiian sunshine. It feels so lovely. I take pictures, and hit SEND.

Easter morning, I wake the kids for sunrise service on the beach. We gather our Starbucks at dawn and walk the cool morning sand a distance, passing a circle of guitar-

431

playing worshippers sitting on a grassy slope, and eventually we come to a beach-side church service. We sit in plastic chairs in the sand, and a voice drones from the giant speakers. The kids look at me respectfully, yet imploring. *Please, Mom,* I read in their eyes, *do you really think this is God? Do you really feel something . . . anything . . . here?*

They're right. I feel nothing except obligation, and I want to feel Love. The message is vague, the songs too white and too high, there isn't enough hippie in the attitude, too much polo shirt, not enough fringe, and so we wander back to the guitar group, which is now baptizing a man of fifty and two teenage girls dressed in white. They enter the ocean waves and Hawaiian music is strummed, and people sing, and I feel God dance on the thrum of the ukulele, I feel Love sway with the hula sounds, and I begin to feel a small prick of light. First one head, then another, and then a salty third is ocean-dunked and reemerged, and clinging clothes misshapen by the wet stumble back to the strumming circle, all smiles and congratulations and born again. We are welcomed in, but not fussed over, and one of the teenage girls is crying. Her mother is praying. We drink coffee and eat their muffins, and sip cold apple juice.

"Mom," Julitta says, "is Jesus real?"

"What do you think?" I ask. I don't want to feed her my answers. I want her to come up with it herself.

She ponders. Then: "Yes. In our hearts."

"Yes. I think so, too," I say.

"Do you think He will make you get Alzheimer's? Like Nani?" she asks.

I am quiet.

"Why did Nani get it?" Her voice is tiny now. Soft and curious and scared. "Will I get it?" She holds her breath.

I look out at the waves. "I pray not," I say. "I don't think so. No."

"Will you?" She barely whispers.

I want to say, "Just shoot me if I do." I think I heard my mother say that once. But I know what my daughter wants. She wants to see me forever safe, forever happy, forever a bunny in an oval egg preparing for a pink tea. I say, "I will work very hard from now on for a cure for Alzheimer's, Julitta. I don't want to ever forget you."

I rise from the sand, and grab her hand, and say, "Let's swim!" We all run holding hands into the water. My head begins to clear. The fog begins to lift. Maybe that will be my siphon, my leaf blower, to join the forces of Alzheimer's research and blast an end to this horrid disease. We rise, and we rise, and we rise, and we rise, in the waves, together.

■ ■ ■ ■

EPILOGUE

■ ■ ■ ■

As winter comes to an end in the beautiful New York Catskills, there is a magical moment when the sap miraculously starts to flow through the maple trees on my property. The daytime temperatures rise above freezing, causing every fiber of the bark to breathe a sigh of relief. Then, the nighttime temperatures plummet, causing the wood to harden once more. I love that moment, that exact second in winter, when the frozen world first begins to thaw. The seasons imperceptibly shift, as if spring ponders, one groggy morning, whether she wants to wake up or not. She opens a sleepy eye; it doesn't last long, perhaps a brief day or two, but in those precise moments, deep in the rich earth, microbes begin to stretch, seeds begin to warm up, bulbs begin to stir, sap begins to run, and soon, soon, spring turns over and throws the snow-white covers off her blanketed grounds and gets out of bed.

Rip Van Winkle wakes up.

In that small, mystical synapse of time, the maple sap flows, and my children and I tap the trees around our lake with delight as we gather the sweet elixir that will soon be boiled down for syrup.

This yearly miracle was going to be captured in an episode of *The Flower Path*. The kids would have gathered the maple sap and boiled it down, Mom would have shown how to use maple leaves in an arrangement, or how to dry and press them for greeting cards, but we never got to it. This was one of many opportunities robbed from us. The thief — you know his name — had been planning this robbery for a long time. The thief stops in for dinner regularly now. He tends to hang out longer than he is wanted. We don't exactly welcome him, but we have come to accept him — what else can we do? He is a regular guest at our dinner table, plucking memory from the desert dish like a plum. Mom gets tired of fighting with him as the day comes to an end. She just wants to sleep. I'm afraid of this thief, and often I don't know how to go forward. I don't know how to make everything okay again. I feel as though I am frozen in the second before the sap begins to run. I know, for my mother, there will be no "spring awakening." *No one* wakes up. The tapestry unravels. The threads dangle.

My mother has been so many things in her life: from daughter to mother to teacher, traveler to activist, and more. She has inhabited each position, each identity, each season and stage of her life with grace. Even the "stages" of Alzheimer's she manages with grace. Stage 4 Alzheimer's, stage 5, stage 6, and stage 7. I know it's cowardly, but I don't want to know where she is. I don't want to attach a number to her. These are *not* the stages of her life I want to talk about. This is *not* the season I want to remember.

Her legacy cannot be Alzheimer's.

"What else, Mom? What else do you want people to know about you?"

What is the legacy my mother imagines? I wonder.

She slowly responds, carefully forming each word: "Well, what's important that people know about me is: My children. My travel. And flowers. And I want to always be helping my children. And helping people."

It strikes me that over the years, when I've sometimes lost track of my mother's thread in relation to *me,* it is in her relationship to herself and to her community where true growth and exploration were happening.

439

While I was struggling in New York to "make it" as an actress, I lost track of her rise — like the bamboo in the backyard, I hadn't stood still long enough to see her grow. But others *had* seen it, and I now discover these events of my mother's life like unearthed pieces of her tapestry; they come together in stories her friends tell, in pictures I dig from the bottom of a box, in scrap bits of mementos or her scrawled Spanish lessons. Her womanly graduation photo in front of the china cabinet reminds me that she was educating herself, putting herself through college and studying at night and on weekends so that she could graduate with an Associate of Arts degree, which she did, at fifty-seven years old. Her Spanish books remind me that she learned the language well enough to spend a study month in Mexico, where she lived with a host family who spoke no English. And her ikebana community informs me that Mom was an activist. An activist?? My *mom*?? I've learned that in the early 1990s, Mom had made it her mission to reactivate the Fort Worth ikebana Chapter 38, which had dissolved several years before. I'm stunned that I didn't know that. I feel guilty; I didn't see it happening . . . I was busy with my own life, preparing for my first Broadway play . . .

how could I have not known this? I thought *I* was the activist — marching in the gay pride movement with my fellow *Angels in America* cast in New York City. But no. I learn that Mom was already marching in her *own* way in Fort Worth. Her students explained that Mom had by this time earned four levels of teaching certificates, her present level being First Somu in the Sogetsu School, and she wanted to continue learning and growing, but she had nowhere to study. So she had banded together with some friends and students, writing letters and insisting on meetings, and, with the support of the local ikebana community, finally convinced the Ikebana International Headquarters in Japan to reactivate the chapter. They had begun with twelve members, and Mom had proudly watched their numbers grow.

In 2012, Mom was honored with a lifetime achievement award by her ikebana group, Chapter 38, as they celebrated their twenty-year anniversary. Our entire family gathered. Seeing her in the midst of so many friends, all expressing how much she had changed their lives, it was clear that Mom's legacy would *not* just be her children and grandchildren who surrounded her during the ceremony, but also the legacy of building a place where arts and harmony and peace and beauty could all come together. Mom was delicate that day; her cognizance floated in and out of the flurry of speeches. She wasn't sure of all the names of her longtime friends; she wasn't sure of the import of the events around her, but we were. And though it saddened us, we were there to celebrate, and all of her children were bursting with admiration and pride.

The celebration was just that — a celebration of all that my mom was, and all that my mom is. We celebrated the past and present, but the future is unknown. I have never made peace with the unknown.

Later that night, in the quiet of her own home, Mom calmly said, "People often tell me things I used to do . . . but I don't remember any of them. I'm afraid I am losing so much of my memory."

"How do you feel about that, Mom?" I ask.

"Well, it's nice to know. It's good because these are things they actually saw me do, so I know it's true."

Yes. It *was* true. She *had* done these things. Mom had come full circle. Her grandmother and her mother would have been so proud. She had brought home to Dallas–Fort Worth the riches of her time spent in Japan, where she had enjoyed the greatest adventure of her life. In doing so, she had made many "friendships through flowers" — which is ikebana's motto. And she had culturally bonded countries and cities through the art of ikebana, which is its mission. Our fierce, kind, capable, and creative mother had, in her own quiet way, changed the world around her, and made it a more beautiful and pleasing place to live.

The unknown is what we battle now.

Not long ago I Skyped with Mom and read her some passages from this book.

"Oh, it's wonderful. It's good for the women. It's helping them. And it is something, the whole arrangements, that come from inside me. They express something inside me about my day."

Recently, my sister Sheryl asked Mom what the Japanese word *"ikimashō"* meant. She said, without hesitation, "Hurry up." She was right. She had learned that expression thirty years ago.

It's time for me to *ikimashō.* I have come to a blank page, the end of the book. I stare for hours, and then call my mother. I'm afraid to stop, afraid to leave something out, afraid to let go.

"Hi, Mom. Whatever you are thinking

about, I want you to tell me. Whatever you think about your children or your travels, or life, or God, or love; whatever you think about sex, or food, or aging; whatever you are thinking about, anything, I want you to tell me. Okay?"

I am FaceTiming with her, and I can see that she starts to say something, and then stops.

"God . . . ," she says.

"Do you think about God?" I ask.

"Yes."

"What do you think about God?"

"Love," she says. "Love. It happens to everyone. The better the thoughts, the better the thinking."

When all is said and done — even without memory — what still exists is love. It is omnipresent. It transcends place and time. It is her true nature. Love.

I remember one Sunday not long ago, when, with the help of her caregiver, Rose, I'm dressing Mom for church. Pretty gold top with a cowl neck, stretchy black pants, earrings and necklace, makeup, curled hair. Her skin is soft and clear, her eyes gentle, her spirit trusting. She smiles at me, perhaps not really sure of who I am, but feeling happy to be with me. It comes and goes,

444

her recognition of what is around her, and, minutes later, she says "Marcia!" as if she had just discovered the thread. She remembers my face on the tapestry.

We get in the car, turn on the radio, and sit in stunned silence as Sarah Vaughan begins to fill the space with a soulful, glorious song. I'm sure she is singing to us. She knows we are listening, and she is singing to Mom, and to me, and to Rose as we drive to church on Sunday morning.

"Eeeverything must change . . . nothing stays the same," Sarah moans in velvet notes, drawing out the A's of *chaaange* and *saaame* in long and rolling drifts. Her voice is full and throaty, and when she sings the second verse *"Everyone must chaaange . . . nooo one stays the saaame,"* she clings to the notes, wringing them out in a soft vibrato.

I slow the car down, not wanting to miss a word.

"The young become the ooold, and mysteries do unfoold, 'cause that's the way of tiiime . . ."

"That's for sure," Mom says, her eyes glancing out the window as the Texas landscape swishes by. "That's a beautiful song," she says. I turn it up.

Sarah's voice begins a haunting build:

445

"There are not many things in life you can be sure of except rain comes from the clouds, sun lights up the sky . . ."

Mom looks out the window and stares up at the sky.

Then, when Sarah's voice hits *"and hummingbirds do flyyy,"* Mom responds quietly, "I have a hummingbird."

The song hits me in the heart, as if we're being given a lesson in how to go on with our lives, and Mom and Rose and I drive on, through the one traffic light, past the tumbleweed, feeling like we are in church already, in the car, listening to Sarah's wise and painful voice sing out, while Mom responds to the lyrics.

Sarah sings *"Winter turns to spring,"* wrenching the notes of "spring" in a halting plea. Mom says, "yes it does," and she whispers along with the song, *"seasons always change . . ."*

Mom looks at me on *"a wounded heart will heal,"* and I smile at her. She smiles back. I reach across the coffee cup holder in the car, remembering orange hibiscus in a brown coffee mug, and I hold her soft, cool hand.

"Wounded hearts *do* heal," I think. Especially with mothers who hold you tight, and braid your hair, and caress your heart with gentle counsel.

I see Rose in the rearview mirror, staring out the window, blue above, and big white clouds blanketing the sky.

Sarah's voice goes high to meet the Texas sky, high and wide, on *"mysteries do unfold."* Her voice is soaring now, at once painful and yet joyful, soaring up into the Texas clouds. She sings "fly," again and again, "fly-yyyy, flyyyyy, huuummmingbirds do flyyyy," and her voice flies away on "fly" . . . and Mom flies with her. She flies, right up into the sky, and holds Sarah's hand — soaring with angels and birds and joyful voices, looking down on all the people below. Mom is laughing, her hair streaming out behind her, her golden cowl neck ripples like gossamer wings, and she is watching herself, and me and Rose, from above as we drive to church. "Yes, sun *does* light up the sky," she says, laughing, the clouds between her teeth. She is lit up like the sun, flying with Sarah Vaughan in a big blue Texas sky.

We pull into the parking lot, and I have to wait a minute to get out of the car. Sarah knows this. She finishes her anthem.

"And music, music makes me cry . . ."

Mom smiles as we wheel her through the parking lot. She cups her hands around her now white hair so it doesn't get messy blow-

ing in the soft breeze; she adjusts her earrings and fiddles with the gold cross on her
neck that once belonged to her mother.
Then she closes her eyes, basking in the
warmth of the sun.

The clouds bounce around the steeple
top, the sun lights up the sky, and we go to
church.

Be in the moment, now. That's where my
mother is. In the moment. Still teaching,
still yearning, still loving.

Shin, soe, and *hikae.* Heaven, earth, and
man.

ACKNOWLEDGMENTS

This book has many contributing voices, and I am deeply grateful for each and every one of you. You have inspired me, pushed me, and assisted me in both large and infinitesimal ways, reminding me that it takes many steps to complete a journey, but not one step can be missed. Each of you has taken a step with me, and so the completion of this book has *your* spirit dancing around in the pages, along with my family's . . . keeping my mother company along her Flower Path.

I am deeply grateful to Sandra Prachyl of Ikebana Chapter #38, who advised me on many occasions. Also, much gratitude to Sharman Palmer, Mary Lib Saleh, Betty Neese, and Margaret Woodlief, Mom's band of activists who helped reinstate the Fort Worth chapter. I would especially like to thank the ikebana community in America and Japan for planting the first seeds of *shin, soe,* and *hikae* in my mother's life, which then gave her the creative tools to express herself, and to bring tranquil beauty into our lives. Thank you to the Southlake Garden Club, and especially to Denise Stringfellow.

This book would not have come into being without my friend, Alvin Sargent, who one day shared his extraordinary gifts of the pen and inspired me to write. Alvin said, "Write in twenty-minute stretches," and he read every single word, giving me feedback and encouragement. His is a class worth taking!

Thanks to Dr. Wendy Walsh, who introduced me to the wonderful people at Dupree Miller.

Thanks to Lacy Lalene Lynch and Jan Miller for finding the story in the narrative. Lacy, thank you for waiting patiently, pushing positively, and walking me through necessary improvements, even at midnight.

Thank you to all the people at Simon & Schuster and Atria Books. This book would have never been possible without the commitment, logic, and patience of my editor Rakesh Satyal, and without the heart of Judith Curr. Writing this book has been an adventure unlike any other, and I am still stunned that you thought I could do it.

I am an actor, and so I understand stories by reading them aloud, and feeling how the words fall in the room, how they feel on my tongue, and how they dance in rhythm with the characters. That means I had to read, a lot, to anyone who would listen. So . . . thank you all for your ears!

Thanks to my daughter Eulala Scheel, who listened to me read and read and read. And to my twins, Hudson and Julitta, who, between listening, made their own dinners many nights so I could continue writing. To Ashleigh Falls, who loves and feels words, and made me feel mine were worth listening to. To Natalie Peyton, who gave me a poem, and listened and edited with me. To my second son, Dan Murphy, who remembered with me. To Kelly DiPaola, who keenly pushed me and honored me with perceptive suggestions. To Maryellen Mulcahy, who is the backbone of everything I do. To Carri McClure, who jumps hurdles and makes the impossible possible. To Camryn Manheim, who makes me a better person.

Thanks to Amy Lederman, Harry Ford, Boris Kodjoe, Rebekah Jones, Leesa Carter, Deborah Koenigsberger, Augusta Allen-Jones, Jocelyn Flores, Ashley Guillem, John Peyton, Bridget Peyton, Stephanie O'Brien, and Thaddaeus Scheel for listening.

Thank you to all caregivers, everywhere, for your heartfelt work, and especially to Lisa and Rose, for your love and for all you do for Mom.

Finally, thank you to all the scientists and researchers and doctors in the Alzheimer's community. Please find a cure. *Ikimashō.*

I am the most grateful of all for my first loves and my deepest childhood connections: my siblings. Leslie, Sheryl, Thaddeus, and Stephanie, thank you. We were always our own neighborhood.

ABOUT THE AUTHOR

Marcia Gay Harden is an actress of the stage, screen, and television. She originated the role of Harper Pitt in Tony Kushner's *Angels in America,* a performance that earned her a Tony Award nomination. In 2001 she won an Academy Award for Best Supporting Actress for *Pollock,* and in 2009 she won a Tony Award for Best Actress in a Play for Yasmina Reza's *God of Carnage.* Her films include *Miller's Crossing, The First Wives Club, Mystic River* (for which she received a second Academy Award nomination), *Into the Wild,* and *Fifty Shades of Grey.* Her television credits include *Law & Order: SVU, The Newsroom, How to Get Away with Murder,* and *Code Black.* She holds a BA in acting from The University of Texas at Austin, and an MFA from the Graduate Acting Program at New York University's Tisch School of the Arts. She lives between Los Angeles and New York with her three children, two cats, and a dog. The fish stays in LA.

Learn more from TheOfficialMarciaGay Harden.com and follow her on Twitter @MGH_8.

8/18